Hurry Home Wednesday

Setting type on the Intertype.

Hurry Home Wednesday

Growing Up in a Small Missouri Town, 1905–1921

Loren Reid

University of Missouri Press
Columbia & London
1978

Library of Congress Cataloging in Publication Data

Reid, Loren Dudley, 1905–
   Hurry Home Wednesday.

    1.   Reid, Loren Dudley, 1905–   2.   Gilman City,
Mo.–Biography.   3.   Gilman City, Mo.–History.
I.   Title.
F474.G4R44   977.8′17 [B]   77–25401
ISBN 0–8262–0247–0

For acknowledgments and illustration credits,
see pp. 287, 290.

Dedication

To Mother and Father, who started it all

To Dr. Swint and Mrs. Noll, who helped bring me into the world

To Don, my only brother, companion, and coconspirator

To Theodore Gilman, New York banker, who gave the town its name

To the Quincy, Omaha, and Kansas City Railway, which provided a reason for the town and kept it going

To Bessie, Bony, Edith, Esther, Flora Maye, Florence, Fuzzy, Hobart, Jasper, Shorty, Tom, Tompy, Vera, and other schoolmates

To Mr. Broadbeck, Miss Lois, Miss Norwood, Mrs. Oliphant, Miss Sloan, Miss Terry, Superintendent Vogelgesang—our teachers, the loyal opposition

To Ed Clark, Ed Hull, Fred Lightfoot—printers and operators—who taught me various printing-trade mysteries

To Dr. Quinlan, who filled so many cavities, and Drs. Magraw and Gardner, who practiced bravely in an age of calomel and Epsom salts

To Mr. Burrell, Mr. Dunn, Mr. Eckles, Mr. Haines, Mr. LaMastres, Mr. Lierley, Mr. McClary, Mr. McClelland, and other advertisers, family friends, and Gilman City boosters

To Charley Hurst, Bill Middleton, Carl Price, and Tom Welden, rural carriers who got the mail through, rain or shine

To grandparents, uncles, aunts, and cousins, for boundless affection

To Ellen, John, Steve, and Tony, who grew up frequently saying, "Tell us a story," and then, "Write it down"

To all good people who have a bit of small town in them
and

To Gus

Preface

For fifteen years Gilman City, Missouri, was the center of the universe to me and the other 617 people who lived there. As the saying goes, the horizon was the same distance in every direction. The town was on the main line of the mighty Quincy, Omaha, and Kansas City Railway, which we called the O.K., and had good dirt roads connecting it with New York, New Orleans, and San Francisco.

At the time I was born into Gilman City society, of parents who ran the newspaper and later the post office, the town had great possibilities. Year after year, its population increased steadily. I was fortunate to have lived there at the peak of its glory. When I moved away, at the age of sixteen, it began to decline. Other reasons were that the roads were improved, and people who shopped in Gilman City began to take their patronage to larger places. Next thing the railroad was abandoned and the newspaper folded. The Gilman City of today is an entirely different kind of community from the one in which I grew up.

In a sense Gilman City was, when I knew it, forty years behind the times, so that today I sometimes feel as if I were a hundred or more and grew up in the latter part of the nineteenth century. In that respect my small town was like everybody else's small town, all taking a long time to catch up with the calendar. Yet in my mind it is still busy, active, thronging, politicking, merchandising; the home of twenty or thirty different kinds of businesses and professions; noisy with the clanging of school bells, off-key church bells, and the hoo-hoo of train whistles. I can still hear dray wagons rattling along like barns falling down; automobiles making crudely muffled explosive sounds even with the cutouts closed; horses, cattle, and hogs, whinnying, mooing, and grunting in the nearby stockyard.

I saw Gilman City not only as a schoolboy but as an active member of the newspaper and post office family. Between the ages of eight and sixteen I hand-set type, ran an Intertype, printed letter-heads, bank checks and sale bills, sold ads, wrote news stories about accidents and funerals and golden weddings, and, at school, debated and orated. I carried papers and got acquainted both with the patrons and the rural mail carriers of the post office. So I was even then not only onlooker and participant but also reporter and recorder.

I saw a way of life that has disappeared: the golden days of a busy and promising midwestern town that set out to be a community of a thousand and almost made it.

L. D. R.
Columbia, Missouri
April 1978

Contents

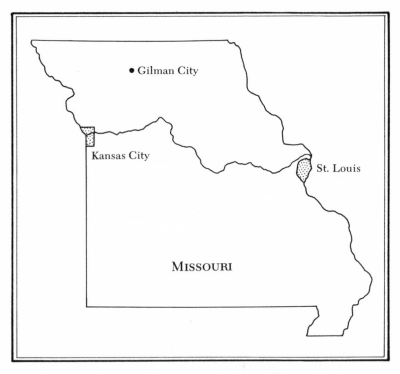

Map of Missouri showing Gilman City and other well-known localities.

1

The Birth of a Town

When I think back to what it was like growing up in a family that owned the newspaper in a small Missouri town, life seems to be mainly one Wednesday after another. Wednesday was Press Day, the day we printed the *Gilman City Guide*, folded and addressed the papers, and took them in bundles to the post office. Just like any other calendar, our week had Mondays and Tuesdays, but they were spent getting ready for Press Day. We also had Thursdays and Fridays, but they were spent cleaning up after Press Day.

Wednesdays seemed to us to be what Saturdays were to the department-store people, plus what Sundays were to the church people. Our Wednesdays didn't stop at midnight as a proper day should but generally slid over into the next morning. Two-thirds of the work of getting the *Guide* assembled and printed seemed to be done on Wednesday.

My kid brother Don and I had firm instructions to show up every afternoon right after school, but on Wednesdays we had to hurry it up. As soon as we hit the office, where Father and Mother had been working full tilt for hours, we tossed our caps on the nearest typecase and began our regular assignments: counting sheets of newsprint, gassing the engine, and setting odds and ends of type for ad copy that had come in at the last minute. Any of these jobs, however, might be interrupted by an even more urgent request like "Son, go over to Haines's and get their ad proof, they haven't brought it back yet, but before you do that bring me a small *m* and a capital *X* from the 18 point DeVinne and also some thin spaces." So we halted the counting of newsprint at 314 or wherever, marked the place, and did the other stuff.

Wednesday, Wednesday, Wednesday. . . .

Those years Gilman City, Sugar Creek Township, Harrison County, was a town of about six hundred. World War I was still in the future. Nowadays when I drive through a town that size

I see just filling stations and a garage or two, a place to eat and to buy groceries, a feed store, and perhaps two or three other stores. We had all of that plus a railroad, often with four passenger trains a day, and twenty or thirty businesses and professions from drugstores and blacksmith shops to doctors and veterinarians. We even had a three-story hotel.

And we had a weekly newspaper. You may think it surprising that a town the size of Gilman City had one, but it would have been even more surprising if it had not. Most towns had newspapers; a town of a couple of thousand had two or even three. Trenton, twenty miles east, with fewer than six thousand people, had two weeklies and a daily.

Sometimes I talk to people about my hometown and they ask, "Where is Gilman City?" Most small-town and country folk have that problem because even when you answer your questioners, they know little more than before.

So all of us have figured out a way of answering this question. I begin by saying that I come from northwest Missouri, a statement that generally yields an encouraging nod. Then I name larger, nearby, county-seat towns, moving outward in a broadening spiral until I see a glimmer of recognition in the questioner's eyes.

Gilman City, I say, is near Trenton, Bethany, and Gallatin. If his eyes are a blank, I quickly add Maryville and St. Joseph; if I get no returns with these, I throw in Kansas City and St. Louis. At some part of the list, however, he will nod and smile. Maybe he will say, "Well, it must be near Higginsville," which, at least, keeps the conversation alive while I try to locate Higginsville in my mind.

Once, talking to a Dubliner who seemed to have relatives everywhere in America, I had to go all the way to Chicago. "Oh, Chicago!" he exclaimed, his face lighting up as if he had seen the living cross of St. Patrick.

One usually does not begin an autobiography by telling about the founding of the town where he was born, but since this town has so much to do with this story, and with the story of anyone who grew up in any small community, I need to start with Gilman City and how it happened to be.

Not until recent years did I realize that Gilman City is only eight years older than I am. I was one of the first two-score youngsters born within its limits. When my playmates and I toddled off to elementary school, the high school had not yet graduated its first native-born senior. Moreover, I did not suspect that Bill Noll had built the town's first buildings; that Bill Dunn had owned one of the first two department stores; that Ben DeWitt had left a nearby farm to become one of the first carpenters and contractors. I knew them as middle-aged, established citizens of Gilman City, not dreaming that they had actually seen the founding of the town.

Gilman City came into being because of the construction of a thirty-four-mile stretch of railroad track.

In the late 1890s it became apparent to two groups of people studying the railroad map of the Mississippi Valley that if a few short gaps could be filled in, the agricultural wealth of northwestern Missouri, southern Iowa, and eastern Kansas and Nebraska could be moved to the rich markets of the East, West, and South at tremendous profit. Circulars spoke of the vast interior basin in which lay Missouri, Kansas, Nebraska, Iowa, and southern Minnesota, the greatest food-producing region on the face of the globe.

Foremost among those considering these glamorous prospects was a Kansas City capitalist named Arthur E. Stilwell. Stilwell was an extraordinarily imaginative and persuasive man who had been active in putting together the Kansas City, Pittsburg, and Gulf Railroad to give Kansas City a direct route to the sea. For the southern terminus of this line he spotted long, narrow, shallow Lake Sabine, between Galveston and New Orleans, running parallel to the Gulf of Mexico and just a few miles north of it. His plan was to build a city on the north side of this lake, connect it to the Gulf by a canal, and thus provide an inland port, sheltered from the severe storms that lashed Galveston and New Orleans, yet actually closer to Kansas City than either of those ports. His enthusiasm was so contagious and his arguments so persuasive that he had little difficulty selling bonds both in this country and in Europe. Modestly he gave the proposed city his own name, calling it "Port Arthur."

Port Arthur, however, was to be only the beginning. Once there, shippers on the Kansas City, Pittsburg, and Gulf would have ready access to the rich, coastal markets of the East at a cost less than by rail. And there was still more; beyond those markets lay Liverpool, that magnificent port of western England, gateway to

Britain herself, and, for that matter, to Europe. And why stop at Europe? Once you reached one ocean, all oceans lay at your feet. Beyond the Gulf lay the Atlantic, and beyond the Atlantic lay the Indian, which lapped Calcutta, a market without known limits.

To all this, the Kansas City planners added ecstatic visions of imports. From the South would come yellow pine, rice, fruits, fish, and not only these immediately consumable items, but the crafts and arts of Europe and Asia as well.

The whole railroad world, including the Baltimore and Ohio, the Santa Fe, and twenty other lines, was watching the development of the Kansas City, Pittsburg, and Gulf. Everybody saw, for example, that the new line would be a formidable competitor of the Illinois Central, operating between Chicago and New Orleans.

The planners were not worried that Port Arthur was only a village, and that port facilities and the ship canal project were just getting underway. Stilwell and his Kansas City associates, knowing that New Orleans was shipping twenty to twenty-five million bushels of grain a year and Galveston five million, saw only a rich, profitable market. They declared they would build their own fleet of cargo vessels if necessary, and if their new canal were not deep enough would build lighters to transport cargo from the port to their ships lying in deep water. Moreover they would build refrigerator cars and ships to transport Kansas City dressed beef to London tables. Eventually they did do all these things.

This enterprise was fueled not only by their hopes of profit but also by the blazing, competitive, midwestern spirit. Kansas City would become a bigger railroad center even than Chicago. If the Santa Fe also came into Kansas City, and if other rumors materialized, it would have absolute railroad supremacy. Its stockyards, then the world's second largest, would become the first. Midwestern farmers and businessmen, moreover, would be forever emancipated from paying tribute to Eastern transportation and shipping interests.

Thus blossomed the Kansas City-Gulf-Overseas part of the scheme. But there was more. Looking to northwest Missouri, Stilwell and his associates saw that if they could build a short, seventy-five-mile stretch of rail from Kansas City northeast to Pattonsburg, they could connect to the Omaha and St. Louis line and thus offer the upper Mississippi Valley the shortest possible route to the Gulf.

A second group of capitalists viewing the map was based in Quincy, Illinois, just across the Mississippi River. Quincy, located near some of the richest, most productive farmland that the Lord ever created, had long had a bridge across the Mississippi. In those days a city with a bridge could and did lay claim to traffic on both sides of it. Quincy planners thought of two bright prospects. One was to lay track fifty miles east to Beardstown, Illinois, and link with the Baltimore and Ohio, giving them an outlet to the Atlantic. The view west was still more attractive, however, since they could envision a railroad through to Denver and on to the Pacific. Actually they had already made a beginning on this western project and had built tracks a hundred thirty-five miles west to Trenton. They had spent hundreds of thousands of dollars of their own money on the enterprise, securing other hundreds of thousands from Missouri towns and counties through which the tracks passed. At the height of this venture, however, the depression years of the nineties caught up with them, making their bonds impossible to sell either in this country or in Europe. So they had had to stop at Trenton.

Now as the Quincy people listened to Stilwell, they saw they were being given a second chance to fulfill their dreams. By extending their track at Trenton a mere thirty-four miles westward to Pattonsburg, they could link up with the Omaha and St. Louis already there, and also with the new track being built to Pattonsburg from Kansas City. Once at Pattonsburg they could ship to the Gulf, or to Omaha, and thus to the Pacific—a dogleg, to be sure, but the more they dreamed, the shorter and flatter the dogleg became. Moreover, they could still build that fifty-mile stretch east and join hands with the mighty B. & O. and so to the coast. Dollars were heaped in bushel baskets in the streets of eastern cities, waiting to be scooped up. Obviously, here were the makings of a great Atlantic, Pacific, and Gulf railroad—centering on Quincy.

To the Quincy people, the Kansas City dreams were a secondary operation. Quincy capitalists were not awed by the big city. When their new line was open, Kansas City would simply be a good place to buy tobacco and chewing gum. Kansas City

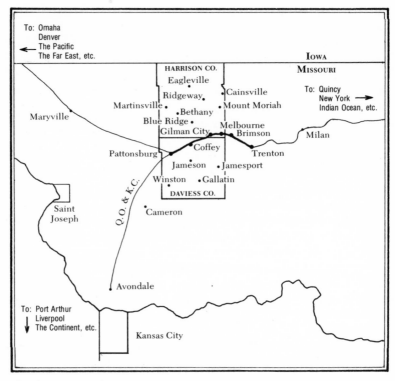

The thirty-four mile gap.

would be a mere whistle-stop on the way to New York, Liverpool, and points east.

To both groups the thirty-four-mile gap between Trenton and Pattonsburg assumed enormous importance. The engineering problems of shooting the gap were minimal since the country was flat prairie, and the streams, though numerous, were not formidable.

Nor were these possibilities lost on Trenton businessmen. Trenton was a well-established Rock Island town, famous in northwest Missouri for its alert citizens. The businessmen of Pattonsburg, already on the Wabash, and nearby Bethany, on the Burlington, were also following developments closely, ready to move in with checkbooks. The Quincy, Omaha, and Kansas City railway, which years before had been halted at Trenton, was again on the march. In the minds of the fired-up northern Missourians, the Quincy, Omaha, and Kansas City was viewed as the Quincy, Omaha, Kansas City, Atlantic, and Pacific. Or as the Quincy, Omaha, Kansas City, San Francisco, Hong Kong, Liverpool, and Calcutta.

At this point Theodore Gilman, an astute New York financier, entered the picture. He was a member of the banking house of Gilman, Sons, and Company, being one of the sons. Since Quincy railroad ventures had suffered various financial reverses, Gilman now emerged as chairman of the executive committee representing the bondholders, which undertook not only to revive but to extend railroading in northern Missouri. The committee's first task was to build the thirty-four-mile gap, and to do this it needed to acquire right-of-way, sites for offices and shops, and other facilities.

Gilman and his associates traveled in regal splendor in their own private car, complete with staterooms, a kitchen, a bar, and a sumptuously furnished lounge. The local businessmen of Pattonsburg, Milan, and other points were invited aboard, wined, dined, and allowed to feast on maps, blueprints, and columns of figures. In return for modest subsidies, Gilman's committee dangled enormous prizes: one fortunate community would be awarded the roundhouse and machine shops, and another the general headquarters office. Even Kansas City was interested in the latter. At Trenton the committee dickered for free rent of an office building, right-of-way for tracks and sidings, and depot space. At Milan it talked maintenance and repair shops. Hundreds of jobs were involved. Everywhere local citizens could visualize the possibility, through the thirty-four-mile link, of moving Trenton, Pattonsburg, and even tiny Brimson and Coffey next door to the Gulf, the Atlantic, and the Pacific. The profits could be enormous. On a good day, for example, a thousand loaded freight cars went through nearby places like Galesburg, Illinois, or Burlington, Iowa.

Gilman, who was then in his fifties, a native of Illinois, and educated at Williams, was both courteous and persuasive. By late 1896 his committee was able to let contracts, first for grading and bridging the link from Trenton to Pattonsburg, and later for laying the track.

The actual labor of building the new railroad proceeded at astonishing speed, especially when viewed by our generation that has become accustomed to seeing state highway departments spend a couple of years on the grading and construction of a thirty-mile stretch of superhighway. As soon as contracts had been let, Trenton filled up with wagons, carts, scrapers, pile drivers, picks, shovels, timbers, horses, and men. Although there were no bulldozers, no trucks, no chain saws, not even gasoline engines, a crew of two hundred speedily cleared the right-of-way of trees, raised the low spots, lowered the high spots, bridged the streams with heavy poles and timbers bolted together, and thus created a passable surface for the rails and ties. Grade requirements were generous—later, as boys walking miles of track, we could easily spot "uphill" and "downhill" stretches. Despite winter weather, the roadbed, begun in the fall, was finished by February 1897.

That spring a crew of two hundred workers boarded a specially designed train and began the job of laying the track. To the mind that thinks efficient assembly-line procedures began with Henry Ford, the ingenuity of the tracklaying crews is astonishing. A locomotive, bearing the gaudy name "The Picturesque Hills of Chariton," pushed, ahead of it, nine flatcars, loaded with ties, rails, spikes, and plates. On either side of the cars was mounted a chute, running from back to front, with horizontally placed iron rollers every few feet. On one side of the car, ties were pushed forward on these rollers to the front of the train; rails moved forward on the other side.

A hundred men were organized as a tracklaying crew, to handle ties and rails, and another hundred as a surfacing or finishing crew. In the tracklaying crew, two men grabbed a tie and carried it forward, handing it to two other men who positioned it on the newly graded roadbed. After a few ties had been placed and temporarily anchored with shovelfuls of dirt—proper ballasting came later—two sets of eight men grabbed rails and laid them in place, while other men positioned iron plates under the rails and drove spikes to anchor rails and plates to ties. The men worked like drilled soldiers, carrying, placing, and leveling the ties; carrying, placing, and spiking the rails. As soon as a section of rails was in place, another man raised a red flag, and "The Picturesque Hills of Chariton" pushed the flatcars ahead so that the process could be repeated.

Behind the train followed the finishing crew. These men drove more spikes, bolted the rails together with plates, further leveled the surface of the roadbed, and in general took out the kinks. When the train had consumed its stock of ties, spikes, plates, and rails, it backed up along its newly laid track to Trenton, where it took on fresh supplies. The competitive spirit led the crews to try each day to beat their own best record, and, if possible, to equal or excel standing records of other crews.

These thirty-four miles were laid in twenty-five working days, at a cost of $11,000 per mile. Service from Trenton to Pattonsburg began at once, at "shipper's risk," a necessary condition, since the track was new and the telegraph line was not yet in. Later heavy rains washed out parts of the new track, but that contingency was taken as a matter of course, and section gangs speedily repaired the damage. Flooded rivers also took out scores of wooden bridges, but that again was a problem anticipated and readily met. My uncle, Lon Reid, for thirty years foreman of a bridge gang of the Rock Island, eventually supervised the replacing and rebuilding of hundreds of washed-out bridges.

While the railroad was a-building, Gilman and a group of Trenton businessmen, principally Albert Fisher, a real-estate developer, and W. O. Garvin, had spotted a place for a brand new town, midway between Melbourne and Coffey, six miles from each. In those days, railroad companies routinely looked for sites for new towns, a project that quickly yielded high profit. Organizing a Town Site Corporation, Gilman and his associates bought a ninety-

acre tract from John Dorney, one of the county's prosperous farmers, and had it surveyed into business and residential lots. The new
streets were generously wide; each block also featured a fourteen-
foot alley bisecting the block, to serve as an access to buildings and
homes.

They could have called the new town Tombstone, after the
small creek nearby, but these founders had a brighter vision and
named it Gilman. Later, with radiant optimism touched with subtle humor, it was called Gilman City. If Missouri could have a
Kansas City on its western edge, why not a Gilman City at its
northern reaches? In the true spirit of the dreamer, they called the
principal intersecting street Broadway. Perhaps Theodore Gilman,
the New Yorker, looking over the staked-out cornfield, named it
after the original, far-famed Broadway. With mounting pride the
founding fathers lent their own names to other north-south streets:
Fisher, Cook, Garvin, Thompson, Dorney, Markey. Quickly running out of founders, they took up the problem of naming the
east-west streets. When you have to name a lot of streets in a hurry, you fall back on a set scheme: Maple, Cherry, Washington,
Adams, or Connecticut, Pennsylvania, and so on. They decided
simply on First, Second, and the alike, following the pattern of
New York and other famous cities.

A choice lot on Broadway—a single block from the main business district—was to be my birthplace. Just to think about it boggles
the mind.

Everybody was optimistic about the future. Newspapers in
the Quincy-St. Joseph-Kansas City triangle carried stories about
the new metropolis.

Word spread that on a certain day in May 1897, lots would be
offered for sale. Fifty buggy loads of prospective buyers swarmed
along the twenty miles from Trenton, the sixteen miles from Bethany, the thirteen miles from Jamesport, to look over the new site,
its streets and lots neatly staked out. Others came from Bancroft,
a promising settlement a mile south, which had just been missed
by the new railroad. There were no sidewalks, waterlines, sewers,
telephone or telegraph poles. Even the railroad had not yet been
completed, though each day the crews got a mile and a third closer.
Prospective buyers did see facilities for hitching their teams and
tanks of water for the horses. The Dorneys had erected a tent to

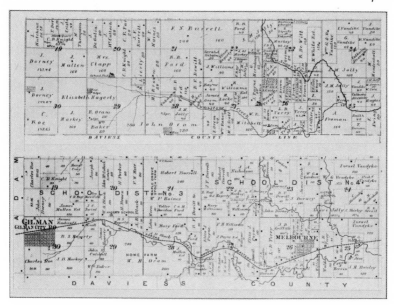

Sugar Creek Township, before and after the coming of the O.K. (for a short time known as the Omaha, Kansas City, and Eastern), and the founding of Gilman City. The township was heavily settled long before the railroad was built, with numerous small farms. The new town was carved out of part of the farm of John Dorney, shown in the southwest corner of the township. The town of Melbourne was for a while a competitor, but the promotion was less successful; some thought Melbourne lots were too highly priced. Tombstone Creek, which the O.K.'s tracks cross six times, was a major obstacle. After leaving Melbourne, the O.K. had to contend with Sugar Creek itself.

provide food and drinks, and with the help of neighboring farm families served the visiting VIPs the best of the region's produce, in an atmosphere of excitement and expectation.

The visitors milled up and down the streets, trampling the young cornstalks, viewing each lot with reference to the new depot. One prospective buyer saw a place for a dry-goods store; another for a lumberyard; others for blacksmith shops, harness shops, a barbershop, a hardware store, and even a hotel. In three hours, at prices averaging $40 per lot, $3,500 worth of lots changed hands, mainly to men who planned to build on them. Others bought as a speculation. Gilman, Fisher, and others reserved choice lots for themselves; their names were still prominent in the weekly lists of real-estate transactions twenty years later. The boom was on. One reporter observed that if the sale had been vigorously advertised, it would have attracted five hundred buyers.

Buildings began to be erected and firms went into operation, in order of the needs of the day.

The first business to open was a lumberyard, the lumber and other materials being hauled by team and wagon from Bethany. A sawmill and a brick kiln were also established, sand for the latter also being hauled. A general store opened to sell groceries, clothes, and miscellaneous notions and sundries. As one general store would not be enough for a community that was certain to grow, a second opened up. Wooden shacks housed a barbershop, a harness shop, a blacksmith shop, a flouring mill, and a livery stable. The community quickly raised $700 to build a depot; the fact that it had no benches in the waiting room caused grumbling, but it served for a time. Westward along the right-of-way were built a coal chute and a water tank for the locomotives and stock pens to serve the region's livestock breeders.

A few weeks later a heavy windstorm blew over most of the shacks, but the owners took the destruction in stride and rebuilt. A town with a new railroad doesn't give up easily.

When the iron horse poked his nose into town on August 10, 1897, he found all of the amenities waiting for him. Everybody turned out to see the first entrance of the Quincy, Omaha, and Kansas City Railway, even then known as the O.K. Ivan Ray, then a small boy, was one of those who rode on that first day. He told me that he and his mother had bought tickets for Trenton, to the east, boarded the train, and were surprised when it continued west. The conductor explained, however, that he had decided to go on to Coffey before turning back to Trenton. So from the outset the O.K. was free and easy with its schedules.

A new telephone line from Bethany, and new telephone and telegraph lines from Trenton, linked the town with the whole civilized world. Trenton and Bethany men founded the Gilman Bank, with a capital of $10,000. Had it been named even a few weeks later, it would certainly have been called the Gilman City Bank. A two-story hotel was started. Men spoke of organizing a baseball team. The *Gilman City Guide* issued its first number in

December. It did so well that for a time a second newspaper was contemplated. And why not? Throughout the settled part of the nation newspapers were popular—Missouri alone had more than a thousand, adding twenty or twenty-five new ones every year. Actually the *Guide* had two or three competitors that in turn opened an office, collected advance subscriptions, and then quickly folded.

The town went after a post office; families had to have a better address than merely Sugar Creek Township and a mailing facility closer than Blue Ridge, which was halfway to the county seat, or even Bancroft, a mile south. Several Republican aspirants competed for President McKinley's signature on a postmaster's commission. A post office was open for business in just a few months, the new postmaster augmenting his income by operating a hennery in the same building.

In the spring a chapter of the Odd Fellows lodge was installed and a school district organized. Retired couples moved to the new town, contracting with Bill Noll or Ben DeWitt to build their dwellings. Talk started about building a railroad spur going north to Blue Ridge and on to Iowa, thus connecting Gilman City with the Burlington system.

Gilman City was located so close to the southern edge of Harrison County that, if the state had been tilted a little, the whole town, railroad and all, would have slid into Daviess County.

Actually both Harrison and Daviess counties were entering a period of remarkable prosperity. Harrison was leading every other county in the state in eggs, butter, poultry, cattle, hogs, sheep, horses, mules, corn, oats, wheat, hay, grass seed, lumber, game, hides, wool, tallow, molasses, cornmeal, ship stuff, and hoop poles. Its leading citizens quoted official figures to support these claims. Daviess, a smaller county, was fully as prosperous. One Daviess County farmer living close to Gilman City had sixty thousand bushels of corn cribbed on his barn lots.

Building in town was well underway when the residents, full of enthusiasm, saw that the upcoming Fourth of July would be a good time for a celebration. Col. William Jennings Bryan, who had lost his first race for the presidency the preceding November, was supposed to be the main speaker, but couldn't make it. The speakers who did appear painted pictures of a bright future, if, in the oratory of the day, everybody put his eye on the future, his shoulder to the wheel, and his nose to the grindstone. Theodore Gilman was present—this time he came not only in his own private car but also over his own tracks—and gave the town a large silk flag, which he personally hoisted from the roof of the new Hotel Gilman. When the Spanish-American War broke out, Gilman's flag would be raised with cheers whenever Admirals Dewey or Hobson reported a naval victory.

Unfortunately, Gilman's own connection with the new railroad barely lasted until Thanksgiving. After his initial success he had wanted to build an independent line from Kansas City to St. Joseph, but Stilwell had opposed the move. The result was that Gilman was ousted as chairman of the executive committee and Stilwell assumed the presidency of the Quincy, Omaha, and Kansas City. Gilman returned to New York and from then on was more involved in banking and finance than in railroading. He interested himself in the problem of panics and depressions and evolved a concept that can fairly be said to have led to the Federal Reserve Bank system. Although he lived to be eighty-nine, dying in 1930, I am morally certain that he never again returned to Gilman City, unless quietly and privately to look after his real estate.

Three years after Gilman's ouster, Stilwell himself was booted out by New York interests. He turned his attention to building a railroad into Mexico, to which he gave the imaginative name of Kansas City, Mexico, and Orient. The residents of the new community in the middle of the thirty-four-mile gap were too busy to worry about changes in the railroad's high command.

Just as an individual has roots, so has a town. The first people to settle in Gilman City moved in from nearby farms and villages. Missouri in the decade of 1890 to 1900 was already well settled; she was in fact the fifth most populous state in the nation. Seventy percent of her American-born residents were native Missourians; another 20 percent were born in Illinois, Kentucky, Ohio, Indiana, and Tennessee. The people of Harrison and Daviess counties had almost exactly the same background. Imagine a taproot growing deep in Missouri soil, with laterals stretching eastward through the states named just above. Smaller roots reached to Virginia, Pennsylvania, and New York.

Those early settlers who moved to Gilman City had come from the land and were proud of it. They thought of their origins as being in counties, not in nearby towns or cities. As their obituaries and family histories proclaimed later, they were born in Grundy County, Missouri; or Adams County, Illinois; or Fayette County, Ohio; or Montgomery County, Indiana; or Bourbon County, Kentucky; or numerous other Missouri or eastern counties. When older settlers passed on, survivors prepared lengthy tributes, which were published in the small town papers. As an obituary contains the details that the family wants most remembered, one set of facts that invariably appeared dealt with origins.

A few examples from the largest families, the Wards, the Weldens, and the Orams, will illustrate.

The Weldens traced their ancestry to Jonathan, born in Pittsylvania County, Virginia, in 1776. This single sentence connects Gilman City with the birth of the republic: Pittsylvania County, its county seat being Chatham, named after William Pitt, Lord Chatham, hero of the Stamp Act repeal. On their way to Gilman City, various Weldens moved through Kentucky, Indiana, and Illinois. The Orams came from Maryland, then westward through Ohio. The Wards traced their origins to Virginia, Tennessee, Ohio, and Illinois. These families became involved in nearly every phase of the community's livelihood: they farmed, raised livestock, went into business, held office. Many of the older ones were present at the creation of the new town.

Among the Missouri-born Gilman Citians was a black girl, who worked in the Dorney and Markey households, later owning her own house and lot; and a black barber. The largest black community, however, was in the county seat, where there were more jobs and a school for the children.

So much for the American-born residents. Where the Gilman City community differed from Missouri generally was in the number and origin of foreign residents. Less than 10 percent of Missouri's residents were foreign born; the corresponding figure for Harrison and Daviess counties was less than 2 percent. Statewide, the foreign-born group consisted of Germans, Irish, English, Swedish, and French, in that order; in the two counties the group consisted of Germans, English, Canadians, Bohemians, and Irish, respectively. The small numbers indicate that immigrants did not penetrate the northern reaches of the state to any great extent. Moreover, there were no mills or factories to recruit foreign-born workers.

Of the relatively few Gilman City families headed by foreign-born parents, the Irish were the most influential. Among them were the Dorneys, already mentioned; the Markeys, perhaps the wealthiest; the Reillys and the Honans, active in banking and other business enterprises. They, with the Dohertys and others, founded St. John's Catholic Church.

At one end of Main Street was Edward Parker, born in Brighton, England, where he had learned the watchmaker's trade. He came to America in 1882, worked in Michigan, Illinois, Kansas, and Nebraska, and settled in Gilman City the year it was founded. At the other end was M. Wetzler—I never knew what the "M" stood for—who owned the Boston Store. He was born in Austria; as a boy he immigrated to New York and learned the dry-goods business; later he moved to Chicago, heard about the new town, and went into the dry goods, gents furnishings, and grocery business. For several years the *Guide* was housed on the upper floor of his building.

Among others in the foreign-born group was a Frenchman—a stonemason who had learned his trade in the old country. South of town was a German farmer, who, when only eight, crossed the ocean in a sailing ship. At the age of thirty he came to Daviess County from Illinois. He died in 1911, at the age of seventy-three. I was then old enough to shake hands with him. So there you have it. The older generation that today crosses the Atlantic in six hours or less, overlaps the generation that crossed the Atlantic in six weeks or more. It also overlaps the generation that moved across the central states to found new towns like Gilman City.

The early settlers were a hard-working lot. They were relatively young; three-fourths were forty or younger. They wanted to build a decent town. When they heard about plans to establish a dance hall, a gambling parlor, and a saloon, they discouraged the promoters. Yet they liked sports, shows, games, and fairs. Almost from the outset the town had four churches, each with a small but loyal congregation. The census enumerator reported no one who could not speak English; fewer than a dozen who could not read and write. He did identify three men, all landlords, who said they could read but not write, which leads to the interesting speculation that they could not write out a bill but could read a check.

Families had come to this part of mid-America chiefly because the soil was fertile and because small streams were plentiful. After farmers and livestock growers came merchants and artisans, and still later bankers, physicians, and other professional people, so that town and countryside residents could find nearly everything they needed in the way of goods and services.

Since the new town was not aggressively publicized, either in America or Europe, early settlers had come from relatively short distances. Even the few who came from overseas pursued about the same kinds of livelihood as those who had come earlier. As a result, the early growth of the town had not been spectacular but it had been persistent. One astute reporter who saw the streets staked out, the arrival of the O.K., and later the construction of residences and business structures, declared that in five years Gilman City would be a town of fifteen hundred or two thousand people. Few on the spot would have doubted him.

Southeast corner of Main and Broadway streets. Gilman City's first two-story building housed Austrian-born M. Wetzler's "Boston Store." On a tree-less prairie, a structure like this was a landmark that could be seen for miles. Built by B. R. Harmon, it was long known as the Harmon Building; the second story was the first home of the *Gilman City Guide*.

2

I Make a Well-Recorded Arrival

Gilman City's first six years were so full of activity that Al Bowen, the *Guide*'s editor, decided the time had arrived to write the town's history. He printed short biographies of the leading citizens in his June 19, 1903, edition.

The census taker had recently counted 447 inhabitants, but in the vocabulary of any small-town weekly that figure rounded out nicely to 500, or, as Bowen stated it, Gilman City would soon be the second largest town in the county. He had solid evidence. He noted that Gilman City, located halfway between Quincy and Kansas City, furnished more traffic for the O.K. than any other station between these points. He knew that the Farmers Telephone Company had started on its second hundred telephones. He could proudly state that twenty new residences and six new brick buildings had been built within a year, adding up to more construction than at anytime in Gilman City's history. And when he heard rumors of a new railroad from Columbia to Trenton, then to Gilman City and on to Bethany, he commented that as Gilman City was halfway between Quincy and Omaha, the O.K. would probably move its machine shops, with its 200 employees, from Milan.

Here was an issue of the *Guide* that townspeople could mail to relatives and friends, thus encouraging new residents. And when the city fathers were able to count as many as 500, Gilman City could move from the status of "village" and become a town, thus passing another milestone. The first 500 would be the hardest, but then the town could really take off.

Among the first businesses were those of several Bancroft merchants who moved buildings and all to the new town. Baptist and Catholic churches were also moved in from the countryside. In those days the hauling of frame structures was commonplace; they were secured to heavy timbers, these in turn to rollers, and the whole pulled by teams. Seeing this fleet of buildings inch across the prairie was an intriguing sight. Occasionally the telephone man was called in to move a line temporarily until the building passed by. I have seen this done a dozen times. At the new location the building was set on a new foundation, the cracked plaster touched up, and other repairs made.

Main Street those early years consisted almost entirely of wooden structures. Those not moved in were erected with incredible speed; a few days was sufficient. In later years Ben DeWitt was to build an eleven-room country home in sixteen days. Of course there were no complications with wiring, plumbing, or built-ins. A business establishment needed only counters and shelving. As the years passed, empty lots were filled with brick structures. Whenever fire took out a wood building, it was usually replaced with brick.

After two or three years, local families that had lived in Sugar Creek and adjoining townships many years, began to buy the established firms and start new ones. The Gilman Bank, originally established by Trenton and Bethany capital, was taken over by the Reillys, Markeys, and others. They had the available capital and their knowledge of farm and livestock financing seemed appropriate for managing deposits and loans. Ira Oliphant, who had been born in Indiana and moved west with his parents, went from a farm into real estate and insurance. The Boston Store and the Gilman Mercantile Company were training grounds for young men who first worked there, then went into business for themselves. In short, news items reflected many changes, as people traded farms for a business interest or half-interest, bought into or bought out partnerships, and moved from one line of work to another. For example, Bill Haines came from the farm, opened a drugstore, sold it, went into the furniture business, and still later secured a license as embalmer. Any given store might sell unusual combinations of merchandise; a drugstore might stock drugs and toilet articles, but also might have wallpaper and even carpets. The owner of a hardware store might sell out and buy a grocery store, no doubt reasoning that if he could sell Moon buggies and Great Western Endless Apron Manure Spreaders he could sell anything. Men with funds bought businesses and had others operate them. At various times Bill Noll, contractor and builder, owned a meat market, a hotel, and a hardware store.

Another circumstance that encouraged change and variety

was the ease of admission into what are now tightly regulated professions. One did not need a credential to sell drugs; in fact, the *Guide* occasionally published an ad by a registered pharmacist listing the advantages of having prescriptions filled by him instead of by the unregistered dealer down the street. One of our physicians had worked for a while in a doctor's office and, after a short course in a medical school, had hung out his own shingle.

Going into business was relatively so simple—a roof overhead, counters, shelves, and a minimum of special equipment—that anyone with enterprise and a little capital could do it. No one seemed to bother with market surveys—if he felt the urge, he went ahead. At one point Gilman City had two drugstores, and then the Williams drugstore moved in from Blue Ridge. Eventually only two survived—one of them being the newcomer. In the next six years, two-thirds of the business firms were either abandoned or changed hands.

A different kind of restlessness was shown in a general shifting of the population. Some residents moved on, attracted by still other new towns farther west and by the prospect of picking up cheap land in the well-advertised government lotteries. This movement accelerated as the years went on. Americans were on the move. Instead of paying $25 an acre for land in Sugar Creek Township, the enterprising might acquire a quarter section of raw land out west for $1.50 an acre. The O.K. offered special one-way tickets—$20 or less—for colonists and settlers. Of course, many drew a blank in the lotteries, or a title to what one described as "sandpile number 9," but others were more fortunate. Occasionally the *Guide* printed an enthusiastic letter from a former resident who liked his new home. Gilman City lost a promising real-estate dealer to "Muscoge," in Indian Territory, later Muskogee, Oklahoma; a bright young lawyer to Riverton, Wyoming.

Editor Bowen saw that a way to hold old residents and attract new ones was to encourage new industry, suggesting such enterprises as an ax-handle factory, a cheesemaking establishment, a creamery, and a harness factory. Strangers had come to town, he reported, making inquiries, but had left without taking action. The *Guide* itself was doing a fine business. Every issue carried one or more half-page or quarter-page ads plus smaller ads. Often 75 or 80 percent of the paper would be filled with advertising, a proportion that would make most weekly publishers radiant. But Bowen himself began to get restless.

That historical issue of the *Guide* and other kinds of information reached the Reid family, twenty miles to the south. The Reids, like many of their neighbors, had come to Daviess County by way of Virginia, Tennessee, and Kentucky. As one of the boys, Dudley, had been crippled in early life, he could not pursue the family career of farming. He turned to books, developed an interest in writing, and became a reporter for the *Gallatin Democrat*. Friends encouraged him to buy the *Winston Sentinel*, ten miles away, so he became an editor and publisher on his own.

Gradually he became competent in not only the editorial but also the mechanical aspects of newspaper publication. When he was thirty-two, he married a Daviess County farm girl, Josephine Tarwater. As both the *Democrat* and the *Sentinel* had regularly exchanged issues with the *Guide*, he had been able to follow the growth of Gilman City. Moreover, he knew Bowen, as both had learned their trade at the *Democrat*. When, in November 1904, Bowen offered to sell the *Guide*, he found Dudley Reid to be a responsive listener. Here was a chance to get in on the ground floor of a larger newspaper in the new town. After a buggy ride to Gilman City to view the plant, he signed a contract and became the *Guide*'s publisher. Later he and a relative drove two farm wagons, loaded with the new couple's possessions, across open prairie and over dusty trails to the seven-year-old town.

For a while he lived at the Gilman Hotel, which later he described as a frame building having a lobby with a few cane-bottomed chairs downstairs and six or seven rooms upstairs, but before long he found a house to rent at five dollars a month. Josephine joined her husband at Gilman City, resumed her career as housewife, and began to learn the editorial and mechanical side of newspapering.

That sets the stage for my arrival.

One of the nice things about being born is that for a time you are at the absolute center of the universe—a small universe, perhaps, but the center. Before the event, a few people look forward to it with mounting excitement; at the moment itself the best available brains are at your disposal; and even for a while afterward your needs and wishes are commands that must be obeyed. Your sovereignty is wiped out when the next baby comes along, but while it lasts, it is glorious.

At an unrecorded moment in February 1905, Mother must have felt me stirring around inside and realized that I was actually on the way and would make a personal appearance on this planet late in the summer. I do not know what Father said when she confided in him, but I suspect he said "God Almighty" in sheer awe. Father's vocabulary completely encompassed such an expression, and more when necessary, and this situation was one he had not faced previously. No father ever fully understands his connection with the birth of his child, regardless of what the books say. If he builds a bookcase, he understands *that*—the measuring, the sawing, the fitting, the nailing, the varnishing—but never his share in the creation of a baby. Too much happens with too little effort on his part.

Mother always thought I should have arrived in mid-August, but first babies are notoriously late, and actually I chose to arrive on August 26 (a Saturday), the weekend of the annual Gilman City picnic. Fully five thousand people came to town to greet my arrival and to attend the picnic while they were waiting. At the intersection of Main and Broadway the heart of the picnic featured the merry-go-round and its calliope, the crack of rifle shots at the shooting gallery, the cries of merchants vending hot dogs and fluff candy, and the yells and shouts of five thousand people enjoying themselves. Hundreds of teams were hitched at the available posts and racks. Special trains unloaded visitors at the depot two blocks away. The streets were six inches deep in dust in some places, and three inches in all the places, and the weather was hot and sultry. In short, it was August.

For her physician, Mother had selected Dr. J. C. Swint, genial, likeable, experienced; black haired, black eyed, black mustached; the official physician for the O.K.; so competent that a dozen years later he moved his practice to St. Joseph, for us the medical center of the world. Anything that Dr. Swint didn't know about delivering babies hadn't been discovered yet. On hand for further assistance was Mrs. Bill Noll, who lived a couple of blocks west. She had been the first to call when the Reids set up housekeeping and was as close to being a godmother as I ever had. She was the queen of Gilman City society. I remember her well as largish, ever smiling, slow speaking.

Mother, then twenty-three, was a hazel-eyed, even-tempered, athletically built beauty. She looked more like sixteen than twenty-three. Her hair was so dark brown that it seemed glossy black and so long that, when she combed it out, she could sit on it. She had more energy than most women, and more patience even than energy. The Lord had been so pleased with his handiwork that when He created her He did not immediately break the mold but struck off three younger sisters: Frances, Sarah, and Grace. The four of them together could create more excitement than you could find at a county fair. They were full of fun and hardworking; they envied nobody, were intensely loyal, and utterly devoted to each other and to their families.

Father, ten years older, was also young looking. Ordinarily he was a man of poise and enterprise but when his family's welfare was concerned he simply came apart and could do little more than fret. In his own account of the birth of his firstborn he appears as one who had assumed considerable responsibility for the event, but I suspect that Dr. Swint and Mrs. Noll dispatched him to the kitchen to boil water so he would be out of the way. Whatever Father did, he did thoroughly; so I am sure he built a fire in the cookstove hot enough to barbecue a hog and boiled enough water in the teakettle, the big dishpan, and the clothes boiler to scald it. What with his own internal temperature, he would never have felt the 90-degree heat outside, or the extra ten or fifteen humid degrees that he generated in the kitchen.

As I have seen three of my own babies born, I can well imagine what was going on that morning in the tiny, southeast bedroom, adjoining the kitchen. Mother's strong, tight-muscled body did not yield easily to the demands of the struggling creature that was about to abandon its aquatic existence and become an air breather. Mainly it was a matter of white-knuckled endurance. Later she told me, "You gave me a hard time, son; I almost didn't get you here." The steam calliope and the rifle shots and the yells and shouts up the street were no comfort. Eventually, eventually I did arrive and was discovered to be a boy.

Mother, utterly exhausted, took little interest in the events that happened immediately afterward. Dr. Swint cleansed his instruments, stowed them in his black bag, and departed, satisfied that both his patients were doing well. Later he sent a bill for $10, and as the physician who delivered my brother, Don, three years later, charged only $15, Father could say that we were two for twenty-five. Dr. Swint had weighed me in at 8¼ pounds, so the charge was only a little more than a dollar a pound—entirely reasonable, I think.

At this point Mrs. Noll took charge, saw that I was mopped and scoured, and wrapped in some of the nice linens that Mother had accumulated. Considering my early involvement with a newspaper office, I have often reflected that a copy of the *Kansas City Star* or the *St. Joseph News-Press* would have been more appropriate. Years afterwards, when I reached the proud and sensitive age of ten, Mrs. Noll could embarrass me utterly by observing that she had often changed my didies. Right now her task was to get me prettied up and displayed to Father. "Lord, God Almighty," he whispered—I suppose. He then banked his fires and threw out all that hot water.

After an interval, Mother was given a chance to inspect her baby. My front side had everything desirable, but when she flopped me over to view my backside, she saw that I had a bright red spot the size of a quarter on my haunch. Mrs. Noll said it looked like a radish, but Mother declared, "No, it's a strawberry."

Mrs. Noll asked, "Why do you call it a strawberry?"

"Because," Mother said, "I have had such a yearning for strawberries all summer and couldn't get near enough." You couldn't give a better explanation.

Following the practice of generations, Mother's mother soon arrived, as it was well known that fathers were incapable of doing anything for themselves when a new baby came.

Grandmother Tarwater was not quite fifty when she made this memorable trip to Gilman City. She had married at the age of twenty-one and in the next twenty years had given birth to eleven babies, losing the first two. She was short, stout, firm, resourceful, with perpetually enduring features. Once when she was in her sixties I said to her, "My, Grandmother, you certainly look well," and she replied, "Oh, son, that's my indestructible Dutch face."

For that matter, Grandmother herself was indestructible, indomitable, indeflectible. Sometimes when I feel myself persistently and stubbornly keeping at a frustrating task, I think the reason is a subtle inheritance from my Dutch grandmother. She was staunch, firm, and, to me, a little forbidding. When she said, "Son, will you go to the barnyard and bring me a bushel of kindling," I was not likely to reply, "Yes, Grandmother, as soon as I finish reading this chapter." I was more likely to say, "Yes'm," and get a basketful promptly, and a heaping basketful at that.

In her own home, Grandmother was one of the first up and the last to bed. She knew the arts of quantity cooking, butchering, and lye soap and lye hominy making; and, in an earlier day, of making candles and of fireplace baking and grilling. Out of her hog-rendering days she salvaged an expression to be used when praising someone for doing a job well: "You got a good scald on it."

Grandmother had had, of course, vast experience with doctors and newborn babies. Both she and Mother lived in the era when *pregnant* was not one of the polite words. A woman was "going to have a baby" or "was in a family way." When her condition became obvious, she was not supposed to appear in public. Although the birth of a farm animal was a commonplace sight, children were told little about the human reproductive process. Grandmother's physician, Dr. W. M. Givens of Gallatin, had a standing proposal to deliver free of charge the tenth baby in any family. Eventually Grandmother's number ten came along, and when she felt the hour was due, she asked her oldest son, Grover, to get the doctor. As Grover did not know about the financial arrangement and probably was not told exactly why he was being sent, Dr. Givens assumed that a child was ill and since he was not free to come himself, he sent another doctor. Grandfather had to pay for the tenth baby after all.

Mother's role in the drama that day was to mount Silver Dick and go after Grandfather, seven miles away on a neighbor's farm. Silver Dick, incidentally, had been in the stable for days—the children could not understand why. When Grandfather arrived, he stood in the doorway of the bedroom, surveyed the scene, and said, "You in trouble again, old girl?" Grandmother often repeated that remark, treasuring it as unusually solicitous. As Grandfather was one of sixteen children, he knew about large and growing families.

Now Grandmother had come to inspect the firstborn of her oldest surviving child. As she held the newcomer, she must have had fleeting thoughts of anxiety and apprehension, wondering whether or not this infant would be one of those that would pull through. She had lost her first baby, a girl, at childbirth. The second, also a girl, survived the hazards of the first summer and was nearly two when the third, my mother, came along. When Mother was four months old, however, the second little girl died; so Grandmother, like thousands of other pioneer women, knew what it was to hold one child in her arms while friends and neighbors buried another. Even so, she reared Mother and her remaining brothers and sisters to full maturity.

This day, however, was one for celebration. When the sun had risen that morning, she was the mother of nine; when the sun set, she was, for the first time, a grandmother. She was entirely delighted with her first grandchild. She noted that he had been born on a Saturday: "Friday's child is loving and giving; Saturday's child must work hard for a living." She was, of course, distressed by the strawberry. "You should have told us, Biddy," she admonished Mother. "We've had lots of strawberries. Now you've gone and marked your baby."

The belief was universal that an expectant mother could mark her baby, and not only in a physical but in a mental way. If, for example, a mother daydreamed about travel when the baby was on the way, she had only herself to blame if the baby grew up to be a wandering son and eventually fled from home. The possibilities for remorse were simply endless.

Occasionally I see somebody with a strawberry on his face and am the slightest degree grateful that mine got stashed away on my backside, out of public view. I am also the slightest degree grateful that my young mother hungered for strawberries and not watermelon. As I grew, the strawberry did also, but faded with the years and finally ended up the size of a man's palm, no longer red but tan. At school when showering in the gym, the other boys occasionally expressed curiosity about it, so in due course I developed a standard answer: "Oh, my mother was ironing my pants one day when I was in them, and the iron got too hot." That response stifled further inquiry.

At every birth, there is invariably a missing grandmother—the father's mother, since the young mother especially wants the companionship and support of her own mother. The father's mother seldom gets in on the beginnings of a baby's arrival. After a time, however, and after the household on Third and Broadway had settled down a bit, Grandmother Reid arrived for her own inspection.

Though I was to know my Tarwater grandparents twenty years or so, I never really knew my Reid grandparents, who were fifteen or twenty years older. Like many of their neighbors, they had Kentucky and Tennessee origins. My Grandfather Reid had died before I was born, and Grandmother Reid a few years afterwards. Grandmother Reid, who had her own quilting frame, made each of her children and grandchildren a quilt. We still have the one she made for me: scores of small pieces of gingham, in red, white, and blue triangles, sewed with hundreds of tiny stitches. It is the single, tangible, personal tie I have with my father's forebears.

Like many of the older women of her day, Grandmother Reid smoked a pipe. She had learned back in Kentucky by filling a pipe for her mother, selecting a red-hot coal from the fireplace, giving the pipe a few good, starting puffs, and then handing it over. At the end of the day's work, among close friends or family, Grandmother packed her long-stemmed, clay pipe with long-green twist, nimbly fingered a coal from the fire, lit up and puffed away. I think of her when I see the ad, "You've come a long way, baby," featuring a pretty socialite with a pencil-thin cigarette. Grandmother could have shown her a thing or two. Father sneaked a puff from her pipe once and said it was as powerful as the kick of a mule.

They named me Loren Dudley; partly in honor of my father; partly in honor of a family friend; partly, as Father once said, in honor of the human race. Mother acceded to the Loren because she wanted a name that could not be easily nicknamed. She thought a nickname was an affront to human dignity. She had been named Josephine but everybody called her "Biddy." One brother, James Carlisle, was "Duck" all his life; another, Thomas Thurman, was "Shack." Father's family had fared little better, with "Mit" for Mildred, "Clem" for Clement, "Lon" for Alonzo, and "Brick" for Ransom. Gilman City had a "Stub," a "Shad," a "Slick," a "Bony," a "Foxy," a "Curly," a "Fuzzy," a "Banty." I grew up never having had a nickname, or at least not a persistent one, and always felt a little deprived. My brother started life as Donald; if anybody had called him "Don," Mother would have removed that person's head. When he reached high school and his classmates started calling him "Don," Mother, to my surprise, then made no objection. She explained to me privately that "Don" was a better name for a grown boy than "Donald," and, besides, it wasn't really a nickname.

The morning after my birth, the dust of the annual Gilman City picnic had begun to settle. Most of the teams were gone and the last of the O.K. specials had pulled out. The merry-go-round and the numerous stands had been dismantled. By nightfall most of the five thousand visitors had departed. Father had the day to rest before climbing the stairs of the Wetzler building to begin the next issue of the *Guide*.

Father's first public duty was, of course, to write two or three columns about the picnic, but his second was to telephone editors of newspapers in nearby towns and tell them about my arrival— this in a day when the telephone was used sparingly. Northwest Missouri was full of small, country weeklies whose editors were a friendly, close-knit lot. A fair amount of each editor's issue was clipped from neighboring papers. So the next issue of the *Guide*, the *Gallatin Democrat*, the *Gallatin North Missourian*, and the *Winston Sentinel* carried a front-page announcement of my birth. The following week their items were clipped far and wide and printed in more distant papers, so that the news was passed along to twenty or thirty other communities.

Some weeks later Father went to the typecases and printed a big batch of checks in red ink, with his picture in one corner and mine in another, captioned "Senior" and "Junior." The check also proclaimed that the *Guide* had one thousand appreciative readers and was hand in hand with the newest and best of everyday. So each of its creditors—the paper house who supplied paper, the drayman who handled it, the agent who insured it—could view our portraits before he cashed the check. Others who have had their portraits on negotiable paper are Washington, Hamilton, Jackson, and Lincoln—not a bad crowd to travel in.

As I said, one of the nice things about being born is that for a while you are at the center of the universe, and if you are an editor's son, the universe is pushed out a little in every direction.

3

The Great Moral
and Religious Weekly

The Indian philosopher Tagore has written about children as movingly as anybody: "Every child comes with the message that God is not yet discouraged of man." I am sure Tagore was thinking of me as well as of all those others. I sincerely believe, of course, that babies are created in Heaven and are transported by God's angels direct to the loving arms of parents. Still, a kind word needs to be said now and then about parents, who cheerfully accept these bundles of perfection and try to do something with them. In short, fathers and mothers deserve equal time.

Father had been born in 1872 in neighboring Daviess County. At seven he had been stricken with tuberculosis of the hip and had undergone such drastic treatment, combining powerful drugs and tight bandages, that although his strong, little-boy system overcame the massive infection, he was left with a shortened left leg. Though he walked with a limp, he was so active mentally and physically that I never thought of him as crippled.

Like any amateur genealogist, I located the family in the census records of 1880, and, in the handwriting of the census taker, were the names of my Reid grandparents followed by the names of each of their six children. Even in that day the Census Bureau wanted to know not only how many bodies there were in the country but also what shape they were in, so opposite the names were columns, to be used as needed, with headings such as "Idiot," "Deaf and Dumb," "Blind," "Insane," and, finally, "Maimed, Crippled, Bedridden, or Otherwise Disabled." Opposite Father's name, in the last column, was a check mark. The bureau did not give Father much of a start in life.

As Father has told his own story in his *Ups and Downs*, I will not repeat it. He hobbled to school a few months of every year. His father and mother did not know what to do with him, since, obviously, he could not make a living at the arduous business of farming. They bought him a violin, thinking he might make a few dollars fiddling at country dances, but he had little ear for music. After hearing his squawks and squeaks they agreed that his career as a musician had to be abandoned.

Even so, Father did an astonishing amount of physical work. He dug postholes for fences, grubbed buck brush, hoed acres of corn, shocked wheat and oats, and hauled enough manure, he claimed later, to cover Daviess County to a depth of six inches. Whenever I complained about my long hours in the printing office, he described his own sunup-to-sundown hoeing in the potato field for half a dollar. Alas, I never thought to ask him what his father told him when he complained; probably sunup-to-sundown grubbing of stumps, trying to snatch a few acres of tillable land from the forest, for half of half a dollar.

Then came the miracle; Father learned to enjoy solid reading. His oldest brother, Lon, took chunks of his own small wages to buy Father copies of Emerson, Carlyle, Shakespeare, Ingersoll, and Dante, seasoned with *Gulliver's Travels* and *The Arabian Nights*. He had a copy of *Plutarch's Lives* that a local bookbinder had wrongly titled "The Life of Plutarch." Emerson taught him self-reliance, and Carlyle reminded him that man's lot at best was toil and suffering, and that the way to achieve happiness was to cleanse oneself of excessive desires. Father also saturated himself with the current conflict between Darwinism and religion.

An older friend persuaded him to attend Grand River College in Gallatin. He traded a buggy to the college authorities as part payment on a year's schooling; later he surrendered the horse and borrowed the rest. College did for him what it should do for anybody; it expanded his horizon, stimulated his imagination, and, on the practical side, built a foundation for a variety of possible careers.

Later, Father got an appointment as an engrossing clerk at the General Assembly in Jefferson City. Engrossing clerks made copies of bills as they were introduced and amended. After the bill had passed both houses, the job of making a flawless copy, without misspellings, mis-strokes, or erasures, to be signed by the officers of the House and the Senate and the governor and to become the law of the land, was given to a higher order of civil servants: the enrolling clerks. An enrolling clerk needed to be not only a better penman than an engrossing clerk, but must have capacity for taking pains. If he copied 3,900 words of a 4,000-word bill and then made a slip of the pen, he would have to redo the whole thing. Often a man would get so nervous, Father wrote, that he wouldn't even be able to lift a spittoon.

Since at that session the enrolling section fell behind in its work, a few of the promising engrossing clerks, including Father, were added to the staff. So, somewhere in the state archives, are bills passed by the assembly, signed by Governor Dockery, and enrolled in Father's neat handwriting. Years later I could observe that his signature, with fancy initial letters, on a check, made out to his son, was a glorious thing.

During his spare time, Father continued to write articles on political and literary topics for the *Gallatin Democrat*, and then moved on to publish the *Winston Sentinel*, and, after that, the *Guide*.

Mother, too, like Father, was crippled. When she was a small girl, she got stuck in the knee with a needle. Infection set in, scar tissue formed, and, as a result, one leg remained shorter than the other, when she grew up. Yet she was active; she plowed and cultivated, cared for farm animals, and could ride a horse better than the Prince of Wales, who was always getting into the world press because of his tumbles.

Mother had had a few scattered months of elementary schooling, but not enough in any one year—she told me many times— to be around for the teacher's Christmas treats. As she enjoyed music, especially piano, she spent two years at Grand River College plus a term at Stephens College; then she returned to the family homestead, and traveled around the countryside giving lessons, sometimes wearing a riding skirt so she could ride "Old Moll" side-saddle, occasionally going in a buggy. She met Father at a neighbor's. He could not get her out of his mind, so after reflection he wrote, in his best enrolling-clerk's penmanship, a fifteen-page letter, the gist of which was, "May I call on you?" and she answered in one page, the gist of which was "Yes." My Aunt Grace recalls going with Mother to Gallatin to get a dress fitted. Mother, too shy to reveal her wedding plans right away, said that she was going to Indian Territory to teach Indians, which seemed to be an entirely believable reason for getting a new dress.

Eventually Father found himself getting a license and arranging with the Reverend Mr. P. P. Doak to be married. At the appointed time the bride and groom drove into the Doak front yard and indicated they would like to be married while sitting in the buggy. Although this procedure was unusual, the Reverend Mr. Doak saw no theological objection, so he read the ceremony, with Mrs. Doak standing by as a witness. Her memory of the event was that she had spent the previous day cleaning house, and the couple had never come inside.

When Father became a newspaper publisher, Mother was too active and too curious to watch from the sidelines and soon learned the various editorial and mechanical arts and crafts that are involved in the publication of a weekly paper. Before long she found herself spending the time between breakfast and supper gathering and writing news and helping with the typesetting and printing.

So it happened that a newspaper office became, for me, an extension of home. The *Guide* may not have been my crib but it was my first playpen, since Mother brought me to the office whenever she came. At first I was stashed in a white pine box that had been used to ship a piano and was given scraps of colored paper to play with. Gradually I was allowed out on probation, which resulted in my spilling a few cases of type, but I learned to coexist in an alluring world of scrap boxes, inky buckets, piles of newspaper, and ad copy lying around on tops of desks.

A family legend is that Mother frequently had to swab down this dusty, grimy, inky creature to see what she really had, a blond or brunet.

After a few months Father sold the *Guide* and bought the *Nodaway Forum* at Maryville, a county-seat town a hundred miles northwest, where Don joined the family. Don's arrival ended my exclusive three-year role of only child, a usurpation I coped with in different ways. For example, one day I masterminded his complete and utter disappearance. Mother searched everywhere, becoming steadily more alarmed, meanwhile paying little attention to me quietly sitting in the front room atop an overturned washtub. After searching upstairs and down, she thought of looking under the tub, and there was her baby, unperturbed by it all, smiling as happily as if he thought he had received special recognition.

In the years of our growing up we got along splendidly, except for the normal amount of brotherly fighting—that is, to say, ten or twelve times a week.

Father's next move was back to Harrison County as proprietor of the *Bethany Democrat*. By that time I was six and was so curious about printing skills that I was given my own type and provided with a composing stick, composing rule, and other tools used by hand compositors. Father had always printed in his newspapers items that he wanted to preserve for all time; we called these back issues, bound in yearly volumes, "the files." In "the files," therefore, were not only selected bits of political wisdom and factual material that he might need for future reference but also notes about his own family. So, according to the files, at Bethany I had two cases of type, knew the names and location of 150 other cases of type in the office, and quite a bit about machinery and presses. I quote this information shamelessly, partly because I did not write it and partly because it deals with a kid I have long since forgotten, who also ran a typewriter and carried on "a prolific correspondence with his numerous uncles and aunts and his grandparents." "The other day," one article concluded, "he set up a stick or two of type on the Junior Linotype." Linotypes still exist by the hundreds, but the Junior Linotype was such a curious antique of a machine, bearing little resemblance to a regular Linotype, and had such a short existence, that if other people are still alive who have operated one they would probably be ninety or a hundred years old.

I became skillful in the art of hand composition, which involves selecting a letter at a time from a case, putting it into a holder called a "stick," and eventually transferring the newly assembled lines to a chase in which they can be locked and printed from. The case is a shallow drawer, subdivided into about ninety compartments, each compartment holding a supply of a single character. A hand compositor therefore needed to know where each of ninety different small letters, capital letters, figures, special characters, and spaces are stored, and handle each with dexterity. Typesetting is an ancient art; what I learned to do in the back office of the *Democrat* was exactly what Ben Franklin had done at Philadelphia, what Mark Twain had done at Hannibal, and what generations of hand compositors had done for centuries.

The result of having my own equipment was that I regularly

Here is a little horse
   Her name is Frank
Donald this is Loren   œ
From Donald Jennings   &
Zero   Quack

This is our Donkey
Our Donkey wants to eat &
We did have some horses
   Balloon.,

At the age of six I blackmailed Father and Mother into giving me four cases of type, promising not to bother the rest of the equipment. Here is the start of a *Graded Series in Reading—Part One.* The spelling is better than the punctuation.

set lines of type, locked them in a small chase, printed copies on the proof press, and showed them to the printers and to my parents. Father preserved several of these creations, samples of which are shown on the preceding page. Thus the accident of environment taught me effortlessly to read and write. I also prowled through the magazines and newspapers that came to the office and absorbed what I could. I wrote letters to aunts and uncles, which, in their boundless affection, they took the trouble to answer.

My development in the spoken word, however, was retarded, especially for a future professor of rhetoric and public speaking. After visiting the nation's capital I demanded of my Aunt Grace, "Is Washington, Dee Tee, a town, a titty, or a tate?" This philosophic inquiry came at the age of six, when boys should have acquired most, if not all, of their speech sounds. On another occasion, reflecting Father's reading to me, I asked this favorite aunt, "Whence did I come, and whizzer am I going?"

California Job Case, $0 90
Most popular of all Job Cases. Note the large cap boxes.
Used exclusively in all our type cabinets
unless otherwise ordered.

A typecase is an ingeniously designed tray in which are put all the different letters, figures, and spacing materials necessary for hand composition. The *e* compartment is the largest because the English language uses more *e*'s than any other letter. Hamilton was a famous maker of newspaper equipment.

When I was seven we moved from Bethany back to Gilman City, the furniture and household goods following in a couple of wagons. Once more Father resumed publication of the *Guide*. Of the four Missouri papers that he eventually owned, he had the greatest affection for the Gilman City weekly. He called it "The Great Moral Rejuvenator," or "The Great Religious Weekly," or, when he was entirely relaxed, "The Great Moral and Religious Weekly." Its columns reported the doings and happenings of the community, plus Father's editorials on a variety of political, social, and literary topics.

The editorial attainments of the Great Moral and Religious Weekly considerably outclassed its mechanical and typographical equipment, where my interests centered, at least at first. The office had sixty, no seventy, cases of assorted type, bearing such names as DeVinne, Cheltenham, Century, Jenson, which were standard for the day, and also Paragon and Chamfer, which any typographer would spot as ancient. Most of these had been in the office since the founding of the paper. Type sizes run from 6, 8, and 10 point—the small sizes used for printing the news—to 36, 48, or 72 point and larger—the sizes used for ads or headlines. A 72-point face is an inch high and might be used for a headline stretching across the top of a front page. To say of an apprentice "He doesn't even know the point system" is to label him as hopelessly backward.

What we lacked were fonts—a font being a set of sizes in one style. We had, for example, 12 and 18 point DeVinne, but no larger sizes; 24 and 36 point Century Bold, but no other sizes, and no Century Italic; we had an odd-sized 30 point Gothic, called a bastard size, a word that Mother hated to utter, but no more Gothic; we had 18 point Old English for wedding invitations or death announcements, but only 12 point to go along with it; we had a splash of 84 and 96 point wood type, also called "7-line" and "8-line" and now collector's items, for screaming announcements like PUBLIC SALE! Most country newspapers, however, were in the same fix. Besides, the fashion in typography was to use different styles in each ad, which today would be like painting a house in several different colors.

Typefaces fascinated me and still do. I take note when a motion picture shows a closeup of a supposedly nineteenth-century newspaper, set in type that was not to be designed for another fifty years. In books I look for the bit that says, "This book was set in Press Roman," or "Waverly," or whatever. As a kid I used to sprawl on the floor with the huge American Type Founders catalog, or the famous blue book of Barnhart Brothers and Spindler, and compose lists of types, rules, borders, and ornaments that we ought to buy for our own shop. What dreams they were! Oh, Barnhart Brothers . . . and oh, Spindler! . . . merrily singing their own song page after page in hundreds of different fonts . . . Old English, Gothic, condensed, bold, italic, 6 point to 96 point . . . finest lead with a touch of copper alloy, highest standard of precision, orders filled same day received, satisfaction guaranteed . . . we will take your old metal in trade . . . don't ask for terms, just write and tell us what you can do.

I could imagine the Barnhart Brothers opening their mail one day and coming across my order. Well, here's a nice letter from Loren Reid, managing editor of the *Gilman City Guide*, listing just pages of stuff . . . wants to take ten years to pay for it. Fine, fine! Spindler, take this well-selected, handsome order and get going on it! Ship it how? By the Quincy, Omaha, and Kansas City Railway, of course—how else?

Well, American Type Founders and Barnhart got little business from us, but we often made a deal with the Dr. Miles pharmaceutical house. This enterprising firm, makers of splendid laxatives, cathartics, and kidney pills, and today of Alka-Seltzer, latched on to the idea that it could advertise widely in the country press, paying for its ads in new type instead of cash. The Miles Company operated its own print shop, equipped with a Monotype, a machine that cast individual type characters instead of whole lines-of-type. Monotype composition was seldom used by newspapers but was often used by high-grade book publishers. The company launched a trade deal advertising program, bartering the type that it manufactured, presumably during slack hours, for advertising space in country weeklies.

Periodically Dr. Miles sent us a list of typefaces, with the offer that if we ran a one-column, four-inch ad each week, we could select, by way of payment, a supply of new type from the sizes and styles offered. As we invariably had extra space, we were eminently ready to deal. The *Guide*'s readers thus had the opportunity to read ads for Dr. Miles's Nervine or Anti-Pain Pills with headings such as "I Suffered Years With My Back," "How Can I Stop These Womanly Pains," and even "I Had Been Given Up to Die by Three Doctors." In turn we got fresh supplies of printing equipment from the maker of these potent remedies. It was fun to open a box of brand-new, gleaming type and distribute it in the cases.

The Great Moral and Religious Weekly also had worktables surfaced with smooth marble tops, called "stones"; a Country Campbell printing press that printed four pages at one swoop, a stage ahead of Ben Franklin's lever-operated press; two job presses for envelopes, sale bills, and such; a paper cutter that would slice through five hundred sheets or more with one mighty heave of a long lever. We carried a fair inventory of various kinds and colors of paper and sizes of envelopes, including paper already ruled for those who corresponded in longhand. In the northeast corner was a pile of newsprint about four feet high, each sheet being as big as four newspaper pages.

The office was heated with a single stove. We stored our coal on the alley side of the building, outside; nobody ever seemed to poach our supply. We had a gas mantle light, suspended from the ceiling, that could be raised and lowered by a pulley. For other work areas we had coal-oil lamps. We had a five-gallon can of gasoline on the premises, and a one-quart brass dispensing can. To get ink off hands, we simply doused a rag with gasoline and rubbed the inky spots. This procedure was believed to cause warts, but warts were a manly thing. We had no running water nor plumbing, but within half a block were two or three privies. Short cuts also existed but these I hesitate to mention.

Father's tools consisted of a battered hammer, a couple of screwdrivers (one without much of a handle), a loose-jointed pair of pliers, a couple of wrenches that never seemed to fit any nut in the establishment, a huge monkey wrench, a saw, and a few other odds and ends. Don and I also liked to do fixing, for which we used Father's tools, and, for a reason which all young people will understand, we almost never returned to the tool box. So the moment came when Father needed the hammer, and it would not be in its proper place, whereupon Don and I were summoned and asked to produce it. Of course by then we had no idea where it was. Don was not only slow in a crisis like this, but seemingly blind as well; and my own reaction was just to trail him deliberately around and around the office, doing time until Father found it himself. Kids have their special methods of survival, so whenever Father demanded that we locate a tool, we merely followed our predetermined, reflex patterns.

In my own home I did things differently since each generation, of course, overreacts to the shortcomings of its predecessor. My kids came along with their skates and tricycles and bicycles, borrowed my tools and failed to return them. "A place for everything and everything in its place" was outworn dogma. When I missed something, I raised the usual rumpus but eventually went to the dime store and bought another. So as my children grew to splendid maturity I managed to keep a hammer, a screwdriver, and a pair of pliers ahead of them. One by one the children left home; one by one the missing tools were retrieved; and today I have half a dozen of everything.

Often when I was alone in the shop, customers would enter and ask for the proprietor. I learned to inquire into their needs and try to help. Maybe they wanted a bundle of old papers with which to line shelves; these I could assemble and tie up, collecting a nickel for the transaction. Or maybe they wanted to sell us a bundle of old rags, to be used for wiping presses; I would gravely inspect their merchandise, select the soft cottons and throw out the hard, stiff denims, and make a cash offer of ten cents; if they agreed, I completed the transaction on the spot. Maybe they wanted 24 x 36-inch colored poster stock cut up into 9 x 12 chunks; I would count the proper number of the big sheets, take them with a yardstick to the paper cutter, adjust the gauges, tighten the clamps, pull down the great lever that I could just reach, trim the edges, and hand them the lot. My friends thought this interesting, but in turn I envied my chum, Shorty McClelland, whose father ran the poultry establishment; he could simultaneously pick up four eggs in each hand, shift them dexterously in front of the candling light, sort out those too far gone even to ship to Trenton, and reach for eight more. We all do what we can with such talents as we possess.

I studied the art and craft of printing from two masters. Ed W. Clark was one of the finest printers that ever graced a country office. He could design a fancy letterhead with rules and borders and ornaments or, with equal artistry, one that was simple and chaste. He loved jobs that involved two or three colors. Such a job would have to be run through the press once to print the blue part; then once more for the red part; and if there were also a black part, a third run. Distances and margins had to be measured accurately, so that, for example, a slogan in blue that was to appear inside a box ruled in red must be so spaced that the slogan was exactly centered.

Ed's masterpiece was the high-school annual, *The Purple and Gold*, which not only had two-color pages and careful presswork with the pictures of the seniors, but a purple cover printed in yellow letters, the yellow being dusted with gold dust while the print was still fresh. All printing offices have sample portfolios filled with their good things, and for years most of our showy samples were the fine work of Ed Clark.

Fred Lightfoot was a younger man. He supported his wife and child on $15 a week, not a bad wage, since even in the big towns printers were glad to get $25. Both he and Ed were generous of their time and showed me a dozen tricks of the trade. For example, if the advertiser wanted a line to run diagonally across the ad, these wily printers would throw the point system out of the window. The white space becomes triangular instead of square, and as the office had no triangular spaces or other filler, Ed or Fred simply chewed gigantic paper wads and stuffed them into the odd-shaped spaces. Ed's were delicately colored by chewing tobacco. The wads would dry hard, firm, and dependable. If, after a chase were locked up, a loose type wiggled, they forced it in place by a "Dutchman"—a wedge made by sharpening a bit of match-stick and tapping it into the tiny crevice.

I shudder to think of the amount of inflammable liquid we had. Our Olds engine ran on Standard gas—the only brand available to us—and for special purposes we had a more highly refined product, "White Rose"; neither was high octane, but either was lethal enough. Don and I often had to fire up a blow-torch or light a gas-vapor burner, and though for these purposes wood alcohol was better, gasoline would do. Often we ended the ceremony, if we were alone in the office, by pouring part of a cupful on the floor—generally a concrete area—touch a match to it, and watch it burn itself out.

Rex Theatre

PHOTOPLAY :: DRAMA :: VAUDEVILLE

⸸ PROGRAM ⸸

HERE!!

Is the Greatest Mystery Story of Them All

The most wonderful of all Photoplay
serials, by the world's greatest
fiction writer—E. Phillips
Oppenheim

The Black Box

FIRST EPISODE

SATURDAY EV'G, JULY 31

**THIS THE GREATEST THRILLER ON THE
SCREEN TODAY. DON'T MISS IT! RE-
MEMBER THE DATE. SATURDAY NIGHT.
JULY 31. THE GREATEST PHOTOPLAY.**

THOMPSON BROS., PROPRIETORS

For a time Slick and Banty Thompson, restaurant proprietors, ran the
Rex Theatre. Serials like "The Black Box" and "The Million Dollar Mystery"
attracted patrons for miles around. The ad is a sample of Ed Clark's typography, showing what could be done with ruled lines, a couple of standard
ornaments, and eight different kinds of type. (*Guide*, July 22, 1915)

I need to tell you about spikes and hooks. On any editor's desk was an upright spike on which he impaled letters, ad copy, or other documents that he wanted to save. Human beings never invented a simpler filing system. Gradually a spike accumulated two or three inches of papers, the ancient stuff sifting harmlessly toward the bottom. Along the sides of typecases were U-shaped hooks that served a similar purpose. These accumulated galley proofs, long strips of paper that nearly touched the floor; schedules mailed by advertising agencies informing the editor which ads were to be run in which issues; copy for sale bills or other jobs in progress; and other vital data. Our gasoline blazes sometimes flickered dangerously near these strips and sheets of paper. Any adult would have instantly seen the possibility of disaster and would have come running toward us at full scream, but we were totally absorbed in our pastime. One day, in some unreasonable, irrational way, the dangling proofs caught fire and the flames were soon head-high. The regular procedure would have been to run into the street yelling "Fire!" which would bring everybody within earshot on the run, carrying buckets. As among those who would appear was Father, I decided we could handle the difficulty ourselves, so we yanked the burning sheets off the hook and stamped out the flames. We buried the charred sheets deep in a wastepaper basket and tidied up the place. We had just missed a catastrophe.

Later that afternoon when the four of us were working, Father happened to say to no one in particular, "I wonder where the ad schedules are." Mother was not able to throw light on the problem. Father asked me if I had seen the Camel or Ford schedules and as that query was merely a vague feeler, I was able to evade it. To my surprise he dropped the interview as nonproductive and started looking elsewhere. Don and I were normally truthful and if he had phrased the question correctly we would have given him a direct answer. If he had said, for example, "Did you boys, while playing with fire, accidentally burn the papers on this hook, in the middle of which were the ad schedules?" we would have given him an immediate "Yes." So much depends upon the way a question is stated.

For a month Father ran his national ads by guess. The irregular appearance of these carefully planned agency campaigns puzzled the New York and Chicago people no end. "Why," they wrote, "did you run our Camel ad captioned, 'There is simply no truth to these vicious rumors' on July 9 when the schedule clearly stated July 23?" Later Don told Father exactly what had happened. About twenty years later.

Fire and flame had a meaning to my generation of young Americans that they do not have today. A furnace, out of sight in a basement, transmitting heat through radiators or pipes, was virtually unknown in Gilman City. With the exception of the Hotel Harmon, our business houses, churches, schoolrooms, and homes were heated by coal- or wood-burning stoves. Unless the fire had kept through the night, each winter morning began with the wadding of newspapers and the laying of kindling. Sometimes the process of starting the fire would be aided by a dash of coal oil, sometimes not. Though we were protected by heavy underwear (the old saying was that kids were sewn into their "union suits" in the fall and the stitches were not taken out until spring), we were well aware throughout the day when the flames ran low and the stove needed coal or wood. I cannot say that it was more tempting for youngsters to experiment with fire then than now, but I do know that children imitate their elders. Then we were continually exposed to fire-building routines. Now we go for weeks without even seeing a flame, much less without building a fire.

Each week we printed not only the current issue of the Great Moral and Religious Weekly, but also letterheads, envelopes, statements, handbills, and even small booklets. A rural community like ours also did a big business in sale bills and in bills advertising the services of a jack or stallion. Much of this work fell to Don and me, as accuracy rather than artistry was involved. The bills were 10 x 15 or 12 x 18 inches, printed in bold type on poster paper of assorted colors. We did not much like sale bills, as they had long lists of farm implements and livestock that had to be set up and carefully proofread. The stud bills we did not mind so much. The name of the jack or stallion—something gaudy like Maximilian 145782 or Napoleon III 204573—would be set in large type, so that part went fast. Then we selected a cut of an appropriate male beast from our slender supply, using reasonable care that a picture of a Percheron stallion did not appear on a poster describing the breeder's prized jack. Next came a few lines of pedigree, which included the animal's dams and sires and their registration numbers. The stated fee was inevitably $10, along with the usual warranty: "Colt guaranteed to stand and suck." Hence if the newborn babe lived long enough to stand on its four legs and take one good pull at its mother's teats, the sire had done all that could be expected. No other explicit guarantee was tendered; nothing like "two years, or twenty thousand miles, whichever comes first." Also always added was: "Care will be taken to prevent accidents, but not responsible should any occur." I always wondered what kind of accidents the owner had in mind, but the matter seemed delicate, and it never occurred to me to ask Father, or even his brother, my Uncle Clem, who owned a jack.

Sometimes the customer gave us an extra twenty-five cents to tack a couple dozen posters on Gilman City's telephone poles. This fabulous pay, however, was not always available, as Father, when in an expansive mood, would sometimes say, "Now, I'll just have the boys tack up a few posters for you, and there'll be no charge."

Occasionally a farmer came into the office when only Mother was on duty, looked anxiously around, and inquired if "the proprietor" were in. Mother instantly recognized the signs; here was a customer in the market for a bill and did not want to do business with a female. Delicate items such as mares or cows that were "recently bred" or that would "foal in the spring" called for language that no gentleman would want to utter in the presence of a lady. Mother asked the customer if he needed some printing, and next, if the printing was a bill, and if so, she indicated that she would be glad to write down the items, explaining that she considered this strictly a business situation, that she had grown up on a farm and knew about farm animals, and, besides, had taken orders for bills many times before. Thus gentled, he would start to dictate his copy, even the "foal" bit and the "stand and suck" bit and the "Care will be taken to prevent accidents" bit.

Mother must have been persuasive to get customers to discuss with a woman the intimate content of a stud bill. The delicacy about farm animals was universal. Certain terms were used by men only among themselves, though they were fully understood by women. Both joined in the conspiracy to insulate these terms from children. Once when I was watching my Aunt Grace help with the milking, my inevitable curiosity led me to ask her why one cow was left unmilked. She could not bring herself to say,

"Oh, she hasn't freshened yet," so she merely said, "She needs a calf." Eventually this bit of dialog reached my parents, who chuckled at the innocence of their offspring.

Father and Mother took special interest in the development of the countryside's livestock industry. A few farms had extensive breeding operations: buying purebred males, gradually upgrading their herds, showing at fairs, and selling promising young animals at special sales. More than once I have heard Father talk to a young farmer who had brought in copy for his first stock bill, relating a few of the outstanding achievements of leading stock breeders, such as the Weldens and Markeys, and noting the steps to success. The secret was continually to improve the herd by purchasing better sires, taking care not to overextend; to keep in touch with research coming from the university; to plan a sale carefully; and of course to advertise it. I suspect the young man sat up half the night talking to his wife about the prospect that Father had unfolded. World War I helped fulfill these dreams, as, first, Allied purchasing officials and, later, Uncle Sam's, supplied a booming market for horses, mules, cattle, and hogs. Eventually, however, a fellow by the name of Henry Ford knocked the bottom out of the jack and stallion business, and with it the printing of the large posters that proclaimed their talents.

These pages will serve as an introduction to what a country newspaper was like. My experience was in the age of movable types, which have been superseded two or three times over by other methods of printing. Today you often see a typecase, bought from a dealer in antiques, hanging on the wall of a home. The little partitions that once held *a*'s, *b*'s, and *c*'s now display small jim-cracks and goo-gaws. What is worse, the cases are invariably hung upside down. When I look at one of these ancient cases, which at one time held the raw materials for printing the good news and the misfortunes that come to a community, as well as its envelopes and posters and funeral notices and wedding announcements, I cannot help feeling that the art of hand composition, which flourished for five centuries, has come to an inglorious end.

Big John

Big John is a dark gray Jack with white points, 15½ hands high, weight 1000 lbs., big bone and a sure breeder. Foaled June, 1906, bred by J. R. Price, Pattensburg, Mo. Sired by Mark Hanna 274, by Phonograph 272. Dam, Big Bertha, weight 1200, by John L. Grandam, Mary, by Liberati.

Big John is known as the A. D. Liesher Jack.

Big John will make the season of 1915 at the W. R. Marshall farm, 5½ miles southeast of Gilman, and ½ mile south of the Corner Church.

Terms: $10.00 to insure colt to stand and suck. Colt to stand good for service fee. Money due when colt is foaled, mare parted with or removed from the neighborhood. Care will be taken to prevent accidents, but not responsible should any occur.

W. R. MARSHALL
Phone 13-18.

Country newspapers printed thousands of bills advertising the services of a jack or stallion. Often, for a dollar extra, they would put an ad in the paper. (*Guide*, May 6, 1915)

On these front pages all type was set by hand. (*Guide*, August 21, October 30, 1913)

4

All For a Dollar a Year

When it came to editing and printing the *Guide*, Father and Mother were the greatest promotional team since Ferdinand and Isabella. Getting a living out of Gilman City was fully as enterprising as opening up the New World. For a subscription price of a dollar a year, they undertook to mail subscribers one issue a week, filled with advertising, news, editorials, and features, so that not only the town but also the countryside knew what was happening. The *Guide* was a weekly persuader, exhorter, merchandiser, and recorder. One who read it regularly knew the character of the town—its achievements and its hopes.

Selling an adequate number of ads each week was the first requisite. Mother was such a dynamic saleslady that Father would not turn her loose on the community more than two or three times a year. She was so persuasive and so persistent that he felt the merchants needed a breathing spell after each of her visits. She was especially magnificent at Christmas, when she would sell every business and professional man a holiday ad in which he could express his sentiments as well as thank the community for its patronage during the year. No merchant found it easy to tell Mother that he did not have any holiday sentiments or that he did not want to say "thank-you" to his customers. Before she had finished with him, he was glad to be let off with a two-column, six-inch ad or even a 3 x 10.

Mother's powerful sales campaign, in fact, swamped the technical resources of the *Guide*. We exhausted our supply of holly border; then our plain rule border; we used up our supply of cuts of Santa, reindeer, wreaths, and filled stockings and had to slip in stars and turkey gobblers from adjacent holidays. The Xs in Xmas and the Ys in Happy New Year also vanished rapidly, so we would have to change her copy from Merry Xmas to Season's Greetings until the Ss and Gs had also disappeared. In order to accommodate her sales, we often found ourselves on midafternoon of Press Day adding extra pages to the paper.

Mother also solicited ads for city or county directories, or for what Father called "special pages." He ruled a page ad into smaller advertising spaces, put a banner headline across the top such as "Dollar Day" or "Bargain Day" or "Turkey Day" and sent Mother forth to sell the idea. Of course, the merchants were unaware that there was to be a Dollar Day or a Turkey Day until Mother showed up with her sample page. Turkey Day, for example, advertised that at two o'clock Saturday a dozen live turkeys would be thrown from the top of the Citizens Bank building to the crowd waiting below. This enterprise was hard on the turkeys but drew a lot of people, who presumably would spend the rest of the afternoon patronizing the advertisers. Eventually stunts like Turkey Day were abandoned but Dollar Day lived on. Mother also sold ads to be printed on the back of cardboard fans, which merchants distributed during the summer months as a good-will gesture. She started out with a few sample fans, lavishly adorned with daisies or asters or perhaps a horse with a pretty lady, and called on business and professional people. After the fans were printed with the firm name, we stapled wooden handles to them. Until well after electricity had come, Gilman City citizens fanned themselves with fans that Mother had sold the merchants.

Father, on the other hand, mastered the slow but persistent soft sell. He reasoned that you should so deal with a customer that you could return the next week. If I have heard him once, I have heard him say a hundred times, "Always leave a person so you can go back and talk to him again." He entered a business establishment and, being crippled, found it easy and natural to sit down near the action. His sales talks were more in the nature of a visit than a business deal. He had always been a lively and agile conversationalist; he could begin a conversation with a stranger, and in minutes have him turned inside out. I have seen him drive into a filling station and leave not only with a full tank of gas but also with full information about the owner's business and politics. So, when making his regular Monday and Tuesday rounds of selling ads, for publication on Thursday, he usually left with something. For merchants known to dislike writing their own copy,

Father produced a sample from his inside coat pocket that he had already prepared. But if the merchant said no, the conversation shifted to a neutral topic and ended on a friendly note. Next week Father could go back.

In an age that appreciates power, it is worth recording that the editor of a country weekly wielded his own distinctive kind of influence. To paraphrase Father's idol, Emerson, the newspaper was the lengthened shadow of the editor himself. Readers were fully aware that the editor wrote most of the paper, so that if a news item expressed a personal opinion, and news items often expressed a personal opinion, they knew it was the editor's.

What enhanced the *Guide*'s influence was that people knew its editor was well informed. Any one who scanned thirty or forty daily and weekly newspapers, looking for ideas, was alert to what was going on. Moreover, Father was one person who was sure to engage nearly every business and professional man in serious conversation every week. By the time he had concluded his ad selling and news gathering, he fully sensed the mood of the town. And if he missed anything on Main Street, he was certain to pick it up later in his other role as postmaster, talking with patrons and with the mail carriers who had made their daily rounds of the countryside.

I have often heard Father discuss with Mother the outcome of a day's soliciting and reporting. If the merchants had had a good weekend, they were relaxed and cheerful and Father could pull from his pockets copy for quarter-page and half-page ads as well as for smaller ones. On those days, to use his own phrase, he wore a smile like a busted watermelon.

On other days one merchant after another told a story of depressed sales, poor crops, low prices for corn and hogs, accounts they could not collect, bills they could not meet. These problems led them to cut down their advertising, so Father's mood, on those occasions, reflected tough going and hard times.

Father could get to the bottom of a situation because he was a good listener as well as a good talker. People discussed their notions freely because they knew he respected their confidence. If a hardware dealer were planning a store-wide clearance sale week after next, Father kept the information under his hat. No

Country weeklies often designed a "special page," featuring a "Bargain Day," selling small ads to the participating merchants. Since every letter was a piece of lead, a printer could spend the best part of the day in putting this page together, and two or three hours putting all the pieces back into the cases. With help from a Linotype, he could do the job in a fourth of the time. (Some of the prices will make a modern reader weep.)

grocer would disclose his Saturday prices for sugar or potatoes if he thought the editor would blab the figures to a competitor.

More than most editors, Father enjoyed a wide acquaintance among county, state, and national officeholders, dating back to when he himself had done tours of duty at both state and national capitals. Candidates, Republicans and Democrats alike, for all kinds of offices, visited the *Guide* office. Favorable lines in the weekly paper might be worth as much as a dozen casual handshakes. Father also knew the editors of newspapers as far away as St. Joseph and Kansas City and most points in between. If, therefore, the town needed outside support, Father knew how to tap it. He would have been a good person to have around in these days of state and federal grants.

These factors added to the credibility of the Great Moral and Religious Weekly. Father was basically optimistic, inevitably taking the long view, but he had a realistic appreciation of difficulties.

Invariably the country weekly is at the leading edge of plans to improve the community. Father supported the issues that were characteristic of that age. On one occasion he advocated more hitching racks for the scores of teams that came to town. On another he deplored the mudholes on Main Street, or urged the importance of keeping sidewalks in repair. Saturday traders should have a rest room, so they would have a few simple conveniences for themselves and their children. Such a facility might encourage shoppers who might otherwise drive to some other town.

Father crusaded for every proposal to organize commercial and good-roads clubs, to extend telephone and telegraph services, and to develop a water system. When a bond issue to improve the electric plant was up for a vote and opposition began to develop, Father wrote: "If a man prefers a dirty coal-oil lamp to an electric light, he has a right to his opinion, but he ought to remember there was a time when a fellow with a coal-oil lamp was confronted by a fellow with a greasy old candle dip who told him the coal-oil lamp was an expensive, dangerous, ruinous thing and liable at any moment to explode." He had, of course, already lived through the candle-dip era into the coal-oil lamp era. Eventually the community voted funds to build the plant. He told the story about the Bethany druggist who had opposed every civic improvement that was proposed, yet still had maintained the image of a community booster. Asked his secret, the druggist confided: "Oh, I come out strong for the new bandstand, or whatever it is. But I fight 'em on the location."

An editor always wonders how much influence he really has. The *Guide* lost out on the public rest room but got the hitching racks. One went past my home, so it was a doubtful asset to the neighborhood. The *Guide* broke even on the mudholes on Main Street, but it did keep people stirred up about repairing sidewalks. Along with other country weeklies it lost the long fight against mail-order houses, which not only survived but also prospered. It argued for an opera house for public meetings and never got one, but the Rex Theatre came to be used for public occasions. Father had to keep reminding people to keep their chickens fenced in.

Father thought he was more than usually successful in his publicity for the periodical votes to increase the school levy. More school revenue gradually made possible a lengthening of the school year, a two-story addition to the school building, and even slightly higher salaries for the teachers. People went out of their way to congratulate him for his news stories and editorials supporting the levy. And, as the passing of the years proved, the school proved to be the town's most durable and unifying institution. If it had been starved out, so that the region's consolidated school had gone to a neighboring town, the loss to Gilman City would have been immense.

The *Guide's* influence was also sharply noted in other areas. Gilman City had always had an enviable reputation as an egg and poultry shipping center. When the Jamesport paper bragged that its leading firm had received twenty-four hundred dozen eggs in a week, the *Guide* retorted that its leading firm received more than that in two days. Even the Trenton paper once admitted that Gilman City shipped more eggs than Trenton, Princeton, or Galt. So one week when Father wrote a short commentary on the excellent business of one of the produce dealers, he was invading sacred territory. The other dealer, angry as a yellow jacket, declared that he would beat Father to a pulp if he wrote another piece like that. Father retorted that as it was his paper he would write whatever he pleased. Although usually he walked without a cane, the next few days he took the precaution of using one. This show of force, roughly equivalent to moving an extra aircraft carrier into the In-

Father owned the *Guide* for twelve of the years between 1904 and 1921. All in all he published four northwest Missouri newspapers, but the *Guide* was his favorite.

dian Ocean, kept his opponent at a distance. On another occasion Father wrote a nice item about a fancy, winding stairway that one of the local carpenters had built for a new home. The other carpenters huffily informed him that any carpenter could build such a stairway, so Father printed a story about winding stairs in general and thus stilled the uprising on that issue.

Although the keen competition invited disputes, and occasional fist fights punctuated other sorts of disagreement, Gilman City on the whole was free from conflict. Political differences freely surfaced, but Republicans had a commanding majority; Democrats who ran for county office usually did so merely to keep the party alive, not from the hope of winning. The town had a strong Catholic group but was not aware of animosity between Catholics and Protestants. Often officers and stockholders of major businesses belonged to both groups.

Basically the community was too homogenous in origin and background to develop much rivalry. There was little if any town-versus-country argument; the interests of the two groups were interrelated. Nearly all of our business and professional men and their wives had, like Father and Mother, been born on the farm. A farmer might sell his farm and buy a business; or, tiring of business, return to farming. Lacking a factory, we had no strikes or other forms of industrial warfare. We did not have mass meetings, demonstrations, or protests. Father freely stated his position on controversial issues, but those that arose were mainly concerned with the community as a whole, not a sector of it.

Scores of events, large and small, reassured Father that the *Guide*'s opinions were reacted to, one way or another. The simple fact was that anything in its columns was read by at least five hundred families, and, since everybody knew nearly everybody else, the information was fully appreciated. Names by the bushel appeared in its columns:

Thieves recently visited the homes of Bonnie Ray and Hobart Burrell, taking their lard, meat, and canned fruit.

T. R. Ray got caught in a corn shredder Tuesday. The cogs of the machine caught the seat of his pantaloons. The doctor took six stitches.

Ward Boyer mashed his foot by dropping coal on it. There was danger from blood poisoning but he is better at this time.

Mrs. Marion Thompson went to Excelsior Springs Monday to drink the waters. She has been in poor health. She will be gone for some time.

The ten pups of L. A. Welden are coming alone fine. All have their eyes open now. A person would have to go a long way to find prettier pups.

There has evidently been some hustling among the leading ladies in the piano contest since last week. The count this afternoon finds the four leading contestants very close together.

An important aspect of the *Guide*'s influence was that it could recognize individual achievement. The small town does not have its "Man of the Year" or "Most Influential Woman" contest, so in its own way the newspaper serves that function. A good week at Dunn's store, a strong financial statement by the Citizens Bank, a farmer who raised a thirty-four-pound turkey, an egg with a double shell, a twenty foot stalk of corn, a half-dozen prime ears of Reid's Yellow Dent with nicely spaced rows and plump kernels, a radish two feet in circumference weighing eleven pounds—all these were worth a few lines of dazzling prose. When banker Nell Williams flashed a new bandanna handkerchief, Father wrote that it was as pretty as a speckled rooster.

Sometimes the achievements were more spectacular. Billy Welden reported that he had sold two loads of cattle on the Chicago market, topping it at $9.10. John Markey reported that he had sold a section of land for $82,000. His father had entered this section in 1857 and nine years later had moved with his family from Adams County, Illinois. This Irish-born family had made good in mid-America. For the record, in the 1970s cattle brought four times as much, and this section of land sold for more than $2,000 an acre.

News columns of the *Guide* struck a friendly atmosphere. The pillars of the community were described as "well-known and successful," "highly respected and prosperous," "popular and widely-known." One man might be described as "a leading farmer and stockman"; another as a "substantial farmer and horse breeder"; still another as "a popular and efficient county surveyor." We had many "progressive and public-spirited" citizens. One who had only a "common school education" could be thought of as having "sur-mounted all kinds of difficulties."

Readers expected accuracy on certain select topics; the printer who allegedly printed that a woman's breast was filled with "rags" instead of "rage" is said to have left town in a hurry. In general, however, the language was oracular and florid. Obituaries mentioned the "floral tributes"; the bereaved was "summoned before the recording angel by the great trumpeter." Before yielding, he had had "a heroic but unequal struggle with the Grim Invader." "Limb" was used, not "leg," whether man or woman was involved. One who made a gallant effort "had spared neither pains nor expense." Usually you partook of a dinner instead of eating it. A birth was a blessed event. If a soldier died, he had "gone West," the splendid euphemism of World War I. A hunter was a Nimrod. A bachelor who finally succumbed to marriage was a Benedict. A livestock car was a side-door sleeper.

A certain amount of blunt language appeared. References to hanging were frequent: an inept public official should be taken out and hanged; for example, "Eben will make a good assessor if he escapes hanging." If a lady were reported as saying to a gentleman, "You're the ugliest man I ever saw," she probably did, and he probably was. For committing various social or political misdemeanors, a man could be called a shitepoke, a woodenhead, a turn coat, a tightwad, a straddler, a skinflint, a white-livered pessimist, or a cheap papier-mâche imitation. At the end of man's and woman's working lives was no "Rest Haven" or "Sun and Fun for Seniors," but only a "poor farm." Work hard and be thrifty, boys and girls were warned, or you'll end up on the poor farm. Time was not always available for niceties. Life was "too short to teach a jack to sing soprano."

When civic progress stalled, Father drew a bead on a whole segment of the citizenry: "If Gilman City really has a single booster, will he please move the dry-goods box on which he is loafing far enough to the right to put it on the tail of the town cat? Something ought to be waked up." When a reader stopped his subscription, Father's ire was boundless. Such a tightwad might waste his substance on many luxuries, "but the home paper—the paper that stands up for his town, for his home people, for himself and his family . . . the little home paper, at a cost of $1 a year, less than

2 cents a week—this is the great, unbearable strain on his pocket-book and it must be stopped."

Father's lively journalistic style led him to be one of the most quoted country newspaper editors in Missouri. One Harrison County historian, Birt S. Allen, called him Eugene Field, Homer Croy, and Ed Howe, all rolled into one. Ed Howe, later the famous editor of Atchison, Kansas, the "sage of Potato Hill," had made his early home at Bethany. Father had known Croy as a reporter when both lived and worked in Maryville. Every Missourian, of course, knew Field.

When Father ran out of news to print, he turned to topics close at hand. He loved Gilman City, Harrison County, the state of Missouri, and the United States in that order; at least he allotted space to them in about that order. He never faltered in his belief that Gilman City would someday have a thousand people or more. And how he loved Missouri. At the drop of a corncob pipe he would offer encomiums on Thomas H. Benton, Champ Clark, Mark Twain, Eugene Field, James A. Reed. From there he would proceed to such Missouri statesmen as A. M. Dockery, Joseph W. Folk, Francis M. Cockrell, George G. Vest. Nor would he overlook Frank and Jesse James. Frank had been tried at Gallatin; Father often discussing the trial. He reveled in Missouri's two big cities, which even in 1910 had a combined population of a million. He would say: "Never forget that Missouri is the only state in the country with two Federal Reserve district banks, Kansas City and St. Louis." For him, currency issued elsewhere in the country was just barely legal tender. Years later I met one of the eastern governors of the Federal Reserve system. "Where are you from?" he asked. "Oh, I'm from Missouri, the only state in the Union with two Federal Reserve district banks." His jaw sagged. "How did you know that?" he asked.

Father knew that Missouri's products were of such infinite variety that Missourians could build a wall around the state and live in magnificent self-sufficiency. Lead, iron, coal, onyx; all kinds of timber; fruit; not just corn, or wheat, or oats, or cotton, or hay, but all of them in abundance; hogs, sheep, horses, mules, cattle, poultry; booming dairy and wine industries; clear, wild-running streams with the largest springs in the world; fertile soil. He also knew that Missouri had more chinch bugs, seventeen-year locusts, and four-inch grasshoppers than any other region; train and bank robbers such as the rest of the world never knew; and could also raise 341 other kinds of hell.

He struck a high note in his first issue. Looking over the young town, then seven years old, he saw, not the dirt streets and board sidewalks, but: 'A broad, rolling prairie of rich, fertile soil, well-watered; spacious and attractive streets; substantial brick and frame buildings; a live, progressive, energetic, and wealthy people." He welcomed every newcomer. He often published a list of people who had left and had returned. He himself had moved away and had come back.

The final note of recognition came when the *Guide* printed an obituary of someone, giving not simply a skimpy account of the names of survivors and the principal achievements of the deceased, as obituaries do today, but commenting at length on character and personality. Again, this practice was in the tradition of the country weekly.

Each of millions of homes must have its collection of yellowed newspapers, its envelopes of clippings, its scrapbooks, even its printed treasures laminated in plastic, as symbols of its appreciation of the hometown paper. Still, the newspaper's greatest influence was exerted issue by issue, in columns that might not have been clipped, both through straight reporting of what went on and by comment upon what should have been happening that was not happening. Scores of small-town newspaper files have been destroyed, but hundreds have been preserved, so that although much of what the common, everyday person did those decades has been lost, a considerable story still remains.

5

Newspaper Publishing:
Family Style

The processes of selling ads, gathering news, and providing editorial opinion consumed time and energy, but the mechanical problems of printing the paper and distributing it were the most persistent and intrusive. Every day supplied little deadlines that were gradually rolled into the one big deadline known as Press Day.

Start with the most relaxing day, Thursday, the clean-up day. The four pages that made up the previous issue, each locked in its own steel form or chase, were laid out side by side on the large tables with their marble-topped surfaces. After scrubbing the ink off the type, sometimes with gasoline, sometimes with lye water, we then returned type, rules, and other materials, piece by piece, to their proper places. These and other duties had to be planned in and around post office, domestic, and school demands.

Many advertisers—Heaven bless each one—ran the same ad week after week. These were tenderly left in place. Even so, great open spaces remained on each page, to be filled with fresh news and ads.

We printed most of our sale bills, stationery, and other jobs Thursday afternoon, Friday, and Saturday. No country editor liked to do job printing the first part of the week when he was deeply immersed in his newspaper. We also set the early news, editorials, and articles clipped from the exchanges, so that by week's end we would have two or three columns of type ready to go.

On Mondays and Tuesdays, Father made the rounds of his advertisers, set their ads, and positioned them on the proper page. Ministers brought in church notes; club and lodge secretaries brought in news of their meetings; hostesses handed in guest lists; school editors wrote school notes. Mother would have written out the news she had gathered from her depot visits. Father and Mother also wrote stories about accidents, weddings, individual achievements and accomplishments. Sometimes I wrote news items. Setting these kept Father and Mother busy during the day and Don and me after school. The open spaces on the pages gradually began to fill up.

Don and I could usually stay at school after it closed on Thursday or Friday, to join whatever fun was going on, and could even remain a short time Monday or Tuesday, but Wednesday was different. Wednesday was the day to finish whatever had not got written, or put in type, on preceding days. Wednesday was also the day to set the ads or news stories that came in at the last minute. And Wednesday had its own demands—the page-size forms had to be put on the big newspaper press and printed.

When Don and I reported for duty on Press Day, we were quickly awash with things to do. Count the required number of sheets of news print for the evening's run. Fill the ink fountain. Make corrections in ads. Locate the hammer or screwdriver. Address the "single wraps," used for mailing copies to distant subscribers. Run down to Robertson and Beckman's and get their ad proof; they've had it for hours. Oil the press. Put stickum on the belts so they'll grip the pulleys.

Meanwhile Father steadily completed the makeup of the pages, filling the remaining spaces with news or ads of the proper size. With luck he finished by supper time. His final chore for each page was to level the type with a wooden plane and mallet. The rat-a-tat of mallet hitting plane as it traveled across the surface of the type was as lively as a snare drum. He invariably ended with extra, joyous flourishes of the mallet that clearly proclaimed, "Well, we've done it again; soon the press can roll."

While he and Mother scanned a final proof of the front page, Don and I scurried to Slick's Cafe for a sack of tenderloin and hamburger sandwiches and, in season, bowls of chili. These the four of us munched together as we braced ourselves for the actual printing.

As the shadows lengthened, we lowered the gas-mantle light from the ceiling, filled and lit it, and pulled it back into place. We used coal-oil lamps for other work areas. What was to follow might be finished in two hours or might take all night. Everything now depended on the Olds engine, the Country Campbell, and the connecting belts.

If human ingenuity deliberately tried to invent a machine that would transcend human patience, his device would look like our four-and-a-half horsepower Olds, which Father had acquired in a trade with Ben DeWitt. It was a handsome beast, not quite waist high, black enamel with two flywheels trimmed in red, one on either side of the single, horizontal cylinder. When the moment came to crank it, we silently gathered around, wondering, hoping, fearing, not quite sure it would start, not quite doubting it wouldn't. Father bent over it, held down the choke with his left hand, fingered the near flywheel for the handle that was recessed and hinged in its rim, and gave it a dozen or fifteen turns. This initial spinning was seldom successful. Father's next spinning was longer and more determined; the Olds usually responded by backfiring, the flywheels suddenly whirling backwards, smoke pouring from the engine's insides. Did we have a long night ahead of us? Mother then took her turn, often without success. Then came the discussion: the engine was flooded; the spark plug should be cleaned; the White Rose had water in it, even though we had strained it through a chamois. The backfiring, however, showed life in the old machine; if it would run backwards, it would run forwards; another spinning of the crank seemed indicated. This time the Olds shook itself, coughed and sputtered, and gradually attained speed. When it ran, its *boom* followed by a *husha-husha-husha-boom husha-husha-husha* was delightful to hear.

The main actor in the weekly drama was, however, the Country Campbell. This two-ton iron monster was eight feet from front to back, five feet wide, and nearly five feet tall. We called it the Big Press. All week long it had stood on its own concrete slab, ignored and useless. During the final hours of Press Day, however, our fortunes and our sacred honor depended on it. And it was somewhat more temperamental, if possible, than the Olds.

A long belt from the Olds drove a main shaft, on which was mounted a series of pulleys from which other belts drove the job presses and the Country Campbell. When a belt broke, as it did at any critical moment or under extra stress, Father trimmed the frayed ends, cut a piece from old belting that had survived other disasters, dispatched Don or me for the leather punch and a supply of rawhide laces, and repaired the breakage. The designs of variegated patching and rawhide strips made what is known nowadays as a collage. For Father, it was making do. Over the years each belt had become mostly patch, with little original fabric remaining. Above the explosions of the Olds and the clatter and rumbling of the press was the flapping and slapping of belts and flying lace ends. A break was not a major calamity, but it brought the printing operation to a complete stop for at least half an hour.

The Olds engine with the main shafting and belts and intermediate shafting and more belts would remind anybody of a nineteenth-century factory. The Big Press itself was so close to the shafting that Father had to work gingerly in and around belts and pulleys to refill or readjust the ink fountain. This adjusting was necessary to keep the pages of the *Guide* from becoming either too dim or too inky. Once he caught his pants in a flapping belt; the pant leg was squeezed between belt and pulley and in a jiffy he was stripped of his trousers. Only the immediate breaking of the belt at the point of a frayed patch prevented a tragedy. While he sat in his underwear, somewhat shaken, repairing the break, we rushed home to get the Five Drops liniment and another pair of pants. The way the incident appeared in the Great Moral and Religious Weekly, however, was: "The editor caught his pants in a belt, which were then run through the press, printed on both sides, and delivered to a subscriber, who said it was one of the best things that ever came out in the *Guide*."

Everyone is familiar, at least in a general way, with the appearance of an office duplicating or mimeographing machine, with its big cylinder about nine inches wide and five or six in diameter, its stack of sheets waiting to be fed, and its mechanisms for feeding, inking, and discharging. The Campbell had a cylinder four feet long and two feet in diameter. Atop the cylinder was a feedboard, on which were stacked the sheets of blank newsprint. Mounted on the cylinder at the edge of the feedboard was a row of grippers, which, like iron fingers, lifted long enough to receive a sheet of paper, clamp down on it, and hold it in place. As the cylinder rotated it brought the sheet into contact with the type pages, which had been freshly inked. The grippers then released, and the sheet was guided to the front of the press and flopped over onto a receiving table. The grippers then seized the next sheet that the press feeder had ready and waiting.

Each sheet needed to be fed snugly against the gauges so that the grippers could get a good grasp. Otherwise the sheet would be printed crooked or even slip off the cylinder altogether and be wound around the ink rollers. Mother, our chief press feeder, stood on a box about eighteen inches high so she could easily manage the sheets.

Starting the Campbell involved putting the first sheet in place, stepping down to the floor, grabbing a lever that shifted the belt from the idle pulley to the drive pulley, and, as the big cylinder started slowly to rotate, leaping atop the box to get ready to feed the next sheet. Feeding involved lifting a single sheet from the top of the pile, flipping it just right so that a cushion of air under it would help float it gently toward the end and side gauges, so that at the proper moment the gauges could lift and the grippers could seize the sheet and whip it through the press.

Once the press-feeding rhythm matched the rhythm of the press—each complete turn of the cylinder meant that another sheet had been printed—Mother could preside calmly over the rumbling and clanking, rubbing and rolling, wheezing and whirring, clattering and flapping. The Campbell, however, was something short of a high precision instrument, so after fifty or seventy-five successful feeds a gripper might not quite hold firm, or the ink might get a little sticky, or Mother herself might miss a gauge by an eighth or a quarter of an inch, so that a sheet would wind up around an ink roller instead of flowing neatly through the press. The nearest observer would let out a yell, Mother would yank the stopping lever, and all hands would spend the next few minutes picking bits and strips of paper off an inky roller.

Father was general overseer. Occasionally he deftly snatched a newly printed sheet and scanned it to make sure no type or slugs were working loose; if he saw something amiss, he waved vigorously, and Mother stopped the press for adjustments. His major worry was the ink-feeding mechanism. Despite his vigilance, the printing might become dim or blurred. We knew nothing about temperature, humidity, static, or drying speed and had no way to regulate these mysteries even if we did. Years later when reading the *Guide* in microfilm, I occasionally saw pages where the photographer had stamped "Poor Quality" on the page before photographing it. He wanted the purchaser, the library, to know that the printing, not his artistry, was faulty. I thought, "Brother, you don't know the half of it." The long nights flashed back and I saw Mother standing on her box, the image of patience and endurance, Father waving his arms when trouble arose, both trying to squeeze a few hundred sheets out of the iron demon, and, please, before midnight.

Yet presses like the Country Campbell, the second generation of presses after the hand-operated, you-ink-them-and-then-roll-them press, had their own place in publishing history. Only a few

Rare picture of the *Guide* office, taken in 1912. At the left is editor Tom Cunningham; in the center, Arabella Idings; at the right Anna Thompson, wife of Slick (Slick's Cafe) Thompson. Even in those days women worked in various crafts and trades. Anna's note on the back of the picture says: "This is the outfit that makes the paper."

The newly installed Campbell press is in the center. The freshly printed papers were flopped onto the table on which Anna is standing. In the lower right-hand corner is the Olds gas engine. The drive belt ran from it to the back wall at the left, then by intermediate pulleys to the drive wheel near the editor's right leg.

On the marble-topped tables in the foreground are chases partly filled with type for the next issue. A gas-mantle light is left of center. Hanging on the wall at the far left is the file of issues printed so far that year.

This picture was taken about four months before Father bought the *Guide* and I began my first year of school.

upon the market in January, 1906. It is, therefore, the most modern of standard manufactured, but the universal popularity of the machine among country pub-
No. 9, or six column
e, the only difference
nces in size.
e market, the Brower
and the most durable.
ter, who can put a job
rower as successfully
n the book of instruc-
d for reference. This
l complete exposition
-ready and running a
nufacturer.

ither time
uch a job.
om fifty to
is included
when other
ed in their

No. 9 BROWER

CHICAGO

Brower Drum Cylinder Press No. 9

recoding gripper studs.

This is not a Campbell, but a newspaper press similar to it. This generation of presses succeeded the hand-lever-operated press, but the manufacturer pointed out that in case the motor "balked," the press could still be operated by inserting a lever in the fly wheel. Newsprint was stacked on the flat surface at the top of the press and fed a sheet at a time. The big drum would roll the sheet against the type and the printed sheet would roll out over the slats at the right and be flipped over onto a table (not shown). Ink fountain and ink rollers are at the left. The press feeder stood on the little platform at the right. This press, like the Country Campbell, would print four pages, each six columns wide. It sold complete for $810.

years later in our Iowa plant I saw a more modern press, equipped with a row of small gas flames; each freshly printed sheet was pulled briskly over the flames, long enough to dry the ink but not long enough to scorch the paper. That arrangement simplified the problem of adjusting the ink fountain. This press also had a throw-off pedal so that, like almost any mimeographing machine, the cylinder could turn freely without printing anything. If the press feeder saw he was about to miss a feed, he stepped on the pedal. The press had its own electric motor with an endless belt that might wear out but wouldn't break. Moreover, the motor was controlled by a hand lever that regulated its speed. Aha, I thought as I gazed at these marvels, that's the way they do it.

During press feeding, Don, posted at the receiving table, kept the freshly printed sheets nice and straight. My job was to cut the printed sheets in half and start the folding. When the last sheet was printed and the Olds silenced, Don joined in the folding, Mother addressed the papers with a hand-operated addressing machine, and Father tied the addressed papers in bundles. When everything was addressed and bundled and moved through the inside door to the post office, we turned out the lights, locked the doors, and made our way home. It might be nine o'clock, eleven o'clock, midnight, or two in the morning. No matter. We had conquered another Wednesday.

For all my growing years and for some years after, Wednesday was stamped on my mind as the day to hurry home after school, the day when other plans must be subordinated to the publication of the paper. Years elapsed before Wednesday could take its place in the week as just another day like Tuesday or Thursday. After we had left Gilman City, and after I had finished high school and college, I confided in Mother, still active in the newspaper business, that I was going to be married on August 28. Her face lit up like a gas mantle and she gave me an enormous hug. Then she stepped back and her face clouded just a little. "Son, that wouldn't be on Press Day, would it?" When I assured her that the twenty-eighth was not a Wednesday but only a Saturday, the glow reappeared, the hug was laid back on with extra warmth, and she savored the full glory and magic of her first-born son about to be married. The only possible obstacle had been brushed away,

6

The O. K.

All these years the Quincy, Omaha, and Kansas City Railway continued to serve the community that was growing up alongside its tracks.

During the first quarter of the twentieth century, Missouri was one of the proudest railroad states of the Union. Father liked to brag about Missouri's railroad system, and had the statistics to support him: eighth in the nation in total mileage. Her more than eight thousand miles of track were enough to crisscross the state east and west and north and south every twenty miles. Missouri's interstate and primary road system today adds up to just about that same figure—eight thousand. If you drew a twenty-mile circle around Gilman City it would intersect not only the O.K. but also the Wabash, the Burlington, and the Rock Island. That was just a starter; all in all forty different systems operated within Missouri's boundaries, plus electric interurbans.

Going east from Gilman City, the O.K. stretched six miles to Melbourne, a small coal-mining settlement, fancifully named after the Australian city; then two miles to Brimson; then nine miles to Trenton, where it crossed the Rock Island; then it proceeded, according to general belief, all the way to Quincy. As I never got that far myself, I cannot say for sure personally, though the *Guide* occasionally printed items about local folk who had made the trip and had got back home again.

Going west, the O.K. passed the water tank and coal chute, then bent toward the south and left the county altogether, stopping at Coffey, seven miles away; then nine miles to Pattonsburg, an important junction point with the Wabash, where one could change for Omaha. Pattonsburg was so close to Big Creek and Grand River, and got flooded so often, that I mainly thought of it as a half-drowned city and was not too surprised to read in the papers a few years ago that it might eventually be abandoned altogether to make room for a lake, a dam, and a hydroelectric project.

From Gilman City to Kansas City was a hundred-mile, four and a half hour ride, with twenty scheduled stops plus half a dozen flag stops. After Pattonsburg came Santa Rosa and Weatherby, and then after an interminable time Avondale, then North Kansas City, which was practically there, and finally Kansas City, which, as we well knew, was the mightiest freight and passenger terminal in the world. If I remember these details, it is because I spent a large portion of each trip poring over the free timetable that one could pick up just outside the lavatory and next to the water cooler. Moreover, well-founded statements from people known to tell the truth asserted that from Kansas City one could take a train, like a flying carpet, to anywhere.

The O.K. was single track its whole length. It operated no limited or express trains; it was strictly local, with stops every few miles, so that anybody who wanted to ship grain or livestock would not have to drive his wagon more than half a day to reach a shipping point. It had no parlor car, no buffet or diner, no sleeper; it was basic transportation. Each train did carry, however, a uniformed representative of Union News, the firm that had the concession to peddle sandwiches, soft drinks, candy, paperback westerns, and miscellaneous magazines.

We were proud to be a station on the O.K. Towns that had been overlooked had little standing; Blue Ridge, seven miles north and west, was nice enough in its way, but as it had no railroad, it became a place that people went through, not to. You could stop to water your horse, or, in later years, to fix a flat tire. Once, his Gilman City chauvinism fully showing, Father described Blue Ridge as having only three residences, a store, and a blacksmith shop, plus a post office consisting of ten mailboxes tacked to a wooden slab.

The O.K.'s six-wheel locomotives ran on coal so soft it could almost be crumbled and sifted like the dust in the streets. Its smoke was thick, black, and saturated with blobs of soot and clinker dust. The mechanics of railroading required that the firebed be well stirred and poked while the train was in the station. Every housewife knew this, so she would hang her wash on the line as early as possible on Monday, being sure to get it down before the noon train—otherwise sheets, shirts, overalls, dresses, and aprons might have to be done over.

Twice a day the O.K. roared in, clanging and belching; No. 1 from the west at two o'clock, No. 2 from the east at noon. At train times, weekdays and Sundays, twenty to a hundred people gathered at the depot: those who were departing, those who were planning to greet arrivals, those who were there to pick up baggage, those who were just there. Sometimes I was on hand to gather news items for the *Guide*, sometimes to pick up bundles of Kansas City, St. Joseph, and St. Louis newspapers, sometimes, along with

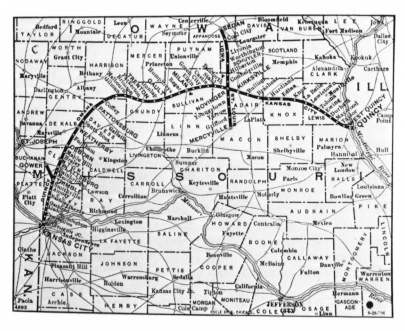

Two hundred fifty-four miles of the Quincy, Omaha, and Kansas City Railway. Railroad timetables invariably included a diagram of the system, each diagram smoothing out the numerous twists and turns that the track itself followed. Towns in capital letters are junction points; the thin lines represent other rail systems. Gilman City itself would have been a junction point if the proposed railroad from Columbia, to Trenton, to Gilman City, and on to Bethany and Iowa had materialized. Gilman City's claim to be the best shipping point on the O.K. between Quincy and Kansas City was not seriously contested, though obviously the claim took in a lot of territory.

Streams like Tombstone Creek and Sugar Creek were the natural enemies of railroads. Heavy rains could wash out timbered bridges and cancel
train service for two or three days. Our favorite swimming hole was on the
far side of the bridge; after the spring rains, however, Tombstone became
too shallow for swimming and in the summertime often dried up altogether.

Tombstone Creek, revisited. Sometimes one returns to a familiar haunt once too often. In better days these roots supported a diving board, from which we could plunge into cool water well over our heads.

other kids, just for the pure excitement. We often laid pins or horse-shoe nails on the track, crossed, so that when the train passed over, they would be pressed into an X, like scissors. Or we bent over and pushed our ears against the rails, listening for the rumble that indicated the train was approaching; we could feel it long before we could either see its smoke or hear its whistle. Always it was more fun to do these things when parents were not around, as then you could hover over the tracks until the last minute. Other adults, however, had a strong protective instinct, and by the time the train actually came into view they laid hands on the kids nearest them and yanked them out of danger, along with language that anyone can supply out of his own historic past. Yet we never had an accident on the station platform, though grade-crossing fatalities were one of the hazards of living—worse than runaway teams—and the *Guide*, along with every other newspaper, frequently carried stories about how a carload of people had been wiped out when automobile and locomotive met at the same point at the same instant.

What with its shrill whistle, its clanging bell, its belching smokestack, its clacking locomotive pulling five or six clattering wooden cars, and its final scream of screeching brakes, the arrival of the O.K. was deliciously terrifying. Actually, at the moment of impact, I suspect the kids were farther from the platform edge than the adults.

Once the train had stopped, with its last squeal and shudder, came a ceremony that I witnessed a thousand times. The brakeman emerged from the leading passenger coach, put down his step box, and helped people off and on; the station agent and his assistant pulled the high-wheeled baggage and mail trucks alongside the express-and-mail car, and unloaded dozens of boxes, crates, empty cream cans, and sacks of mail, including the locked, registered-mail pouch that would have to be personally received and signed for; the local drayman claimed bags, boxes, packages, and cans. Passengers stepped forward to lay hands on their luggage: leather or fiber suitcases with brass locks and corner pieces, further secured with heavy straps, and always a trunk or two. You could travel hardly any distance without a trunk, either a round-topped or a flat-topped one, equipped with sturdy lock and fasteners, and roped with quarter-inch manila rope. Now and then you would see a wardrobe trunk, hinged in the middle. You pointed out your trunk to the drayman, and for thirty-five cents he and his assistant loaded it on their wagon, and before long they arrived at your house and carried your trunk inside, setting it down in your second-floor bedroom or wherever you wanted it.

Nearly everybody among the ones who were arriving or departing knew everybody else. One did not need a claim check for express or baggage. Train crew and station crew developed friendships extending over many years. Always there was a vast amount of laughing and joking, repeating standard gags that seemed to get better at each telling.

After freight, baggage, mail, and passengers were unloaded, the loading began: boxes, egg crates, full cream cans, crates with squawking chickens, tagged sacks of mail. Departing passengers displayed their tickets and verified connection points ("Gallatin? Change at Pattonsburg."). The conductor helped with this process at times, but anyone could see that he was a man with weightier responsibilities: conferring with the station agent, overseeing the loading and unloading, and keeping time on the entire operation. Every conductor radiated the impression that someday he would own the whole railroad.

Hardly five minutes would be spent, but considering that this drama, this slice of life, was to be repeated every few miles, one could see that the trip to Kansas City would require all of the four and a half hours scheduled.

At the head of the train, fireman and engineer staged their own impressive show with fistfuls of cotton waste and big oil cans, attending to critical joints and slides. Not a kid in town but knew the whole oiling routine, and would have done it freely, willingly, and correctly at the slightest beckoning of the finger, with no thought of pay, and would have bragged about it to children and grandchildren the rest of his life. The fireman grandly opened the door to the combustion chamber, revealing its roaring fire, which would spring into new life as he fed it fresh scoops of coal, and belch huge curls of smoke and clinker dust out of the smokestack. The locomotive had its own husky, panting sound, like an exhausted beast recovering from one sprint and catching its breath for the next. The bell, operated by a clever mechanical device, rang steadily.

The station agent's most dramatic responsibility was to stand on the edge of the platform at the approach of each train, holding a message fastened to a loop at the end of a stick; this the engineer deftly snatched as he came in for the stop. The message had all sorts of information about the track ahead and authorized the train to proceed, wait on the siding for a passing train, or slow down for a bridge or crossing where the section gang was working. The conductor also got a copy. On a single-track line one cannot be too careful.

As passengers were in place before mail and baggage, the conductor moved from the passenger area to the baggage area and began to look at his Hamilton or Elgin with the oversize figures, as if to suggest that time was hurrying and the job of loading had better be finished just about now. The O.K. was seldom late except at flood time. Finally everything was finished to his entire satisfaction; he yelled his final "All aboard!" and signaled the engineer that his moment had come. Once the engineer got that signal, the train belonged to him. The tune of the locomotive abruptly changed; drive wheels began to turn, spinning at first but slowly taking hold; slack throughout the train's length would be gradually taken up as the cars began to move forward, one after another, bangety-bang-bang; conductor and brakeman dutifully stood, calm and poised, on the station platform, as the train accelerated; then, at exactly the last second, each grabbed a handrail and gracefully swung upon the steps, climbed them, and closed the door behind him. Even if they had worn capes, they could hardly have given a swishier performance.

Empathically, every kid on the platform also hopped aboard with the same infinite aplomb. After the train had left we hurried to the rails to see what had happened to our crossed pins and horseshoe nails.

At times the station crowd was twice as large as usual, which meant, to seasoned depot watchers, that a casket was scheduled to arrive. Among those silently waiting were women in black, wearing heavy-textured, all-enveloping mourning veils; and men in their Sunday best—dark suits, high collars, string bow ties; one could see reddened eyes and faraway expressions and hear the quiet sounds of grief. The crowd was solemn; the joking and joshing were halted; incoming boxes were handled more quietly and cans did not clink so loud. We stood around watching as the baggage car was slowly emptied of its usual cargo. Eventually the large pine box, containing the casket, appeared. Bill Haines, the undertaker, was on hand to oversee its reception and somberly carry it, with the help of friends, to the waiting, horse-drawn hearse. Gently, carefully, the box was placed inside the hearse, and, as it pulled away, the crowd slowly dissolved. On those days it hardly seemed proper to play with pins on the tracks.

Father used to say that although Bill himself looked as if he had just been lifted from one of his pine boxes, he actually had more loyalty and town spirit than anyone. I was not surprised to read, years later, that when a committee of citizens was selected to meet with railroad officials to get improved service, Bill was among those chosen. The O.K. meant something special to him that it did not mean to anyone else.

Often these boxes came from St. Joe, the principal city in the region for major medical care. Such was the state of medicine that surgery was considered the last resort when all else had failed. People so dreaded the knife that they would not consent to an operation until the ailment was almost past the point of no return. The long train ride to the hospital, a journey involving two different lines and a connection, which would test the stamina of a well person, was an ordeal for a sick one. By the time he got there he could not offer much for the surgeon to work on.

The depot I knew was a sturdy, brick structure, with wide, overhanging, sheltering eaves, the successor to the $700 shack that the community had originally erected for the railroad. A partition divided the waiting room from the inner sanctum. A door led from one to the other, and a window provided an opening for the dispensation of tickets, telegrams, bills of lading, and travel information. Inside was the agent, the local personification of the whole O.K. system, who was ticket seller, information dispenser, and telegraph dispatcher. Others had duties in connection with baggage, express, and freight. Most magical of all was the table with telegraph transmitters and receivers, incessantly clacking away. From a big window facing the track the depot crew had a good view of the platform. In addition there was a ladies' waiting room, that strange relic of chivalry, found universally in depots. Here

women either because of their shyness or their wish to keep a close
eye on young children could elect to sit apart from other travelers.

The public half of the depot featured an iron potbellied stove
with a coal box, coal hods, and shovels. It had two temperatures,
too hot and too cold. To raise the temperature, one scooped in coal.
To lower the temperature, one opened the stove door, which
checked the draft and thus slowed combustion. A huge brass spittoon was nearby, but wherever it was, it was never in the right
place, judging by the spotted areas on the floor. The sign, "Do not
spit on the floor," did not help much. Wooden benches were arranged along three sides of the room. Posters advertising special
excursions, some current and some of remote date, were tacked
on the wall. These featured a picture of a huge locomotive pulling
a string of Pullman cars, with places, dates, and prices in large
letters. For $5.50 the O.K. offered a round-trip ticket to St. Louis;
for $60 a trip to the Golden Gate and back. For only a little more
you could go to the Klondike and participate in the gold rush.
Occasionally I also saw a poster I had printed, advertising a farm
sale or the services of a jack or stallion.

The business that Gilman City generated for the O.K. was
astonishing. A crowd of a hundred—a fifth or sixth of the total population—was not infrequent, since most travel was by rail. The
auto was coming on strong, but, lacking good roads, was entirely
at the mercy of the weather. Any rain would reduce driving speed
to a crawl, and a heavy rain to zero. Every road had mudholes that
in some seasons only a team could negotiate. Of course a sustained
downpour washed out bridges on roads and railroads alike.

During spring and fall seasons, for the convenience of shoppers and shippers, the O.K. put on special trains to serve the Tren-
ton-Pattonsburg section, one arriving at 7 A.M. from the east and
one at 6 P.M. from the west. These bore the stately designations of
No. 4 and No. 3. Sometimes a special left Brimson and Melbourne
at approximately 6:30 P.M., arriving in Gilman City before 7 P.M.,
allowing passengers and crew to go to the Rex, the only theatre
for miles around, to see its two-hour Thursday mix of a newsreel
plus two lively serials. The special stood on the tracks until the
show was over and then took the moviegoers back home.

The depot sat with its back to the town, on an island of hard-

The O.K. depot: waiting room at far end, baggage room at near end. The first train entered Gilman City in 1897; the line was abandoned in 1939 and the tracks torn out soon thereafter. The depot building was sold and wrecked. A church now stands on the old foundations. (From *Gilman City, 1973*)

packed cinders. On the south, or town side, was an excellent place for the marble players, as cinders were nice and smooth and dried rapidly even after a downpour. The two favorite marble games were bump back in which players lined up a few feet from the depot foundation wall and took turns tossing commies, or common marbles, toward the wall, trying to hit any marble there. For a while marbles accumulated, but sooner or later a player would hit one and could then step forward to reap the harvest, leaving behind a single commie as the next target. We played other games, but more marbles could change hands faster through bump back than in any other way. I regularly supplied the other players quantities of fresh, new commies, paid for with the money I earned from my paper route. Every town had a few kids like me: compulsive gamblers, long on marbles and short on talent.

Nowadays people who collect marbles display their handful of prizes as lovingly as if they were rubies. But I knew half a dozen kids who had shoeboxes full of aggies, steelies, moonies, chinas, crockeries—the whole lot—and they had won every one by their own skill, first winning an opponent's commies and then trading him back his own commies for whatever finer specimens he happened to have with him. I further suspect that any of these kids would have traded his whole collection for a controlling interest in a bicycle.

I have already mentioned the water tank at which the locomotives quenched their thirst. It was perhaps fifteen feet high and sat alongside the track, its long spout connected to the bottom of the tank. When the spout was not in use, it was pulled upright, so that tank and spout looked like a giant coffeepot against the sky. Nearby were the stockyards, along a siding on which were always a few open-slatted hog, horse, or cattle cars. The stockyards, extending a fourth of a city block in each direction, consisted of wooden fences, arranged in squares, with gates so that animals in one square could be driven into another or into a passageway and up a chute that led to the cars. The ingenious arrangement of squares, gates, and passageways made it easy for the shipper to grade, sort, and feed his animals as he wished. The solidly built gates were fun to swing on. When the stockyards were empty and when no adults were around to bother, we played a form of tag that we named "bumbrakie." The term must have come from "bum" and "brakeman," so that in our own way we symbolized the perpetual contest between the bums that tried to snitch long, free rides on the O.K.'s freight trains, and the brakemen who just as continually tried to spot them and throw them off.

As the fences were made of smooth, well-rubbed 1 x 4 boards, nailed horizontally a foot or so apart, we could sidle along a lower rail at a handsome speed; and since a horizontal four inch board was nailed connecting the tops of the posts, we could, if we preferred, run along the top. Touching the ground was forbidden.

As in any tag game, one person was "it," and after other players had been given a slight head start, he set out in pursuit to tag someone to be the next "it." If you approached a gate at its latch end, ahead of your pursuer, you could unfasten it and swing away, leaving a gap between you and him. Even if you approached it from the hinge side you could, given sufficient lead, reach the opposite end, and give the gate a push that would swing him away and give you at least a moment's reprieve. By the time we had played a couple of hours, and each of us had slipped into the pens a few times, the floors of which were covered with you-know-what, we were in such condition that only a devoted mother could love on strictly a short-term basis. The Big Boys played bumbrakie on the stock cars, climbing ladders, running along the tops, shinnying along the sides of the slatted cars, and in other daring maneuvers eluding capture as long as possible. I never graduated to this variety, but at the other game, being small, quick, and agile, I was a star. This talent helped offset my frequent inability to hit a commie.

The O.K. was a prime source of news for the Great Moral and Religious Weekly. For a decade Mother visited the depot twice a day, learning who was going where, or who was arriving to visit whom, and picking up other news from her conversations with the town's traveling elite. Hence when the paper came out on Thursday the world would know that Emmett Woltz and Roy Ford had attended the implement dealers' convention in Kansas City; that Mr. and Mrs. Hugh DeWitt were in Trenton Tuesday, where Mr. DeWitt had his teeth extracted; that Misses Stella Gustin and Odessa Warner went to Trenton on Tuesday to visit friends; that Misses Stella Gustin and Odessa Warner returned from Trenton on Saturday, where they had been visiting friends; that Charley Hurst returned from St. Louis, where he had attended the meeting of the Knights of Pythias Grand Lodge as a delegate. Or Lowell Baumgartner, who had spent the last three weeks in St. Clair Hospital, St. Joseph, where he was operated on for appendicitis, had returned home, and was now doing as well as could be expected. That last phrase meant simply that the Lord had not yet decided to reveal what He was going to do about Lowell. Meanwhile, *Guide* readers could marvel that thus far Lowell had survived both the infection and the surgery, and, actually, as I well remember, he recovered altogether and could display a ten inch scar ascending his belly.

Although most trips were social, the *Guide* also recorded students going to and returning from college, patients seeking medical treatment, merchants on buying expeditions, business and professional men attending conventions, enlisted men and draftees going to war, voters attending political meetings. In brief, the O.K. was to Gilman City what automobile and airplane are to cities today. The chief difference was in distances traveled; the outer limits tended to be St. Joseph, Kansas City, Chicago, and St. Louis.

Obviously Mother could case a depot crowd quickly, spot who was leaving, who was there to meet someone, and who was just hanging around. She would not have to ask Odessa how to spell her name, or Charley Hurst where he had been when he stepped off the train. She would not even have to interview Dr. Quinlan, the dentist, because she knew that on Tuesdays he went to Coffey where he had an office and a practice.

In the summer when school was not in session, the job of reporting fell to me. Armed with notebook and pencil, dressed in blue shirt and overhalls (*overalls* was a word we did not use), mop-haired and barefooted, I made the rounds fourteen times a week and got so I could also process a depot crowd swiftly, though I never really enjoyed the assignment.

We learn the hard way. In the earlier part of my career as a reporter, I arrived at the depot one noon and noted that it was unusually full and that the atmosphere was somber, a situation that should have alerted me but didn't. With notebook in hand and pencil at the ready, I approached a kindly looking lady, dressed in black, and asked her, "Are you going somewhere?"

"No, son, I'm not."

"Are you here to meet someone?" I persisted.

After a pause, she answered, "Yes."

Unsuspecting, I hurried on. "Who are you meeting?"

"My husband," she said, in a voice almost inaudible.

"What is his name?" I pursued. She told me.

"Has he been away on a visit?"

"Not exactly."

I still did not perceive that we were on a collision course, but at that juncture a neighboring lady mercifully intervened, took me to one side, and whispered, "Her husband died yesterday at St. Clair Hospital. She's here to meet the corpse."

Ever the alert newsman, I continued: "I'm sorry. Will you ask the family to send us an obituary?" And then, for a reason that I will never understand, I added: "Our readers will be glad to see it."

Next time I entered a waiting room full of solemn people I turned and fled.

Times came when I myself was a traveler. I recall every trip: to Trenton to get my picture taken, to get an earache remedied (a grain of wheat had started to sprout in it), to take an elocution lesson in connection with an oratorical contest; to Pattonsburg to meet, halfway, cousins who were coming from Gallatin to visit us, or to go to Gallatin or Winston to visit grandparents, uncles, aunts, and cousins; to Kansas City, the most thrilling adventure of all. So I have a composite memory of the smoke billowing, the bell ringing, the whistle blowing at crossings, the Union News agent selling candy and pulp magazines, the chatter of trainmen at each stop, the heat, the squeaks, the rattles, the creaks, the clicking of the rail joints, the swaying chandelier, the stuffy smoking room at the head of the coach, the conductor bellowing the name of the next stop, the passengers staggering down the aisles of the weaving cars, bumping from seat to seat, carrying packages and suitcases, the brakeman assisting passengers to descend, the alert eyes of conductor and brakeman on the process of boarding and of freight unloading and loading, the engineer and fireman making their final check of gauges and valves, the collecting and punching of tickets, and the posting of slips above each passenger indicating his destination in an unsolvable code, the perpetual awe of the men who wore their tickets in their hatbands, jauntily, like modern cavaliers —all were a part of the O.K. and of the railroading of those days.

In the early days of railroading, a trip from Kansas City to the west coast required the better part of five days, with stops every few miles, and with special points at which every passenger left the train and ate luncheon at the station. When Father worked for Congressman Alexander, Mother, Don, and I took a trip from Bethany to Washington, which required three days, with a long stopover at Harrisburg, Pennsylvania. There was no sleeper but you could rent a pillow for a quarter.

The limited train, the express, and the through train were far in the future. Most trains were locals, or what the British call "stopping trains," which did indeed stop at every station. The railroads never did solve the problem of a coast-to-coast train. Major routes began or ended at one of three gateways: Chicago, St. Louis, or New Orleans, and everybody continuing had to change not only trains but also lines. The Chesapeake and Ohio once advertised, "Why can you ship a hog across the country but not a person?" This embarrassing question was never answered.

In a decade that embraced a great world war, that is known in the books as the Wilson-Harding-Coolidge administrations, that included Father's and Mother's *Guide* editing and postmastering, that encompassed all but the final year of my grade schooling and high schooling, I lived with the O.K. as I lived with Wednesday's Press Day—its regularity, its routine, its inevitability. The railroad was one of the prime institutions of human existence. When I set out on my last trip, I will take the O.K. to the Big Depot in the sky, stopping at every planet and star and galaxy and black hole, eagerly watching crowds of angels handling sacks of mail and boxes and packages and cream cans. When after all those stops it finally reaches the Pearly Gates, I will once again be completely at home; I will deftly unlatch them in a mighty game of celestial bumbrakie and swing all over God's heaven, leaving the devil behind at a permanent gap that he will never be able to leap across.

7

Life at the Summit

Two years after Woodrow Wilson's election in 1912, Father became postmaster and shouldered postal duties in addition to publishing responsibilities. His credentials were impeccable for this most sought-after political appointment. He knew Congressman Alexander personally, having served as his secretary, and also both Missouri senators. He had strongly supported Wilson in his hard-fought campaign. With these endorsements he might have been an Interstate Commerce Commissioner, but he was delighted to have the Gilman City post office.

We were excited when the U.S. Senate confirmed his appointment, and even more so when his commission arrived, signed personally by the president of the United States and by A. S. Burleson, the postmaster general. I may be the only American who can say offhand, without consulting references, that Burleson was Wilson's postmaster general. Or, for that matter, that Alexander became his secretary of commerce. Every family has a set of names that cannot be forgotten.

The post office was located in the front half of one of Bill Noll's brick buildings, on the southwest corner of Main and Broadway. Father promptly moved the *Guide* to the back half. An inside door connected the *Guide* and post office, so by the simple process of walking through the door Father could shift from editor and proprietor to postmaster, and vice versa.

Gilman City boasted a third-class post office and, as such, was entitled to have not only a postmaster, but an assistant postmaster and other prerogatives. The total volume of business, such as stamp sales and money-order fees, determined the difference between third-class and fourth-class status. At a magical figure I never knew, the line was drawn. As we had no big-mail customers, we had to reach the magic total by a dime here and a quarter there. Our margin of safety was uncomfortable.

Never in the wide world would we ever attain the rank of a

second-class office, but any year we could slip back to the ignominy of a fourth-class enterprise. In such an event, Father's $1,100 salary would be sharply reduced. Moreover, the position of assistant postmaster would disappear. As the assistant postmaster was Mother, and her salary was $400 a year, the possibility of doom was always imminent. Furthermore, Mr. Burleson picked up Bill Noll's tab for rent, but a fourth-class postmaster had to furnish his own quarters, which would have to be something between what we now had and Blue Ridge's ten mailboxes nailed to a slab.

Everything was governed by the P.L. & R., which, as everybody in the family knew, meant "Postal Laws and Regulations." These rules were detailed, demanding, and grim. The larger offices had an overhead, walk-through gallery or tunnel, with peepholes here and there, so that an inspector, unseen and unannounced, could see what the employees were doing. Now and then we heard a sad story about a postal employee who had pocketed a piece of mail and had been personally observed by the hidden inspector. One poor devil was stripped of his pension rights just a few weeks before he would have retired. To me the penalty seemed harsh.

Though our post office did not have a gallery, the postmaster knew that any day an inspector would drop in and would have full access to books and records. He counted the stamps, examined the serial numbers of unused money orders, made sure that the date on the postmark had been changed every day, and that Father had maintained a proper inventory. The inspector then filed a report, certain to contain admonitions and demerits. Although Father was an experienced businessman, dating back to his early government service as assessor and coal-oil inspector, the visit of the inspector was something to have in the back of the mind, like, today, the possibility of being hauled in for an income-tax audit.

A postmaster lived an uneasy existence for another reason. Since his was a political appointment, his tenure hinged upon the outcome of each national election. As long as Wilson and other Democrats were in power, Father could continue in office. If ever the Republicans won the White House, Father's postmastership would abruptly end. Nowadays these matters are determined by civil service, a change that must be a great relief to congressmen who formerly had to choose among various worthy applicants in every community, and, in the process of nominating one postmaster, make ten times as many enemies as friends. People may forget those who do them favors but remember forever those who disappoint them. Father would have added that this quirk of human nature is doubtly true of Democrats.

The office was open weekdays from seven in the morning until six at night, and even on Sundays long enough to distribute the mail. In our home Father was the first to get up, building a fire in the living-room stove in cool seasons, getting his own breakfast, and walking up the street to the post office, building another fire in the stove there. The rural carriers arrived to put the mail they had sorted the previous afternoon into their leather pouches and then started on their routes.

After the carriers had left, the early-morning patrons had been served, and the floor had been swept with sweeping compound, Father had time to write news stories, letters, or poetry. He submitted so many manuscripts that he accumulated enough rejection slips to paper the west wall but eventually made the *Ladies*

This photo was taken in 1914, only a few days after Father was confirmed by the Senate and commissioned by President Wilson to be postmaster at Gilman City. The lady at his left, the mother of two sons ages nine and six, is the assistant postmaster.

The post office was in the front of the building, the *Guide* in the back.

Home Journal, Harper's Weekly, The New Century, and others. From there his poems were reprinted in numerous daily and weekly newspapers.

Father's correspondents included government officials, newspaper editors, and scores of friends and relatives. He was naturally interested in the School of Journalism at the University of Missouri, and once wrote Walter Williams, its founder and first dean, but got no reply. When a second letter also went unanswered, Father took the opportunity when he next printed a short piece about the journalism school to end with the sentence, "We understand the School of Journalism at the University of Missouri is the second best in the whole country." When the dean saw a marked copy, he took one glance at that "second best" and reacted immediately. Afterwards he was so diligent about answering his Gilman City mail that he and Father exchanged two or three letters a year on various subjects.

Father also got to know Floyd C. Shoemaker, for long the director of the State Historical Society of Missouri. Father took care to impress on us that a copy of each issue of the *Guide* must be sent to the State Historical Society for its permanent file. Sometimes press trouble spoiled so many copies that we omitted the more distant subscribers, but the Society was a non-omissible item. Looking through the files recently I saw that in one issue we had forgot to change the date, printing the whole issue under the dateline of the previous week. Mother, however, had corrected in pen and ink the date of the copy mailed to Columbia. She wanted the State Historical Society to have it right.

Today all that remains of twenty years of *Guide* publishing appears on eight spools of microfilm in the Society's newspaper room. One day I spread them out on a table and noted wryly that they occupied about as much space as a Sears and Roebuck catalog. The *Kansas City Star*, however, is meeting a similar fate.

All in all Father got a lot of work done during the morning hours at the post office. By mid-morning Mother had completed her chores at home and had arrived to assume her duties as assistant postmaster. At noon she left to interview travelers at the depot, returning to the post office about the time that the Bob Cole Dray & Transfer Service had hauled the main there.

The post office played an important social function at Gilman City, as it did in thousands of other small towns. Though everybody knew to the exact minute when the O.K. rolled into the station and that mail would not be in the boxes for forty-five minutes or an hour afterwards, the lobby began to fill even before the sacks got to the office. From up and down Main Street and side streets, forty or fifty business people and others left individual shops, stores, offices, and homes for the socializing that accompanied the distribution of the mail. In the lobby, everybody could put aside personal problems for the moment and share in the general good will. While visiting, those who had lockboxes could remove their letters and papers just as quickly as they were distributed. Others would line up to call for their mail from general delivery when the windows opened. The lobby was a combination service club, chamber of commerce. lodge meeting, town bulletin, and coffee break, without membership restrictions, dues, or officers. If Gilman City had a summit, this was it.

The noon mail was the larger, with four or five full sacks and sometimes twice as much. In addition was a sack of first-class mail, and sometimes a locked pouch with registered letters and packets. Immense shipments of catalogs from Sears and Sawbuck, Monkey Ward, and other mail-order houses—known by these names rather than by their formal titles—came two or three times a year. December brought bagsful of calendars, each in its large envelope or long cardboard tube. Any business firm could display three or four wall calendars with large numbers that could be seen across the room. December also brought extra sacks of Christmas mail. In the spring came the free seeds furnished by the Department of Agriculture and sent by members of Congress over their personal franks. Wide, flat boxes containing baby chicks arrived regularly. Something in the constitution of a day-old chick permits its being shipped without provision for food or water. They cheeped and chirped away happily as a fluty obbligato to the comments and greetings coming from the lobby.

Rural free delivery was the greatest invention of the postal service between the invention of the adhesive stamp and the use of airplanes to carry the mail. Twenty-five or thirty thousand rural routes served the nation's farm families at one time or another. But to me the whole vast system was focused on Tom Welden, Bill Middleton, Carl Price, and later Charley Hurst, who served the three routes operating out of the post office.

The primary requisites for a rural carrier were a heart like Barney Oldfield's and a calm disregard for personal comfort. Each carrier had approximately twenty-six miles of narrow, winding, hilly, dirt road that had to be traversed regardless of the weather for $60 a month. The famous slogan of the postal service, "Neither snow, nor rain, nor heat, nor gloom of night stays these couriers from the swift completion of their appointed rounds," was, in the minds of our carriers, translated as referring to steep hills, rutted roads with deep ditches on either side or both sides, bridges that were shaky even in good weather, mudholes that would sometimes grip a horse up to his knees, and temperatures ranging from twenty below to a hundred and ten above.

Father became postmaster at a time when carriers were beginning to use automobiles. The carriers gradually acquired cars but had to keep horses in reserve. On a good day a carrier could cover his route by car and be back well before noon. If he got caught in a rain, however, he would have to add an hour to his travel time. If the roads were so bad he had to use a horse and the familiar, enclosed, four-wheeled cart, he would be gone until the middle of the afternoon. Sometimes, however, when the ruts were deep and frozen, he went on horseback. Horseback travel was especially venturesome for Bill Middleton, carrier on Route 2, who had a wooden leg. If he had to dismount, he found it awkward to get back up on the saddle and sometimes had to wait for someone to come along to give him a push.

Beginning about November, most cars were put in garages and not used until spring made the roads passable again.

The rural carrier was a traveling post office. He not only delivered mail, but picked up letters and packages to take back, weighing and stamping as necessary. He collected CODs. He sold stamps and postcards. He did not actually write money orders, but filled out the application blank and either came back with the money order next trip, or stuffed it in an envelope and mailed it as the patron requested. This variety of services was valuable to farm families, since ordinarily they came to town only on Saturdays.

After the carrier returned to the office, he found the day's accumulation of mail in his bin—letters, circulars, periodicals, packages—the time-honored four classes of mail. He transferred handsful to his worktable, which was waist high and about thirty inches square, with an upright at the back supporting forty or fifty pigeonholes. Once the mail for each farm family was in the appropriate pigeonhole, he grouped letters and papers in bundles, fastening each with a leather strap. The bundles were transferred to heavy leather pouches. Packages were managed separately. In general the mail was arranged in the same order as the boxes on the route.

The arrival of the carrier at the box of each patron was keenly awaited. No one received much mail—perhaps a single letter, a circular, a package, a copy of the *Weekly Kansas City Star* or *Capper's Weekly*—but each bit was a thing of interest. Invariably there was sprightly conversation, and in bitter weather the half-frozen carrier might be invited inside to thaw out over a cup of coffee.

Many boxes, however, were at the end of a lane, away from the home, and the carrier simply left the mail and drove on. As a boy I got to know the carriers well and enjoyed listening to their accounts of the day's adventures. Often they alerted us to news stories about illnesses, accidents, crop conditions, and comings and goings.

Besides the scheduled services, the post-office staff and rural carriers did all sorts of things to make the system work. They decoded handwriting, delivered mail even though the address was not correct, put an extra cord around packages that had ruptured in transit, advised patrons about the best time of mailing, met special requests of stamp collectors, helped with the tangle of overseas mailing, and forwarded letters. They took a personal interest when they were made aware that a patron was eagerly expecting a particular letter. A young man or young woman might make guarded inquiries at the general delivery window about a letter from a girlfriend or boyfriend and show keen disappointment when days went by with no letter. Usually, however, the moment came when Mother could say, "Your letter came today," and share in the smiles that followed.

I was reminded again of this concern of postal employees when one day I received a letter rubber-stamped, "Fell Into the Bay at San Francisco, Calif." I could visualize a conference among the postal employees, wondering how to handle goodness-knows-how-many sacks of mail that had somehow fallen into the harbor and thus had suffered this unusual delay in transit. Someone must have said, "Well, let's just tell the addressees what happened," so that is the way we got the word.

Despite the P.L. & R.'s specific order respecting unauthorized personnel, I frequently drifted into the office while the mail was being sorted. Anyone under twenty-one—much less one only ten or eleven—was strictly forbidden to handle U.S. mail. Although I was eager to help and often did, I tacitly understood that if a stranger appeared in the back doorway, I was to stop my mail handling and drift away. The stranger might be the inspector, who had a hot line to the postmaster general and the four assistant postmasters general, who could reduce Father to fourth class or worse. Gradually I became proficient as a mail sorter. Though Gilman City had no street addresses or box numbers and rural route designations were often omitted, I learned who was town and who was rural, who was regular and who was transient, who had boxes and who went to general delivery. I also learned the carefully prescribed ways of postmarking and bundling mail and what went on eastbound No. 1 or westbound No. 2.

Those were the days when a red two cent stamp would carry a letter and a green one-center a postcard. For a dime one could buy a special delivery stamp, bearing the picture of a man and a motorcycle, that assured personal delivery of the letter. Out of this ten cent fee the postmaster claimed eight cents for the trip. Although the P.L. & R. did not require the postmaster to deliver beyond the city limits, Father often did. One summer day a letter from Chicago came to the daughter of Hugh Markey, who lived well outside of the town in the fanciest home of the neighborhood. Father had such admiration for Markey, a tall, slender, white-haired man, a fine, public-spirited citizen, and a frequent caller at the *Guide*, that he decided to deliver the letter himself, inviting me to go along. I went partly to be company and partly because the Markeys had a white locomobile, with big brass headlights and a wide leather strap around its hood, that I wanted to feast my eyes on.

Despite his bad leg, Father could, and often did, walk long distances, and we strolled over the dusty road for what seemed like miles before we reached the Markey front door. I still remember the graciousness with which the daughter of the house greeted us, telling us that we should not have made the trip since the letter was not all that important, and that she would write her friend and tell him not to write her special delivery. Even so, it is nice to get a letter from your boyfriend on a hot summer afternoon. I wondered if he thought a man with a motorcycle was available at Gilman City for special delivery service, and on the walk home I mentally designed a new stamp, in ultramarine blue, showing a crippled man and a boy trudging down an endless country lane.

As Father kept a running tally of the daily take, he was aware one autumn that postal receipts were declining so steadily that they might sink below the critical point. Actually he could do little to stimulate the sale of stamps. About that time, however, Don and I needed clothes, so Father and Mother picked a couple of dandy suits out of the Sears and Roebuck catalog, quality merchandise at $15 per suit, and made the total remittance in twenty-five cent stamps, the largest denomination the office carried, and sent them along with the order blank. Father had to struggle with his conscience on the issue of buying from a mail-order house, but the situation called for strong measures if Gilman City were to keep its third-class office and not sink to fourth class, and a $30 sale of stamps would materially increase the day's receipts. In due course the suits arrived, a bluish grayish pattern with knee breeches, and Don and I were delighted with them.

Actually nominal remittances in stamps were a common occurrence, as most people did not have checking accounts and did not want to put coins in an envelope. Father was unaware, however, of a postal regulation that required mail-order houses to report, routinely, unusually large remittances made in stamps. Post offices were sometimes robbed, thieves using the stamps as currency. Sears therefore duly revealed that on such and such a day it had received a remittance of $30 worth of twenty-five cent stamps. A check further indicated that the said remitter was the Gilman City postmaster.

In a remarkably short time, the inspector appeared. To me this visit meant simply that I had to keep out of the office until he had left, so I turned to my *Guide* chores, which that day consisted principally of sitting atop a high stool, in front of a case, setting type for the next issue.

The inspector proceeded with his customary rigor, but Father's books were accurate. One of the daily reports showed a heavy movement in twenty-five cent stamps—a denomination that ordinarily was an exceptionally poor seller, as for twenty-five cents you could almost ship a packed suitcase. When the inspector began to question this unusual traffic in twenty-five stamps, Father realized that the visit had ominous significance. He readily admitted that he had bought the stamps himself, the inspector reflecting that $30 worth of twenty-five cent stamps seemed like quite a few. Father, however, saw nothing extraordinary about buying suits for two growing boys and remitting in twenty-five cent stamps. After all, the office did not carry fifty cent stamps. Suddenly the inspector found himself fresh out of all the polite questions and was not entirely prepared to support an inquiry into his suspicious ones.

The inspector turned to other matters but before long quietly entered the office where I was working. He knew about the *Guide* arrangement and that I was the postmaster's son; he spoke in a friendly way and seemed interested in my activity. I felt pleased to be noticed by a gentleman of his eminence and told him that I was setting type. I showed him the location of the different letters in the little boxes that constitute a case of type.

"Well," he said, after my explanation, "you are a bright little boy, to be setting type at your age."

He took such an interest in my typesetting that before long we were chatting intimately.

"I'll bet you have a nice father and mother," he said, by way of openers.

"Oh, yes," I replied.

"I imagine they buy you a lot of presents," he pursued.

"Yes, often."

"What kind of presents?"

"Well, just a few weeks ago they bought my brother and me new suits."

"Did they buy them here in town?" he continued.

"Oh, no," I stoutly denied. "They came from Kansas City. Sears and Roebuck."

Over the inspector's shoulder, out of the corner of my eye, I could see Mother standing in the doorway. Undoubtedly she was emitting all kinds of alarm signals, but, wrapped in the ecstasy of a new-found, highly placed admirer, I disregarded the warning.

The inspector moved in for the kill, offering the notion that if my folks had bought two suits at Sears, they would have had to send a pretty good-sized check to pay for them.

"No, sir," I volunteered. "They sent twenty-five cent stamps."

"That's interesting," he ruminated. "I wonder why they sent stamps."

"Why, they thought it would help increase the business of the office."

"That's right," he observed. "It sure would. Well, you are certainly a bright little boy—a mighty bright little boy."

The inspector returned to the post office to confront my thoroughly uncomfortable parents, who had just seen themselves sold down the river utterly and completely by their mighty bright little boy. Yet, over and above a few words of explanation, he decided to take no official action. Perhaps he acted from a sense of decency; perhaps he felt ashamed of himself for taking advantage of a kid; perhaps he felt pleased with himself for getting to the bottom of the affair. Perhaps he concluded that actually it was no big deal, since the records of the office were in fine shape. Moreover, any kind of long-term view indicated that the needs of the community could not be served by a fourth-class office.

That evening the postmaster and the assistant postmaster reviewed for me personally what I had done. I comforted myself by reflecting that it would never happen again, and sure enough, it never did. In the years to come I bought dozens of suits and dresses for my own children but never paid for any of them with twenty-five cent stamps. What a pity it is to learn something at great trouble and never be able to profit from it.

Some months later Father decided to open a stand in the lobby and sell newspapers, magazines, and stationery. A request to engage in this enterprise went all the way from Main and Broadway to Postmaster General Burleson and back again. The word was handed down that such a modest business would be legitimate—the postmaster general could in no way imagine that it would be detrimental to the best interests of the service, and besides he saw supporting letters from three congressmen and two senators, all of whom knew Father personally. A fancy sign was painted on the front window announcing The Boys' Newsstand, Don and I thus being billed as the nominal proprietors.

Father opened an account with Butler Brothers, a famous St. Louis jobbing firm, and soon was placing orders for pencils, tablets, erasers, crayons, penholders and pen points, and other kinds of interesting merchandise. We helped mark the coded cost price and the selling price on each item, thus introducing us to the basic logistics of merchandising. For the code word, Father selected the name of a distinguished former governor, congressman, Gallatin native, and a second cousin of Mother: A. M. Dockery. This name is nine letters long, each letter different, and to make the tenth, he added "X." From this he could draw a diagram:

A	M	D	O	C	K	E	R	Y	X
1	2	3	4	5	6	7	8	9	0

With this code, an item such as a Big Chief ruled school tablet that cost three cents, which we proposed to sell for five, could be marked D/5. I am sure that Father found occasion, on a visit to Gallatin, to tell Governor Dockery that his memory was perpetuated in the code book of the Boys' Newsstand.

About this time Mother was concerned that her boys had to leave school at noon before the other pupils, rush home, wolf a lunch, hurry to the depot, pick up bundles of Kansas City and St. Joe papers, carry them over town, and rush back barely in time for afternoon classes. She decided the papers could just as well be left on the counter of the Boys' Newsstand and that customers could pick them up when they came for their mail. One by one she buttonholed them and explained the new arrangement. As no one demurred, from then on we simply left the papers on the counter where regular customers could pick them up and others could buy single copies.

So the Boys' Newsstand linked the community intellectually with the best that was published: *Kansas City Star* and *Times*, *Journal*, and *Post*; *St. Louis Post-Dispatch*; *St. Joseph Gazette* and *News-Press*; also *Colliers, Saturday Evening Post, Pictorial Review, Literary Digest*, and Street and Smith's best pulp novels, as well as supplied writing materials on which our customers could write beautiful thoughts.

On a normal day, once mail from the afternoon train had been distributed, Father crossed the frontier to work in the *Guide* and Mother assumed responsibility for what went on in the post office. She presided at the front window like a queen of the realm.

About four in the afternoon the office had its final surge of activity. By that time the carriers would have reassembled to scoop the day's mail from their individual bins and sort it for the next morning's delivery. A host of school kids regularly stopped to pick up the family mail before going home. Rural families could thus get their letters and papers that evening instead of having to wait until the next day. Many town kids also called to pick up the mail for their families.

Mother and the carriers thus added to their acquaintance the children of the community so that they could greet each patron personally. Almost without looking they knew who had mail and who did not, but they always looked. The post-office lobby was the one place in the community where nearly every family checked in daily. Just to be there and see the world go by was an experience.

One day was much like another, but emergencies arose that upset the routines. Any heavy rain would make the O.K. two or three hours late. Prolonged rains washed out so much track, and so many bridges, and so many telegraph and telephone poles, that Gilman City would be isolated for two or three days: no letters, no newspapers, no telegrams, no crates or boxes or packages. Once the first train to get through arrived in the evening long after closing time, but Father and Mother reopened the office, and, with the carriers, distributed the mail—about twenty sacks full. The lobby was jammed with people who had long been cut off from the outside world, who had heard the train whistle, and who knew from past experience that the post office would be open. Nothing in the P.L. & R. said the office force had to do this. What mattered was that if the O.K. could get the mail to the depot platform, the drayman, the postmaster, the assistant postmaster, and the rural carriers would take it from there.

Each day, half an hour before closing time, Mother left for home so that she could start supper. Father then counted the day's receipts and filled out a form that indicated the number of stamps sold and how many remained in inventory, so the government at Washington would know how its outpost in Sugar Creek Township fared.

In the closing minutes of the official day he went out to the street and slowly lowered the flag. This was our own forty-eight-starred flag, not the one that Theodore Gilman had given the town on the occasion of its first Fourth of July celebration. Don and I often helped, and as Old Glory came closer and closer to the sidewalk, we reached to grab the edges so she would not drag in the dust. We learned to unfasten her from the ropes and the proper way to fold her, and to carry her with tenderness into the office. Father then locked the front door, tucked the unused money-order forms, stamps, and cash in a secret place that I still remember but will never reveal, checked the fire, which by now had pretty much died out, and got ready to move toward home and supper, locking the back door behind him. Another day at the summit was finished.

8

Quit When You Feel Like It

In the summer of 1917, an event occurred that made a momentous change in my life—though I was only twelve years old at the time.

That July Don and I had been put on the train for Winston and Gallatin, where we spent two weeks visiting relatives on both sides of the family. Each year we had looked forward to this interlude on the farm, sometimes helping with wheat shocking, sometimes with threshing, and always with miscellaneous farm chores. In retrospect these visits linked us to the agricultural background of our parents. When we returned, we saw that the Great Moral and Religious Weekly had acquired an Intertype. There it stood, in the middle of the floor, the first thing you saw when you entered: a large, shiny, massive complex of machinery. For us the days of hand composition of straight matter had come to a sudden end.

Of the various makes of linecasting machines, the most famous was the Linotype, invented only thirty years previously by Ottmar Mergenthaler, an ingenious, German-born mechanic. The name was aptly chosen, since the machine cast, from its own pot of molten metal, a whole line of type, spewing lines out at the rate of six or more a minute. In fact the name was so descriptive that it became the generic term for various makes of linecasting machines, of which our new Intertype was one. Mergenthaler's machine revolutionized the art of typesetting. A good hand compositor could set a column of type in two hours and a quarter; a good Linotype operator could set the same column in half an hour.

Of all the linecasting machines invented, American printers chiefly used four different brands. The Intertype was easily the second most popular make. Except for simplifications in the keyboard mechanism, it was practically identical with the Linotype. The Linograph, manufactured by a Davenport, Iowa, corporation, was a poor third; it was excessively simplified, cheaply constructed, and soon disappeared from the scene. Father found one in the

Osceola Tribune when eventually he acquired that newspaper, and I struggled with it many months. A fourth was the Linotype Junior, an early model, previously mentioned; it utilized an entirely different principle of handling the individual matrices or molds and was withdrawn from the market after a few hundred had been manufactured. Few printers today, even among the older generation, have ever heard of the Junior. Father had acquired one when he bought the *Bethany Democrat*, and I had set a few lines on it when I was five or six. Because of this trifle I may be the only living person who has actually set type on all four makes of line-casting machines.

The Intertype was such an assemblage of wheels, cams, levers, springs, belts, slides, chutes, and clutches, that it, along with the Linotype, was regarded as the world's most complicated piece of machinery. Yet it was put together so logically and so expertly that it was rugged and durable, given regular care and attention. We called it, simply and reverently, "The Machine." We did not speak of "operating" it, we "ran" it. Whenever any member of the family said, "Mother is running the machine," we understood at once that she was not feeding a press or a folder, but that she was sitting at the keyboard of the Intertype—The Machine.

Our Intertype had been purchased second-hand from the *Trenton Times*. New it had listed at $2,500; Father got it for $1,500, which was what he had originally paid for the *Guide* itself. A young operator and mechanic, Ed Hull, came from Trenton to install it and teach us to run it. The deal was that he was to stay until one of us was competent to take over. Mother had already received lessons while we were vacationing on the farm. Don, sweet, adorable, and nine, was bright, and could read and write fluently, but, more than that, he had an inner wisdom that told him it was not a good idea to get involved in any kind of machinery. The desirable things of life, like baseball, operated without wheels and levers. The coming of the machine almost totally freed him from the typecase, at least for the next two or three years. In his own good time, he became an expert operator but that accomplishment was well in the future.

What made the arrival of the Intertype a turning point in my career was that I gradually learned a craft that supported me through years of college and graduate school. I was always excited by machinery and could hardly wait to take my turn at the key-board. I was further seduced by comments like "Loren has a great talent with the machine," made principally by people like Ed, who would be free to go home as soon as any of us could at least halfway function.

At first, Father was as eager to learn as anybody. I can still see him sitting at the special chair that Ed had designed with a couple of inches cut off each back leg, tucking the great boot that he wore on his crippled foot alongside the machine's pedestal, wrestling its ninety-key keyboard with his two powerful index fingers, strengthened by years of pounding an Oliver typewriter. As the keyboard of an Intertype is power driven, its keys must be flitted over lightly; if a key is depressed too long, the machine de-livers two or three of that character. One hates to try to set "the" and end up with "tthhheeee." With his sturdy fingering, Father hit so many doubles and triples that it took him forever to compose a single line. And once the line is assembled, it must be lifted into a receiver by a gentle stroke of a lever; too light a touch, and the line never gets away; too heavy a touch, and part of it may be thrown on the floor. These mishaps disturb the morning calm and make the hours drag.

Once the line is lifted properly, it moves to the casting part of the machine and actuates its cams and wheels; that side of the ma-chine springs into life, and there is a series of downs and forwards and backwards and upwards with little squeezings and alignings and pumpings and clatterings, and in ten seconds a hot, new slug, a complete line of type, pops into a holder. The casting mechanism then becomes momentarily quiet and still, and the distributing mechanism takes over. Each letter or character, called a matrix or mat, is returned, one by one, to its proper channel in the reservoir (or "magazine"); the a's to the a-channel, the b's to the b-channel, and so on. As the same mats are used over and over, the supply is never exhausted. That feature in itself is a remarkable advantage of machine composition over hand composition.

At times, sadly, a mat gets twisted and fails to drop into its channel; yet by an ingenious device, it can stop the whole dis-tributor mechanism and thus avoid further piling up. The stop makes a little click. Normally the operator is aware of the click, gets up, walks to the back of the machine, retrieves the bad mat,

An improved model (1909) of the Linotype Junior, similar to the one I operated in the *Bethany Democrat* office.

The Junior, quite different from the machine that the Mergenthaler Company made famous, was discontinued after a few hundred were manufactured.

Other typesetting machines invented about this time were even less successful. One ingenious inventor reasoned that a photographic process, rather than hot-metal linecasting, should be developed. The technical problems overwhelmed him but he was, of course, on the right track.

and restarts the distributor. He must, therefore, not be so intent on his composing that he fails to attend to the other sounds that accompany the normal operation of the machine. If he does not hear the click, the situation rapidly deteriorates, one part of the machine after another coming to a halt. To correct the problem then requires additional time-consuming maneuvers. Father could never hear the click.

The Intertype has other ingenious, safety devices that quietly halt it when something goes wrong, thus preventing it from damaging itself. One normally gets accustomed to the sounds of his own machine, just as the driver of a car quickly detects a new or different squeak, scrape, or rumble. An experienced operator can hear the first signs of trouble, either in his own or in neighboring machines.

Hull quickly perceived that Father was not likely to become the regular operator. Father arrived at the same conclusion by a different route; the editor and proprietor had other things to do than to run the machine. The result was that Mother was gradually pressed into service. She could operate beautifully, but she was slow. She more than made up for her lack of speed by her energy and patience—if she could not get finished by closing time she would work until midnight, or, if necessary, all night. Often she went twenty-four hours without sleep. Mother, however, was impatient of daily cleanup and startup routines—without which mechanical troubles of a most annoying kind were certain to occur. Putting the problem in automobile language, spark plugs needed to be cleaned, tires inflated, tank and radiator filled. If Mother dropped a mat on the floor, it stayed there; she was not a good bender or stooper.

One way and another, about the time I entered high school, the machine became my special responsibility. Before long I was setting far more than the best hand compositor. By coming home from school at four and working until six, I could set two columns or more; the whole paper needed only twelve or fifteen. Someone got the idea that it would not be necessary for me to come home for supper; Don could bring it to me, and thus my work would suffer only a brief interruption. Supper was not even started until the post office closed and Father and Mother had got home; my supper would not even be thought of until the others had eaten;

Setting type on the Intertype.

then it would be brought me by the slowest human being in Sugar Creek Township. Food was really of small importance at that age —like other kids, I ate breakfast and luncheon on the run—but I did need to end the day with a full meal. I remember often rising from the machine, stepping to the front door, and looking toward home, a block away, to see if Don were coming—and, sure enough, he wasn't. Eventually, of course, he made it, and my fried potatoes and biscuits and pork chops tasted awfully good.

Father repeatedly said, "Son, quit when you feel like it." And he meant it. If I happened to leave a job unfinished on a Monday, it could be finished on a Tuesday. But something kept me at the keyboard until all of the copy was set. Maybe it was a small, schoolboy responsibility. Maybe it was the news itself—school news, Main Street and Broadway news, items about people who had gone away, or who had come back, or who had been operated on, or had died; letters from the boys in France or Germany, or in army camps where the flu raged; silver anniversary and golden an- niversary weddings and of course the brand-new weddings; the articles about the *Guide* being an independent paper, and that every one should be independent, except at elections, when he should vote Democratic; warnings about the Hessian fly and the chinch bug; the red or white or blue ribbons won at the county fair or the mammoth State Fair at Sedalia; clippings from Jamesport, Gallatin, Cainsville, or Pattonsburg newspapers; blasts against the pool hall and the people who stopped the paper; all the things that people who live in towns that have newspapers can have recorded and can read about, and which people who live in towns that do not have newspapers seldom get to see in print.

Mother ran the machine during the daytime, sandwiching it in and around her assistant postmastering, writing news items gleaned at the O.K. depot, selling ads, and feeding presses. Father also sold ads, wrote news stories and editorials and combinations of both, took orders for printing, set up ads and sale bills and letterheads, kept books, and got involved in community enterprises like the chautauqua, the lyceum, and the annual Gilman City picnic. And also ran the post office in accordance with the postal laws and regulations.

Father was also the principal fixer for the Intertype. Suppose I hit the *a*-key and the *a* did not fall. Or suppose several *a*'s in the *a*-channel came tumbling out. I would summon Father for these emergencies, and he sat down to "study it out." He compared the action of the *a*-key to the nicely working *o*-key next to it; thus, he could likely see what was wrong. Where he really shone was when the solution of the problem required a new part, which, of course, would normally take days to get. To meet these emergencies, he would find a way of repairing the old part with a combination of wire or filed-out sheet brass so that it would operate as it should. His skill in repairing parts even exceeded his skill in patching belts. If he were completely stumped, he would go to the central office and phone a Trenton or Bethany operator, describe the ailment, and learn how to remedy it. The code of newspaper publishers reads: No matter how bitter the competition, you help your competitor to the utmost with his mechanical difficulties.

Gradually I absorbed the secrets of the professional machinist and got so I could fix most things. I acquired a cheap micrometer and learned the mysteries of measuring in thousandths of an inch. Often, however, something would go wrong and I would not be able to spot the problem. In those instances, as a kind of extreme unction, and before I summoned Father, I got a clean wiping rag and an oil can and wiped off the dust, put a drop of oil in each oil hole, gave a turn to each grease cup, and graphited each sliding part. Often this shotgun procedure solved the problem without my ever knowing how.

Machinery is beautiful when it works but aggravating and frustrating when it doesn't. As the months wore on, the Intertype got increasingly temperamental. At times an itinerant machinist came to town, flashed impressive credentials, and offered to clean and completely readjust our machine for $35. I learned a great deal by watching him, so the $35, a prodigious sum, was not entirely wasted. Invariably parts of the machine, at least, would run better than before.

Eventually, however, new difficulties arose. On days when the machine was acting up and the delivery of the evening meal was slower than usual, I dusted off my favorite fantasy, which was to Run Away From Home. I would board the O.K., go to Trenton, get a job on the *Republican* long enough to earn some money, and would then plan to vanish from the earth altogether, maybe going

as far as Quincy. Or I would go in the other direction to Pattonsburg and set type for the *Call*. I had no doubt that I could start a
new career without difficulty. I dreamed this dream a thousand
times; anyway, a hundred. Operating the machine became so au-
tomatic that I could follow other lines of thought while setting the
weekly news.

But there were glorious moments, as when someone came into
the office and stood behind me and uttered luscious compliments
at seeing this youngster, whose feet could just about reach the floor,
command this vast hunk of steel and belts. If he won my favor, I
would show him how the machine worked and even set his name
on a fresh, hot slug. I was often tempted to pick up the new slug,
hold it by its edges and corners in such a way as to avoid being
burned myself, and then offer it to the victim. As he would inevitably start to grab it by its slick, shiny sides—a few seconds
earlier it had come from a pot of molten metal—I would say, "Be
careful, it's hot," just a fraction of a second too late. The effect was
always dramatic; the victim would take something that I had been
calmly holding, and get a shock from suddenly realizing that it
was hot, and promptly drop it on the floor. And my slightly delayed warning got me off the hook.

After I had been running the machine a couple of years, came
an evening I will never forget, though it happened three-score
years ago.

The ninety keys of the keyboard are arranged in vertical banks
of six and horizontal rows of fifteen; five black banks for the small
letters, five blue banks for the figures and punctuation marks, and
five white banks for the capital letters. Instead of using only one
or two fingers of each hand, as I have seen many operators do, I
had gradually begun to use more and more fingers, flitting over
the keyboard and touching the keys lightly, instead of using the
jabbing or plucking motion used by the average two- or four-finger
operator. On this particular evening I suddenly discovered that I
hardly needed to look at the keyboard at all; I had stored away
in my muscles information about where each key is, whether it
was an *r* under my left index finger or an *X* that my right hand
could float to and touch with my right pinky. With the ecstasy of
this sudden insight I explored this new capability and found that

it actually worked; I no longer had to stare at the keys. Not for years did I discover that other experienced operators had evolved their own touch systems.

One summer weekend, after the paper had gone to press and work was so light that the shop was deserted, I decided to give the machine a complete overhauling, cleaning, and oiling. I collected wrenches and micrometer and started dismantling it.

Anyone with ten cents' worth of experience working with appliances or automobiles knows that some bolts can be removed with confidence, since they serve simply to fasten one part to another. Others, however, regulate minute adjustments; they keep a certain part from moving too far, or keep it in alignment with another part. One tampers with these only if he is positive he cannot only replace but readjust. I had one of the famous Thompson repair manuals at hand, but, as with any repair manual, it always had a lot of interesting and precise information that I never needed and was less explicit in explaining the routines that I did need. It was written in a dialogue style in which The Operator took his troubles to The Machinist. (The Operator: "I'd like to see the internal arrangement of the distributor box." The Machinist: "I'll do it now, we have a little time." My Inner Voice: "I don't want to know how it works. I want to know how to fix it.") Besides, the pictures in the manual did not always correspond to this specific Model A, Intertype. Yet we all kept Thompson, or Rogers, or some other guide, at hand; you never knew when it might reveal exactly what bolt to turn and how far to turn it.

I started by removing the parts that one usually removes for routine maintenance and stacked them on the nearby table. Little by little I removed bigger chunks of machinery, gradually getting into territory I had never explored before. In so doing I disturbed some adjustments, even the factory-set adjustments, but I figured I couldn't make things much worse anyway, and would eventually get everything restored, with Thompson's help or without it. Some adjustments, however, I left scrupulously alone, particularly those that regulated the plunging stream of molten lead. You can see a higher intelligence at work here.

In half a day more parts were on the table and on the floor than on the machine, which had been reduced to a skeleton. At this point Father stepped into the *Guide* office, after a morning spent in the post office. He surveyed the wreckage and started to frame a question, but choked up. I could tell from his facial expression that he was contemplating fifteen hundred dollars worth of dismembered and dismantled linecasting machine that had suddenly been reduced to salvage. Once again he started to editorialize the situation, but seemed unable to proceed. I came to his rescue by making a simple, although definitive, comment: "I am taking the machine apart."

As any fool could see that, he did not offer to amplify my statement. He was, after all, looking utter disaster in the face. No one, short of a factory representative or other form of out-of-town talent, could put it back together, unless I could. As he saw no reason for getting his last, great hope upset and bothered, he went back to the post office.

The rest of that day and the next morning as well I busied myself with cleaning rags and pans of gasoline, getting hundreds of parts nice and shiny. I applied heavy machine oil, light machine oil, cup grease, and graphite to inviting places. I filed rough edges. I replaced wheels, gears, cams. I cleaned clutch facings. I do not recall being puzzled at any stage of the operation. Most of the parts would fit only one way; many were interchangeable. A few were secured by dowel pins and then bolted into place; by that statement I mean they could not be put into the wrong place. Some adjustments could be made by trial and error; some with a micrometer after getting the technical data from a manual. Much of the cleaning and polishing was purely cosmetic.

When the machine was reassembled, it beamed like the face of an editor who had just sold a page ad.

I lit the blaze under the melting pot. Meanwhile I began slowly to check out various mechanisms. I turned wheels by hand to make sure they revolved freely. I worked levers and slides. I checked the half-dozen or so safety devices. When the metal was melted, I switched the power full on, hand on the safety lever. I composed a line—not, I am sure, "What God hath wrought," but the operator's great warm-up line, "etaoin shrdlu cmfwyp," the linotype equivalent of the typewriter's "asfg hjkl"; the opening bars of the Linotype symphony. This exercise showed that the keyboard and assembling mechanism were fully operative. Then I looked down at my feet and saw two bolts, six inches long and an inch wide. At least that is the way I remember them. Somewhere they, too, belonged.

Hastily I turned the motor off and began to search for places to insert the missing bolts. I had made the classic goof. I had heard numerous stories from drivers who had tried to repair their own cars and had had parts left over. I could find no place for the bolts to go.

Now the only thing to do was to start the machine and see what popped, snapped, or fell off. I started to cast the line I had assembled, turning the clutch by hand so that the crash would be slow and controlled. Nothing happened, and the shiny new slug emerged perfectly. I held it by its corners and examined it; its "etaoin shrdlu" looked up at me, as if wondering what I was worrying about. Well, I said to myself, the crash has not come yet, but it will be along soon. I switched the motor back on, composed another line, and ran it through the machine under full power, hand poised on stopping lever; nothing amiss happened.

To complicate my reflections, Father, hearing the machine, came in and surveyed the situation, relieved that everything appeared to be under control. No doubt he felt richer by a full fifteen hundred dollars. He did not happen to see the big bolts and I did not get around to pointing them out. He went back to his Oliver.

A moment later the whole keyboard, with its ninety blue, black, and white keys, practically dropped into my lap. Short, stubby dowel pins had temporarily held it in place, but it should have been bolted as well. Given this clue, I quickly found a place for the mysterious bolts. As I gave them the last firm twist with a wrench, I suddenly felt emotionally exhausted. Father had always said, "Quit when you feel like it," and I felt like quitting. Not every kid can tear down a Model A Intertype and flawlessly put it back together. Well, almost flawlessly.

My typesetting career lasted eight years after leaving Gilman City. While attending college, I worked at the *Grinnell Herald*. One summer I was admitted to the International Typographical Union at Chicago, got a job in a composition shop on South Dearborn Street, later at the *Des Moines Register*, and still later at the Government Printing Office. As a graduate student at the University of Iowa, I worked on the *Daily Iowan*'s night shift, alternating typesetting with studies. After I got my degree, I abandoned my printing career. The time had come to quit altogether.

Recently as I was walking past the warehouse of a soft-drink bottling works I saw, through the open door, three Linotypes—dusty, abandoned, jammed, and crowded together. I stood beside them and silently paid my respects. It seemed as if someone had said, "Take this Linotype and put it in the warehouse—and while you're at it, take these other two." The machines were truly ancient —if they had been Packards or Stutzes they would have been called classics—but here they were standing in neglected majesty beside tins of printer's ink, also of the kind used long ago, cartons of old correspondence, and odds and ends of printing machinery and spare parts.

I stared a long time at the nearest old veteran and was tempted to dust its brass, shine its nickel plate, graphite its slides, oil its bearings, and give its grease cups a couple of twists, but managed to restrain myself and the urge went away.

As I stood there, I had an appalling thought. These machines, each at one time more costly than a six-room house, were now utterly worthless. I fancied myself hunting up the owner and saying to him, "Could I have one of those Linotypes you're storing in the back?" He would have said, "Yes, of course, and if you'll take all three, I'll pay the hauling charges." I recalled the man who had up-ended several Cadillacs, burying them partly in the ground, and fancied myself collecting half a dozen Linotypes and stringing them across my front yard—letting them stand as a symbol of the linecasting machine, the work horse of sixty years of printing and publishing.

I also reflected that there were still thousands of men and women who, in their youth, had mastered the ins and outs of The Machine in a country newspaper office. Like many other institutions that we grew up with, however, hot-metal linecasting, after serving with distinction, has been replaced by more sophisticated systems.

9

The Miracle Mile

At the time, none of us thought of Gilman City's business district as a Sunset Strip, Golden Triangle, or Miracle Mile.

Actually, it was that and more. To be sure, to add up to a full mile you would need to walk both sides of Main Street and throw in explorations on Broadway and Cook. But between Jim Crump's blacksmith shop at one end and Tom Patterson's at the other you would pass fifteen or twenty different businesses. You could get medical, dental, and veterinary services and buy real estate and insurance. Bill Noll or Ben DeWitt would build you a home or a business structure and Ira Hurst would paint and decorate it. Mose LaMastres would tailor a suit of clothes for you.

When the time came to join that great Miracle Mile in the sky, Bill Haines would prepare your remains for their final, earthly habitation. Any of four ministers would preach the sermon. Father would write a glorious obituary, I would set it on the Intertype, Mother would feed the press, and Don would fold and wrap the paper.

Where today can you find a community with a population of 618 that can spread before you such a feast of goods and services?

Our world was divided into two groups: the advertisers and the non-advertisers. For us the few non-advertisers hardly seemed to exist; the only human being lower in the scale was someone who did not take the paper. Father argued that business and professional men should not advertise merely to sell potatoes or services; they should advertise because the newspaper boosts the town, its churches, schools, and civic activities, and one who did not advertise simply did not properly support the community.

We treated advertisers with the utmost courtesy. Don and I were under strict instructions to address adults as "Mr." or "Mrs.," particularly if they were advertisers. Everybody called the local dairyman "Joe" or "Uncle Joe," but to us he was Mr. Bogue. Everybody called the restaurant owner "Slick," but to us he was Mr. Thompson.

The word for *shopping* was, of course, *trading*, because most customers hauled in eggs or other produce and traded for merchandise. We did a fair share of our trading with the firm next door, "Eckles and McClary, Plain and Fancy Groceries," a faithful advertiser. This store was housed in a narrow building; the two long sides were lined with shelves, and in front of the shelves were counters. On the shelves were rows of cans, jars, and boxes. In the center of the room were barrels, larger boxes, and crates of potatoes and other items sold in bulk.

I can see myself entering the store and walking on its wooden floor down to the middle of its right-hand counter. One of the proprietors steps up to wait on me, and I say, "Hello, Mr. Eckles." Probably no one else will call him "Mister" that livelong day; to everybody else he is "Ralph." Consulting a list that Mother made out, I ask him for two cans of tomatoes. We walk to where the tomatoes are, I in front of the counter and he behind it, and he gestures toward various brands and sizes. For "various," read "two or three." I indicate a size and he places two cans on the counter. In like manner he personally collects each item on the list. In moments of doubt he is pretty certain to know Mother's preference. Soon he has a small heap of items on the counter, some of which he may wrap separately and tie with a string, others of which go directly into a sack. Nobody waits on himself; everybody is waited on.

Many items are sold in bulk. Cookies and crackers come in large boxes or barrels. Flour and sugar come in barrels; each customer's order is individually scooped into sacks and weighed. Lard is scooped from large tubs. Bacon is sliced to order from a slab. Cheese is sliced to order from a wheel. We spoke of it as "rat trap cheese" as if it were a single word. Eggs come in wooden, thirty-dozen crates; each egg is carefully removed and put in a sack. Potatoes, carrots, lettuce, radishes, are sold unwashed, tops and all, much as they came from the garden. Coal oil comes from a barrel at the back, pumped into a container that you brought yourself. If your spout does not have a lid, Mr. Eckles will pop a potato over it. If you need wicks, he can supply you. Coffee is ground to order.

Vinegar is stored in an upright barrel with its own pump. Candy, in a glass case, is assorted and weighed to your order. You can have horehound or peppermint sticks, wrapped in waxed paper, chocolate-covered caramels, chocolate creams of assorted colors but similar flavors, brazil nuts immersed in white icing, white or chocolate fudge with peanuts, various kinds of hard candies, a monstrosity on a stick called an all-day sucker. A candy bar called the "Oh Henry" makes its appearance about this time—perhaps the first of the candy bars. This delicacy, selling for ten cents, was fully four times larger than the current Oh Henry. Oranges and bananas are available in season. Bananas come in long, cylindrical crates just as United Fruit packed them in Central America, and clerks can tell hair-raising stories about sometimes discovering a tarantula along with the bananas.

Eckles and McClary, Plain and Fancy Groceries, had no refrigeration, though pond ice, cut in the winter and stored in sawdust, was available. Stores felt they could not be finicky about the quality of the produce the farm folk brought in. Despite our continual "swat the rooster" campaign, most eggs were fertile and quickly spoiled; one in every four became inedible. Much butter was not attractive; what the stores did not care to sell locally was shipped to the Trenton creamery for recycling into "creamery butter," obviously a dubious product. Milk could not be kept around very long. Most of us believed that store cookies, imported from Kansas City, were compounded of rancid butter, sour milk, and far-gone eggs.

Each store, however, had its favorite suppliers who took pride in their product. Mother would caution me to ask for "good butter," or to inquire, "Has Mrs. Sawyer brought her butter in?" Bread, unsliced, was delivered in huge trays; each loaf was wrapped to order. We called it "light bread." We had a choice of Banty Thompson's, baked down the street, or Holsum, already wrapped, shipped in from Kansas City.

When I had secured the items on Mother's list, plus the addenda that she had shouted after me, I settled up. A few of the larger stores had a central cash register, located at the back or on a mezzanine, and in that situation the clerk took your money—probably a couple of silver dollars—put it with an itemized sales slip in a container the size of a tomato can, fastened the can to an overhead pulley arrangement, pulled a lever to give it a smart impetus that zipped it along a taut wire to the cashier's cage. She made the change and sent the can whizzing back to the clerk. He verified the transaction and handed you your change and a copy of your slip. As Eckles and McClary did not have such a device, Mr. Eckles personally rang up your sale and personally handed over the change. As you began to pick up your assortment of cans, sacks, and tied packets, he would point to one sack and remind you, "Those are the eggs."

Across the street was William D. Haines, Furniture and Undertaking. For many years he was the town's eligible bachelor, but he eventually married, and his wife, Minta, also became a licensed embalmer. Some families had a delicate preference that deceased females should be attended by a female rather than by a male embalmer, so Bill and Minta could honor those sensibilities. I overheard a lot of undertaking talk. Once Mrs. Haines told me that she had done especially well with a girl who had been badly torn up in a car accident. In every profession people take pride in their work.

Next door was the Gilman Mercantile Company. The hardware store of fifty years ago was greatly different from one today. Inside the main door was a glass display case filled with twenty or thirty different pocketknives, priced from ten or fifteen cents to a dollar or more. Everybody carried a pocketknife; I used mine mainly for mumblety-peg, that timeless game of knife-throwing maneuvers, each maneuver ending by burying the point of the small blade into the soil. The loser had to pull a well-driven peg out of the dirt with his teeth.

Next to the glass case were the long counters. Behind them, mounted on the walls or stored in banks of small drawers, were tools, bolts, screws, and other small items. Across the room were horse collars; hanging from pegs were sets of gleaming black harness; in tubular containers were buggy whips; on nearby shelves were saddles. In the middle of the store were various brands and styles of heating stoves and kitchen ranges; nearby were coal hods, shovels, pokers, and lengths of stove pipe. You could pick out a nice lap robe or horse blanket. You could buy pumps, either lever or chain operated, but little else in the plumbing line, since indoor plumbing was practically nonexistent.

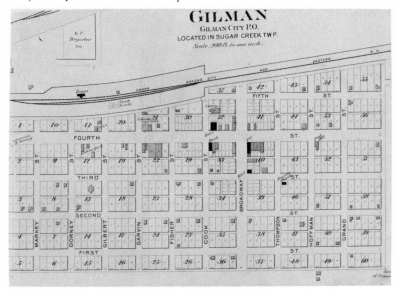

This plat was drawn when Gilman City was a year old. The business buildings, shown by shaded areas, were mainly wood. What the founders show as Fourth Street came to be known as Main Street. When the original depot, shown here at the head of Dorney Street, burned down, it was rebuilt at the head of Cook Street. People had complained vigorously at having had to walk so far and then having to cross the tracks to get to the depot.

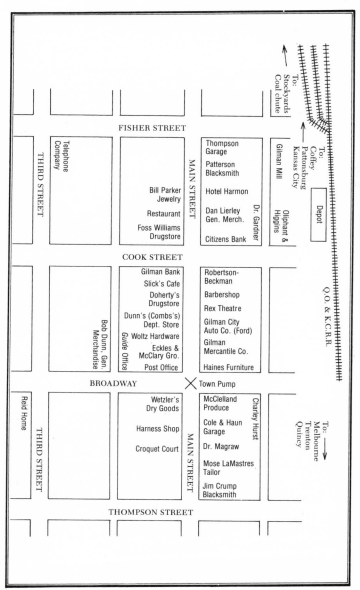

Diagram showing Gilman City's streets and principal firms for 1913 through 1921. Since changes of ownership and moves were relatively few, they are not indicated.

North side of Main Street; Cook Street intersection in the foreground. *Right to left*: Robertson-Beckman, general merchandise; Welden Barbershop; Rex Theatre; Gilman City Auto Company; Gilman Mercantile Company; W. D. Haines Furniture and Undertaking. Taken for the *Purple and Gold* 1917 Annual.

These buildings faced, on the south side, the Gilman Bank, Doherty Drugstore, Slick's Cafe, W. H. Dunn's Department Store, Woltz Hardware, Eckles and McClary, post office.

The two banks at opposite corners of Main and Cook were both regular advertisers in which I took a special joy, as they almost never changed their ads, which meant that I never had to bother with any resetting or altering. Each had a capital and surplus of $25,000. I had a mental reservation about the Citizens Bank, as we printed their checks, and that turned out to be a standby job that filtered into my spare time. Printing bank checks would not have been such a troublesome job had we not had to figure so closely on the price, to compete with out-of-town bank supply houses, that we had to use skimpy margins, which complicated the presswork. A wide margin gives press grippers ample room to hold the freshly printed check tight so it will not stick to the type or roll up on the ink rollers. Moreover, the checks, after being printed, had to be bound in books of fifty, which called for the cutting of cardboard backs, facing one edge with binder's cement, and putting the lot under heavy weights until the cement set. Sometimes the bank suddenly ran out and sent in a hurry-up

Town pump (post office in background), on corner of Main and Broadway. Merchants and customers got their water here. A galvanized tank nearby gave teams a chance to quench their thirst. Ordinarily a tin cup was available but was hardly necessary; if you held one hand under the spout and operated the handle with the other, you could get all the water you needed, and then some.

Alley behind the *Guide* (*extreme left*). The buildings in the center re-placed those burned down in the mid and late twenties. Early in the town's history, this alley, on a typical Saturday, would be filled with teams; then with a mix of teams and cars; still later, mostly with cars.

request for checks; this request could easily come on a Friday or Saturday, and thus cut into ball-playing time.

Thousands of veteran bankers can describe the small-town bank of their younger days. When you opened an account you were given a passbook in which was written the initial deposit and a pad of counter checks—not coded. If you made a deposit and did not bring along your passbook, the banker entered the amount on a deposit slip, giving you a carbon. Every few weeks you took your passbook to the bank and had it balanced. Two or three days later you recovered it, now showing all debits and credits, with fancy red or black ruled lines, and also your current balance; inside were the checks you had written, the whole packet secured by a rubber band. The bank was not fussy about overdrafts; notices were sent more to inform than to warn. *Minimum balance* was a term still to be invented. On any visit you might be waited on by the president himself, or the cashier. Most sums were figured in the head, although the bank had a lever-operated adding machine with as many keys as a Linotype.

Suppose you made a purchase and did not have a check: no matter, the merchant was certain to have pads of checks available for every bank in his trading area. If he inadvertently ran out of "Melbourne Bank" checks, he offered you a "Gilman" or "Citizens" bank check, and you penned in the alterations. Occasionally the rotogravure section of a Sunday paper printed a picture of a check that had been improvised on a strip of birch bark, or a piece of cardboard cut from the lid of a shoebox, that had passed merchant, bank, and clearing house, and had eventually made its way back to its maker.

As the popularity of banking expanded, with nearly every member of a family having a personal account, old procedures were, one by one, abandoned. Still, I remember that Father and Mother sometimes gave us $10 gold pieces each for Christmas, and it was nice to march to the bank and have $10 written in your own passbook.

Those who appreciate the ambience of a deluxe hotel would have loved the Harmon. It had opened its career with magnificence and splendor on Columbus Day in 1911. A hundred commercial men from nearby towns and cities were offered free tickets to the banquet, and to a man they showed up. Once there they had a chance to inspect a hot-and-cold water system that had no equal, even in the largest cities. They could further note that a public bath graced each of the three floors. Moreover, the bay-windowed, sumptuous front rooms of the second and third stories had private baths. The guests were so closely knit to each other and to their customers that they had an evening of fellowship long remembered. Though the hotel could not have had many more than thirty rooms, travelers were so accustomed to doubling up, even with strangers, that every one found a place to sleep, either at the hotel or in the homes of friends.

Gilman City's three-story brick hotel was a major showpiece that added to the attractiveness of the town for salesmen and other visitors. For years the O.K. selected the Harmon as the site of its noon luncheon stop; one could see the passengers walking from the depot to the hotel for their quick twenty-five or thirty-five cent lunch. Commercial men, toting their heavy sample cases, could call on customers that afternoon, complete their business the next morning, and take the train to the next town.

At least one other establishment had a hot-and-cold water system without equal: Len Welden's two-chair barbershop. Once inside, the customer saw a sign, "Bath, 25¢," and although I never took one there, I occasionally heard someone in the partitioned-off space merrily splashing away. A sink in the corner of the main room was useful for rinsing after a shampoo; while the patron, carefully toweled, bent over the sink, the barber poured warm water from a pitcher over the patron's hair to get the soap out.

Each of Len's regular customers had a mug, bearing his initials in gold letters, on a shelf behind a glass-doored cabinet. I used to sit and read the initials on the mugs, trying to figure out their owners, and feeling pride at seeing Father's "D.A.R." among the rest. For a dime one could enter this world of hot, steaming towels; rich, foamy lather; and astringent, sweet-smelling, creams and colognes. The barber began by getting his customer comfortable, then leaning the chair all the way back; lathering his face and swathing it with towels so hot they had to be applied slowly and gently; then the customer could close his eyes and relax, or study the ads painted on the ceiling. Next the barber selected a razor from his assortment and tuned it on a strop, stroking first one side and then the other. After removing the towels he surveyed the scene and figured out his plan of attack, re-lathering where necessary, then stretching the skin here and pinching it there so he would have a taut working area. If he nicked the skin, he staunched the flow with a bit of alum rubbed off his large, smooth chunk. When he had finished and had applied cologne and powder, the patron was elevated to an upright position, cleansed, refreshed, invigorated. A good barbershop shave would last two days, sometimes three. I never enjoyed a barbershop shave until long after I had left Missouri, but few things in this world were more relaxing.

Gilman City always had two, and sometimes three, barbershops; and much of their custom came from men who could leave their businesses during the early morning hours long enough to patronize their favorite. In those days the world was full of kings,

Bill Noll, Gilman City's biggest builder, constructed the famous Hotel Harmon in six months. Originally estimated to cost $8,000, because of improvements and alterations it came in at $15,000, an early example of a cost overrun. It was certainly the finest hotel in a twenty-five-mile radius and probably the finest on the O.K. between Quincy and Kansas City. Eventually it was knocked down, but for more than forty years it stood as an indication of the faith that B. R. Harmon, one of the first settlers, had in the future of Gilman City.

princes, dukes, and counts, but none of them could get finer treatment than was dispensed in Gilman City's tonsorial parlors.

My own experience was different. At stated intervals Mother ordered me to get a haircut, an operation I dreaded for two reasons: the job took forever, and, what was worse, during the ordeal I was subjected to caustic, professional observations about the quantity and quality of my hair.

No barber really relished my patronage. As I was too small for the chair, the unlucky one who drew me got a board, put it across the arms, got me seated atop it, and surrounded me with his white cloth, tightly tucked in at the neck. As he gingerly combed the tangles, he made such comments as "Look at this kid's hair," in a tone of voice he could easily have used if he were calling attention to the tail of a stallion, Napoleon III, for example. "Did you ever see anything so tough and wiry? Ruin a man's shears." The other barber agreed, shuddering, thankful that he did not have to cut that kid's hair, and at times customers in the room would describe people they had known who had unmanageable mops.

When the unhappy barber had finished his chore, he sprinkled half a can of talcum onto his brush and whisked it vigorously around my neck and across my face, creating a fog so powdery that I had to hold my breath until he unfastened my shroud and set me free. He took the fifteen cents I proffered him with the air of a man who had done his share of penance for the day. To add to his discomfort he knew he had to do a first-class job, because Mother would give me a careful inspection when I returned to the office. She always wanted her boys to look well groomed, at least periodically. If she did not approve his handiwork, she would call his shortcomings more or less to public attention next time he called for his mail.

In the middle of North Main was the Rex, the only movie house in our end of the county. It offered shows every Thursday, Friday, and Saturday nights, starting at 7:00. Lyceum lectures, declamation contests, or political meetings were scheduled at random on other evenings. Two hundred people could be accommodated. An investment of fifteen cents for a ticket and a sack of buttered popcorn—the profit from the delivery of newspapers to five customers for a week—was eminently sound.

The Rex showed only the finest movies: "The Iron Claw," for example, the exciting narrative of the terrible revenge of a man whose enemy had crushed his hand, compelling him to go through life with a steel hook instead of a thumb and fingers. The hand-mangling scene was so vividly portrayed that you could feel your own fingers being crunched. The revenge was even more delicious to watch. Every Thursday brought two-reel serial installments, featuring Pearl White, Ruth Roland, Warner Oland, and their famous contemporaries—in other words, the absolute best. Each installment ended with the hero or heroine in a desperate situation: Warner Oland as Wu Fang, the Chinese tong leader, tossing the hero into a tank in which an octopus was clearly seen threshing around; Pearl White, bound to a log in a sawmill, the log moving slowly toward the giant ripsaw; Ruth Roland, long-lost Inca princess, about to be sacrificed to the Sun God when she was accidently discovered not to be an average American girl but the princess (ironically her royalty was revealed when, while traveling in Central America, she accidentally brushed back her dark bangs, disclosing on her forehead a tattooed Rising Sun almost as big around as a Spaulding baseball).

You left the Rex on Thursdays in quite a state of mind, what with one person facing an octopus, another a ripsaw, still another death at the stake. You would certainly be back the following Thursday with a fresh sack of popcorn to see how each one resolved this terrible predicament, and, incredibly, carelessly, fall into another just as dangerous.

Once Don was so terrified that he crawled under the seat so that he would not have to view the carnage. Under the seat he found another young, tender body. I was astonished to discover that this other person was me.

One Thursday afternoon Don fell out of a big maple tree in our front yard and was knocked totally unconscious; Dr. Gardner was immediately summoned. When the doctor arrived we watched and wondered, all of us tense, helpless, frightened, noting Don's pale face, his labored breathing, the occasional twitching of his eyelids. Little could be done except carry him inside, lay him on a bed, and wait. With the others I stood beside his bed for the rest of the afternoon. My first thought was that he would recover, but my second thought, I blush to say, was to hope that he would recover by 7:00. When he failed to do so, I wrestled with my conscience a full minute and then, without saying anything to anybody, slipped away to the Rex. One of the serials was to come to an end that very night. Father shortly missed me and knew exactly where I had gone. I had hardly got halfway through the first reel when he was at my shoulder, explaining gently that since my one and only brother was desperately, critically injured, and since we did not know what the outcome would be, I should join the rest of the family for the bedside watch. So I tore myself away from the theatre, disappointed but dutiful. In less than an hour Don regained consciousness, was disturbed that he had missed the serial, and still wanted to go see it. As a precaution, however, he was kept abed.

Next morning he was his bright, sunny self. Luckily his head had hit neither the edge of the sidewalk nor the protruding roots; he had missed death by inches. I asked him what he would have done if I had fallen out of the tree and was still unconscious at show time, but he sagely and prudently refused to answer.

I write, of course, about silent movies. The Rex had a single projector, which meant that the show had to stop for reloading after every second reel. Frequent film breakages also stopped the show. A slide then appeared on the screen bespeaking the audience's indulgence. If the breakdown were serious, house lights would be turned on so patrons could buy fresh supplies of popcorn. At times the projector was as troublesome as a Country Campbell. A pleasant part of the evening was the piano music provided by one of the high-school girls. She would either follow the sheet music that had been specially written or improvise with suitable mood music from her own small but select repertoire.

Gilman City's one filling station bore the trademark of the Standard Oil Company. The first pumps were operated by a crank; a certain number of turns added up to a certain number of gallons. A scale on the pump indicated the amount. Later the crank-type pump was replaced by a lever-action handle, which pumped the gas into a glass container holding as much as ten gallons; after the container was filled and the customer could see how much gas he was going to get, a lever was pulled and he could see the fluid being drained into his own tank. A nearby, hand-drawn sign proclaimed, "Free air." Many years were to elapse before I knew what "free air" meant.

From the beginning, the filling station established a tradition of service. Few American business firms exceed what we now call the "service station" in the friendliness and competence with which the customer is served. "Foxy" Lawrence, who had once been the town's night watchman, and now Mr. Rockefeller's personal representative as proprietor of the Gilman Oil Company, was in the tradition that built the industry.

Our Miracle Mile as I first knew it was strictly a daytime operation. Although electrically lighted communities had been known since before the turn of the century, Gilman City did not get its power plant until the fall of 1914 when I was in fifth grade.

For months we watched the building of the small, square brick structure northwest of town and the installation of the big engine and dynamo. We saw workers stringing wires down streets and alleys. At strategic street corners they installed low-power lights. One by one houses and businesses were wired. Wiring consisted simply of installing drop cords, with old-style, pointed bulbs hanging at the end. Our house had five rooms, hence five bare bulbs, one in each room; no outlets, no wall switches. The *Guide* had half a dozen lights hanging from the ceiling, and a simple, knife-style switch to serve the big electric motor with which we had joyously replaced the Olds.

The plan was that electricity would be available at sunset and turned off at 10 P.M., six evenings a week. A single engine cannot supply uninterrupted, twenty-four-hour service. On Saturday evenings the power was to run until 11. Ten minutes before shutoff, the lights blinked a warning blink. Our school parties ran merrily until the lights winked; then came the grand rush to get the girls home. Afterwards the boys made their way home by available moonlight; if no moon, they felt their way in utter blackness.

So that housewives could do their ironing, the city fathers originally planned to have power available Tuesday morning, the traditional ironing day. Father and Mother, however, reflected that Wednesday morning would be much more useful for the *Guide*, as it was our busiest day. The outcome was that Mother pushed a petition getting signatures suggesting Wednesday. With her skill at persuading, she had little difficulty getting the necessary signatures. Thus she succeeded in overturning the lifetime ironing habits of the women of the community. A placid majority often falls before a vigorous, motivated minority.

Business establishments profited greatly by electric power, especially during the long winter evenings. As the stores were open from six or seven in the morning until late at night, they had the convenience of electric lights instead of coal oil or gas-mantle lights. No one ever needed to put an "Open" sign in the window. Stores were nearly always open, to accommodate the need of families without refrigeration—in other words, almost everybody—to shop nearly everyday.

Otherwise, the Miracle Mile had little night life. Slick's Cafe was often crowded with young men, there for a cherry coke or a malted milk, but by the time the lights blinked, streets and stores were pretty well deserted. I recall no electric signs; the neon light was still to come. An utter novelty was to spell a word, like "Rex," in light bulbs. The business districts of nearby county-seat towns, however, were brightly lit. Kansas City was incandescent splendor. Years later on my first trip to New York, the high buildings impressed me most of all, but, after them, the flood of light. When lights were blacked out during World War II, New York streets looked more and more like those I had grown up with. Most people my age remember their first airplane, but only those who grew up on the farms and in the small towns removed from the mainstream of progress, can recall seeing a whole town wired with Mr. Edison's dazzling invention.

That part of the Miracle Mile between Cook and Broadway—a single block plus the adjacent corners—was the home of the largest business establishments, such as some of those I have just described. Here, and in a few smaller offices just off Main, were found Gilman City's leaders—those who did most of the town's planning.

Father's news stories often mentioned Ira Oliphant, active in real estate and insurance, who served several terms as mayor and was often a Commercial Club or school-board official. Another was Charley Hurst, also a real estate and insurance man, who was clerk of the town for more than fifty years and wrote its ordinances. Father's list would also have included three or four bankers, among them Charley Burrell of the Gilman Bank and Charley Oram of the Citizens Bank, whose names often appeared as treasurers of the

Commercial Club, the school board, and the chautauqua and annual picnic.

Father noted others who gave time and energy to the town's
enterprises. Charley Neff, head of the Farmers Telephone Company, illustrated the kind of help that a dedicated person can give
a community. Once the Commercial Club appointed a committee
to recommend the best route between Gilman City and Gallatin,
and to mark the turns by painting stripes on telephone poles. In
turn the committee delegated this task to Neff, who met with the
Gallatin group and marked the trail. Everybody realized he was
an ideal man for the job since he and his workers had set up a
telephone pole in every lane and road for miles around. Often,
driving across country, I would come to a crossroad and not
know whether to turn or go straight, so I would stop the car and
explore the possibilities on foot. Before long I would come to one
of Neff's painted poles, and, heartened, proceed on my way.

When the town needed a manager for the new light plant,
Father recommended Neff because of his experience and judgment. Although Neff concluded that running one utility was
enough, he used his connections to secure poles for the light plant,
saving the town several hundred dollars. On another occasion
he personally circulated a petition to raise funds to prosecute
anybody who tried to smuggle liquor into Gilman City. Father,
commenting that hundreds of people sought the advice of this un-
assuming, level-headed man, called him a wheelhorse in every
worthy cause.

Bill Noll was another stalwart; Father called him "the father
of Gilman City" because he had built so much of it. Bill's father,
Jacob, born in Prussia, had moved to Bethany when the county
was young and had started a brick kiln; when Gilman City was
founded, Bill moved to the new town and opened a brickyard. He
found Gilman City a town of wooden business structures and left
it a town of brick, in all erecting twenty-three buildings. I have
already mentioned that at one time or another he owned three
different businesses. To fill in his slack time, he served for a while
as alderman. Father thought Bill was one of the best boosters the
town ever had.

Nell Williams, cashier of the Gilman Bank, and one time postmaster, thought the O.K. should make its noon-day stop at Gilman

Interior of Slick Thompson's cafe, taken about 1906, when he was in the grocery as well as in the restaurant business.

The foreground shows the wood floors that were found not only in the small-town stores but also in big city establishments. The serving area at the left is covered with linoleum. The shelves of groceries at the right are reached by the ladder that ran on its own track. At Slick's right elbow are the rolls of wrapping paper that nearly every store had to have.

At the extreme left is the corner of a fancy marble-topped bar, in front of a large plate-glass mirror, equipped for serving malted milks, ice-cream sodas, soft drinks, and, for those in need, Bromo-Seltzers.

City, instead of Coffey, so that passengers could spend their lunch money on Main Street. Working almost single-handedly, he got railroad officials to agree. When the community needed a band-stand, Neff offered to donate the poles, and Noll to build the roof. With that backing it was easy to raise money to finish the job.

For special expertise, others were available. Eldon Davisson, paperhanger and plasterer, and also musician, was the leading spirit in getting the band organized. Doc Quinlan, the dentist, managed the baseball team. Tom Norris, coal and feed dealer, was well informed about the needs of the school system at the time when teachers and students needed a new building. An abundance of farming and stock breeding talent was available; for instance,

Slick's Cafe

The Thompson family (Slick Thompson at right, Banty at left) founded the fast-foods business in Gilman City and was associated with it longer than anybody else. Aunt Fanny (not in picture), mother of Slick and Banty, opened a boarding house on East Main, feeding the town's earliest businessmen, residents, transients, and railroad workers. From the boarding house to the restaurant and bakery business was an easy step. Slick's was a popular meeting place as well as eating place. The elderly, like those in the background, congregated in the daytime; the young men took over during the evening hours.

Most of all I remember Slick's tenderloin sandwiches. For a dime you could get a thick, juicy slab of pork tenderloin, served in a bun as big as the side of your face. (From *Gilman City, 1973*)

Billy Welden, who had also once been president of the Gilman Bank. Another Gilman Bank president, Frank Ray, was for years a stock and grain buyer; by paying top prices he strengthened Gilman City's long-standing claim as the best shipping point between Quincy and Kansas City. Two others enjoyed a wide personal following but declined a community office: Slick Thompson, who ran the town's best restaurant, and Warren McClelland, a relative newcomer, who became the town's leading poultry dealer.

Once a proposal gained the support of the men I have named, it had a strong chance of success. Apparently the community then perceived the proposal as noncontroversial and let it sail through on a light vote. An increase in the school levy once passed by a vote of sixty-seven to sixteen; electricity was voted in by eighty-one to thirty-six. Thirty-five or forty votes would elect a mayor, a member of the school board, or a township official. To carry the town, however, for a political office, when feeling ran high, required two hundred votes or more.

Most of these leaders were old-time residents, dating back either from the first wave of businessmen who had founded the town or from the second wave who had bought them out. I remember them as being in their forties or early fifties. I was in and out of their offices frequently, delivering papers, picking up ad copy, waiting while they scanned proofs, or getting information for a news item. They were approachable men who invited confidence and respect. I find it easy to believe that the community supported certain measures because this group supported them, and difficult to believe that any proposal could have passed if this group opposed it.

One persistent problem was to get people to work together. In the quarter century that it had already existed, Gilman City had seen three commercial clubs come and go. Once Father decided to stir things up. "Gilman City needs a booster," he wrote. "While she really needs two or three, she could put up with one as a sort of 'nest-egg' booster." He continued by listing the town's most pressing needs. This bluntly worded statement attracted prompt attention when it hit the mails one Thursday morning. People discussed the notion in the post-office lobby, at Slick's Cafe, in the banks. What started as casual joking and ribbing took shape as conviction that action must be taken, so Mayor Oliphant called a public meeting to organize, once again, a commercial club. This time, perhaps, the idea would take hold for good.

I remember a couple of men coming to the *Guide* to discuss publicity for the meeting. We all know, they said to Father, much must be done. The town needs more electric-light service. An opera house would bring two shows a week, drawing customers for miles around. We need better roads and better trail markings for those we do have. We must attract farmers; one reason previous clubs died out is that we couldn't interest the farm people.

Father took notes, made his own suggestions, and before long his typewritten copy appeared on my tray at the Intertype.

Twenty-five men attended the opening meeting at the Rex Theatre, and elected grocer Ralph Eckles as chairman, and Father as secretary. In his opening comment, the mayor said we all had too much selfishness and indifference. Charley Hurst declared we must join together in a general boost or there would be a business burying soon. A farmer stated that "whatever was good for the town was good for the farm." "This one sentence," the *Guide* reported, "hit the nail square on the head, put the whole story in a nutshell, and left no room for argument."

The group decided to hold an oyster and coffee banquet the very next Saturday. The clincher came when the businessmen agreed to pick up the tab.

Three hundred people attended. Before the feast, they listened to visitors from other clubs stress themes of cooperation. After the feast, they selected twelve for the board of directors. As usual, most were long-time residents: Oliphant, Oram, Honan, Neff, Norris, and others. The collective judgment was that these twelve were outstanding community leaders.

The board met weekly at Oliphant's office. It reviewed the many suggestions presented to it: a park, an opera house, a bridge-repair program, and a trail-marking project. It decided to hold further public meetings, featuring a banquet or some other attractive event to maintain enthusiasm.

Lacking an immediate crisis, however, members began to lose interest in the club. Less and less of its work was done at large gatherings and more and more by individuals. It did succeed in getting better markings for existing roads. When the issue of improving electric service arose, the mayor did most of the leg work as an individual rather than as a member of the board. Plans for public entertainments were put aside. Before long the club had subsided. Initially, however, it had aroused more spirit than the town had seen for a long time. The discussions, moreover, gave at least three hundred people a notion of what a commercial club was like.

I recall that on one occasion Tom N. Witten was invited to address the community on his favorite topic, "The Trenton Idea." I heard the speech, though in restrospect it seems unusual for a high-school boy to attend a lecture about improving the town's business. Witten had been a hardware man at Trenton many years; eventually he became president not only of the Missouri Retail Hardware Association but also of the National Federation of Implement Dealers. The approval of one's peers is a string of merry-go-round tickets a yard long. The Trenton idea was that business men should work for the good of the town as well as for their own good. If a customer enters your store seeking a hundred gallon stock-watering tank and you do not have one, send him to your competitor. Better keep the sale in Trenton than let it go out of town. Your competitor will be pleased and next time he will refer to you a request he cannot fill. Witten's talk was filled with specific illustrations. On occasion I meet the Trenton idea today, and when I do, I recall that speaker and that attentive audience of decades ago.

Tom Witten spread his wise doctrine many years. When he met his death in a tragic car accident, Trenton closed the doors of its business establishments for his funeral, a thousand people being present. In its off-and-on existence, the Gilman City Commercial Club tried to reflect Witten's ideal of community spirit.

If one wonders why leaders in any small town do not do more than they do, or why followers do not support more enthusiastically than they do, one finds the answer in a simple statement: people have different degrees of disposable time and talent. Most of the community's residents labored from early in the morning until late at night. Merchants personally waited on customers, just as Father personally set ads or sold money orders. Not everyone had the time to take a petition up and down Main Street to raise funds for an opera house or bandstand. Certain kinds of talent were altogether missing; no one had a background in industry, or had the personal connections helpful in recruiting small factories to increase the town's resources.

I do, however, recall one incident of a different sort that not only captured the fancy but also challenged the judgment of both the town leaders and the community itself, as well as the countryside.

In the spring of 1917 a nice-appearing, soft-spoken man in his late thirties stepped off the train from Kansas City and checked in at the Harmon, no doubt delighting the innkeeper with the information that he planned to stay a few days. From there he fanned out onto our Miracle Mile, starting with the professional men and moving on to the merchants, introducing himself as a representative of the Cushing-Webb Oil Company of Oklahoma.

The stranger told an exciting story of the millions to be made in oil, starting with the narrative of the millions that had already been made in oil. He had a map showing the location of the productive Cushing field, with dots indicating the size of its many gushers. The choice acreage that he represented hovered above, as the company's geologists confidently believed, a seven thousand barrell a day vein. A sheaf of letters from Stillwater banks and from various Oklahoma financial interests testified to the integrity of the company and to the accuracy of its statements. The sell was soft and gentle. Shares were $30 each, but no attempt was made to take orders on the first call. The stranger made his pitch, asked a few questions about other prominent men of the town, and left to call on other prospects. The sucker was left in a mild state of shock.

This was the time that Wilson was telling Congress that sinkings by German submarines was a war against mankind, that the world must be made safe for democracy, and that it was a fearful thing to lead this great, peaceful people into war. Europe had then been at war three years, and Allied agents had combed northwest Missouri, buying horses and mules, buying hardwood timber for artillery wheels and spokes, buying food and feed. Farm incomes were rising, businesses were perking up, land values were increasing. The *Guide* was running more ads and bigger ads than it had for quite a while. Everybody had a little more money on hand than he was accustomed to. It was a heady feeling. And here was Cushing-Webb, offering a chance to get in on the ground floor. To be sure, there were risks, dry holes had been dug before and would be again, but then . . . .

Within twenty-four hours the whole business district was aware of the stranger's visit. Everybody was talking oil. Father and Mother were among those honored by a call. I heard part of the sales talk. Afterwards they conversed excitedly, their spirits exalted. "Just imagine," Mother said, "if they did strike oil and we made some real money." "Even if they got only five thousand barrels a day," added Father, "that would be pretty good." And so on, into the night. What if . . . just suppose . . . imagine.

In another twenty-four hours rumors of a different sort flowed through the town like oil through a pipeline. This individual had bought shares, and so had this one, and that one. The rumors were readily confirmed by the proud possessors of the shares. Then at some point another, entirely different, line of fantasying took over:

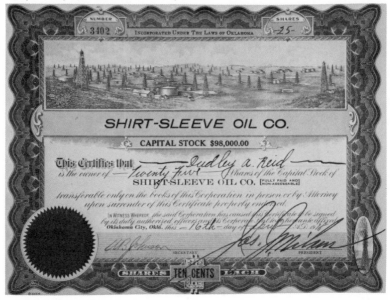

In the spring of 1917, the oil fever hit Gilman City.

What if Jones bought shares and struck it rich, and we bought no shares and were left out? Here was a thought to make strong men and women shudder. No one with idle money could look such an outcome squarely in the face.

When the stranger returned, Father and Mother bought shares.

After Cushing-Webb, came salesmen from the Benton Oil and Gas Company and the Acme Oil Company. In a sense, these companies honored Gilman City by showing that the town was worthy of their attention. Our capitalists were as good as anybody's capitalists. One company I particularly remember, with its big ads in the *Kansas City Star*, was the Shirt Sleeve Oil Company. This firm bragged that it invested no money in expensive office furniture; it had no highly paid, half-idle executives; instead, it was operated by hard-headed, practical, oil men who worked in their shirt sleeves. Father and Mother bought shares in Shirt Sleeve. And The Labette Oil Company. And The Franklin Oil and Gas Company. And the impressive TexOkla Oil Company capitalized at half a million—twenty Gilman banks.

The weeks that followed were sweet and wonderful. Someone, maybe a Honan, maybe a Markey, maybe a Welden, got the idea of getting on the train and going to Oklahoma, to visit the headquarters office and see for himself. He was received royally, shown around the place, driven to the field where the drilling would start any day now. He was shown copies of the *Oil and Gas News* and was further exposed to glowing reports of strikes that had been made by other companies, whose "structures" were similar to our "structures." After he returned, others made the trip. Each of these capitalists, returning from oil country, stimulated the dreams of others.

Little or no oil was found. Father and Mother were taken to the tune of two or three hundred dollars, which for them was a serious loss. For their investment, however, they enjoyed weeks of royal fancying. I can still hear Mother saying, "Oh, son, just imagine—if after all our years of hard work we did make a little real money!" One unexpected return on their investment was to keep them out of the stock market boom of the mid-twenties, so that when so many went down to disaster on that bleak October day,

Father and Mother were high and dry on the sidelines, with little
to worry about except bank failures.

Still . . . what if . . . suppose . . . just imagine.

Gilman City's Miracle Mile shrugged off its setback and went
on about its business. And I have called it a Miracle Mile only
partly in fun. Like a thousand other Main streets in a thousand
other small towns of that era, its leaders did what they could to
compete with other communities for the region's business. Meanwhile, day by day, its business district served an amazing variety
of human needs. On a short walk you could buy a live chicken,
change your currency for silver dollars or twenty dollar gold pieces,
buy custom-designed millinery, or a shirt with a detachable collar,
fill a prescription, have a tooth pulled, or order fancy letterheads
and envelopes. Some of these commodities and services are to be
found today only in larger communities. And some have disappeared altogether.

10

Our Imperial Home

Gilman City's residential district hugged Main Street like a semicircle, bellying toward the south.

A boy's home is where his family is, and so mine was partly the post office and partly the *Guide*, but at other times it was a five-room yellow bungalow with a fancy cupola, a large bay window, and a wide front porch, located on the southeast corner of Third and Broadway, a block's walk from the *Guide*. Huge maple trees lined the sidewalks on the north and west, and two rows of pear trees and a few cherry trees filled most of the space next to the alley on the south.

Father first purchased the house in 1904; it was here that I was born. Later we moved to Maryville and Bethany, but in 1912 returned to Gilman City. Father had a chance to buy the house again and we lived there eight years. More of my childhood was spent there than anywhere else; it was, to use Wordsworth's phrase, my imperial home.

Our house had no water pipes, and, since we had moved in before electricity came to Gilman City, no electric wires. Each room had its own door; in winter we could cluster around the stove and shut off the rest of the house. In the kitchen were a coal-oil stove—a vast improvement over the wood-burning range—a cabinet for dishes and utensils, and a table at which we ate. In the parlor were an upright piano, a sofa that could be unfolded into a bed, and sectional, glass-front, bookcases. In the front room were a couple of rocking chairs and a sturdy oak dinner table. In the living room were a few straight chairs and a coal or wood-burning stove. In the bedroom were two double beds and Father's huge trunk. At strategic places throughout the bedroom and kitchen he had installed shelves; he loved to carpenter and was always discovering new places to put a shelf. Around the front of the house was a large porch, covered with wild cucumber vines that Mother planted anew each spring. Behind the house was a red, iron pump, the source of our water supply. Nearby, suspended from the limb of a huge box elder, was a bag swing, stout enough to support as many kids as could climb on.

Along the alley were the smokehouse and privy—later we added a garage. Alleys were a feature of Gilman City blocks; business people and residents alike could dump their ashes, cans, and other junk in huge piles along the alley, and in the spring hire a man with team and wagon to haul everything away.

Monday was the universal wash day; either you rubbed clothes against a washboard, after soaking them overnight in a large, copper boiler, and next day boiling them, or you operated a washing machine that ran by pushing a lever back and forth. The hanging of clothes on the line was managed so as to avoid the hours at which the O.K. arrived. Given a prevailing wind, the O.K. could generate enough smoke and ash and chunks of soot to ruin utterly most of a community's Monday morning wash. Tuesday was the standard day for ironing.

Spring cleaning was an institution. When the weather became warm, the stove was dismantled and stored in the smokehouse, the pipe removed, and the zinc on which the stove had stood was taken out. Immediately the front room appeared to double in size. Carpets were taken up, revealing newspapers that had been laid down under them a year before, which Don and I would have to inspect with great care, especially cartoon strips along with funny papers that happened to have been interred. We were not in so much of a rush as Mother was to get the carpets hung over the clothesline so we could start beating them with wire beaters. Curtains were taken down, washed, starched, and put on the stretcher. Finally the carpets were brought back in, laid down over a layer of fresh newspapers, tacked in place, and furniture appropriately rearranged. In the winter season, the housewife struggled with coal dust and ash. In the summertime, the problem was street dust. She had to do the best she could by tearing strips of newspaper, soaking them, scattering them over the carpet to catch the dust, and then using a broom. No one had a vacuum cleaner. One way or another she got the house clean and sparkling—at least for a short time.

As a family, we were away during most of the daytime hours, either at work or at school. Breakfast consisted mainly of toast and milk. Luncheon was often navy bean soup, cooked with salt pork. Potato soup was occasionally substituted, but that was really for special occasions, like being ill. Any sick person was put on a diet of potato soup. If a friend or neighbor became seriously ill, Mother, busy as she was, prepared and delivered a nice kettle of potato soup, and I suspect that she thus did a great deal to counteract the calomel, salts, or castor oil with which the patient had been doped. I was fully grown before I realized that one could be sick and not have to eat potato soup, or that one could serve and enjoy potato soup without having a fever.

At noon Don and I came home on the trot, devoured our bowl of soup while standing at the table (I have little memory of sitting for meals), hurried to the depot to grab the papers off the noon train. After delivering them to our subscribers, we rushed back to school, hoping that we could enjoy at least a few minutes of recess. More often than not, however, we would be late; in fact, Father had arranged with the teachers for us to be excused if we arrived after the bell had rung. When our teachers checked their rolls and

My imperial home, about 1914; Father on the front porch. Lightning rods were a standard fixture. In later years the cupola was removed.

saw we were absent, they knew that probably the train had been late that day but that we would be along soon.

Every autumn, Father lugged home a large pumpkin and he and Mother sat up half the night baking pies. When we awoke in the morning, both tables would be covered with twenty or thirty pies—and we could hardly find room to eat our breakfast. As no restrictions were imposed on consuming the pies, the whole lot would disappear in a couple of days. When Tarwater or Reid relatives drove from Daviess County to spend a Sunday with us, bringing all sorts of country goodies, Mother's contribution was an enormous dishpan full of fruit salad; cut-up oranges that had spent the previous night soaking in sugar; sliced bananas that had marinated in homemade cherry juice. The sugar, Mother explained, tempered the tartness of the oranges, and the cherry juice added character to the bananas. Our uncles, aunts, and cousins exclaimed at this mountain of fruit salad, declaring that we could never eat it all, but soon after the main meal, gigantic as it was, people began to slip into the kitchen for a refill of Mother's salad, and by late afternoon the whole dishpanful had vanished. Nobody dieted; I think that word was invented long after I had grown up.

My uncles and aunts reminisced about the glories of the fireplace cooking they had grown up with—beef, turkey, venison, biscuits put in a cast-iron covered pot and heaped with red-hot coals—but I find it hard to equal Mother's pies, fruit salad, and especially fried chicken with mashed potatoes and cream gravy. Her cream gravy was so delicious, poured over biscuits, that for a time you forgot the fried chicken on your plate. But not for long; fried chicken those days meant homegrown fowl, freshly dressed.

Like everybody else, we raised chickens in the backyard. Chickens were, in fact, so numerous, and so difficult to confine, that the town council had passed an ordinance, something like a leash law, with pains and penalties to be heaped on those whose chickens strayed from home. Neighbors had an unwritten code that each would raise a different breed, to keep flocks from becoming mixed. Mother opted for Barred Plymouth Rocks; one neighbor raised White Rocks, and still another Rhode Island Reds. And as if we did not have enough chickens in our own block, across the street were two poultry houses, each with endless crates of hens and roosters awaiting shipment to Trenton or Kansas City.

When Mother did not have chickens of her own to kill, she visited McClelland's, reached into the crates and felt the ribs and legs of the most promising specimens, and indicated to Mac which two or three she wanted. He skillfully pulled them out of the crate, took them to his front office, and tied the legs of each one with a length of binder twine. They cackled and squawked and protested considerably at this outrage, but Mother patted and stroked them and calmed them down. Later she carried them home by their tied legs, wings slightly distended, heads lifted up so they could see better, clucking gently as if things would not be too bad after all.

Actually the poultry season started by Mother's going to Bill Dunn's department store and arranging with Clyde Hagerty or some other clerk to be on the lookout for Mrs. Taylor's eggs. Mrs. Taylor raised Barred Plymouth Rocks of state-fair quality, charging $1.50 for a setting of fifteen carefully selected, fertile eggs. Those she did not sell she brought to Dunn's store, where they were retailed like ordinary eggs for fifteen cents a dozen. The day would come when Mother would acquire three or four settings of gorgeous looking brown eggs and put them under a like number of broody hens, who would set up business in our coal shed. About the twentieth or twenty-first day the chicks began to emerge, and soon the backyard was dotted with baby chickens. We fed them baby-chick grain; then, as they grew bigger, cracked corn and shelled corn, all from the Gilman Mill, along with garbage and table scraps. Chickens, of course, will eat anything. As they grew to fryer prize, they appeared on our evening menu—the young roosters first, the pullets later. The pullets that escaped would join the winter egg-laying flock, providing us with several fresh eggs a day.

Over near Coffey was a farmer by the name of J. N. Bush, a former Hoosier, who had a five-acre patch of watermelons and mushmelons (muskmelons or cantaloupes to you, kind sir or madam). Every week in season we paid him a visit. Father and Mr. Bush preceded the merchandising with talk about Indiana oratory. Bush had heard Benjamin Harrison and Daniel Vorhees clash in the courtroom and had himself been a schoolboy debater, so he and Father had much in common. From there they went on to Midwestern oratory in general, discussing Ingersoll, Bryan, and other great Midwestern speakers.

Loren and Don Reid, ages fifteen and twelve.

After the oratory and political talk came the melon talk, which was just as fascinating. Bush knew each melon just as a shepherd knows each sheep. He went from vine to vine, us in close tow, giving promising specimens a friendly stroke, saying, "Most people would sell you one like this, but it needs two more days on the vine," or "Here's one I'm taking to the Bethany fair." He never thumped a melon; in fact, he considered it an affront to his professional judgment if somebody asked him to plug one. He simply felt it, ever so gently, and if he pronounced it ready to go, it was. For a dollar you could drive away with five big watermelons, plus one or two extra that he would throw in, and for half a dollar you could buy enough mushmelons for a church social.

We never returned from the Bush patch until late afternoon. By then Mother would be home from the post office and we would go to the backyard and guzzle melon until suppertime. Father carved all hands a big, end-to-end wedge, and we pitched in, no fork, and, of course, no salt, devouring the melon and blowing out the seeds. Fifteen or twenty Plymouth Rocks gathered around us, excitedly cackling and complaining, gobbling the seeds and pecking at the rinds, and before long we would have dispatched half a dollar's worth of Bush's beauties. Supper afterwards was a pale and inconsequential thing, we were so stuffed. Come bedtime and we scurried to bed, washing our feet under the pump if Mother insisted, otherwise if she did not.

During the night certain penitential acts had to be performed. The human system has its own special way of reacting to watermelon thus consumed and ingested, and in the dark hours we frequently passed one another on the way to the backhouse. But to this day I love watermelon, cold, sliced, eaten on the patio, and it does not take much effort to imagine Father and Mother and Don there also, and the flapping, fussing, Plymouth Rocks, and as a voice overall the words of J. N. Bush, late of Indiana, more recently of Coffey, Missouri, proudly saying that the great Thomas A. Hendricks had once judged him in an oratorical contest, and that this here melon, Dudley, is one that I was going to take to the Bethany fair, but I want you and your family to have it.

Ours was a reading family. We had a better library at home than was available at school. We had seven priceless volumes of Mark Twain, in the red-backed Harper edition, a set that Father had got as a premium for subscribing to a magazine. I did my reading and studying stretched out on the floor, alongside a coal-oil lamp, or, in later years, under a bare bulb hanging from the ceiling. Give me *Huckleberry Finn* or *Life on the Mississippi* and a stack of crackers, and I would be absorbed for hours. Those precious books have disappeared from our family holdings, but I am positive that wherever they are (I think in the Osceola Public Library in Iowa) they can be identified by the simple process of giving them a good shake, and cracker crumbs will fall out. I loved *Pudd'nhead Wilson*, that strange story of the two babies changed in the cradle, who therefore grew up in entirely different environments, the switch being finally detected by Pudd'nhead's lifelong habit of taking and filing everybody's fingerprints. Another favorite was *Tom Sawyer Abroad*, which almost no one reads today, with its aerial voyage, during which Tom and Huck discover that Illinois was not pink, as the map clearly indicated, but green, like Missouri. For years I was not able to read *The Man That Corrupted Hadleyburg* without breaking into uncontrollable laughter. One day, however, I discovered that I could read it without laughing at all and was saddened to realize that something had gone out of my life, and I did not like any better whatever it was that replaced it. Father also secured a copy of Victor Hugo's *Les Misérables*, and though it was miserably printed on cheap paper in small type, I started reading it one evening and got completely hooked. I always read with such intense concentration that I became transported to the scene of the action.

A stone's throw to the east of our house was the large, white-frame Baptist church. Originally it had been built southeast of town and was one of the buildings moved bodily to Gilman City when the streets were first laid out. I went to Sunday school there regularly, largely because I was caught up in a contest for best attender. Our teacher offered a dollar Ingersoll watch to the pupil who had the best record, and a friend, Garland Miller, and I settled in like grim death to win the prize. Our Bible lessons started with Genesis and we went all through to Leviticus without missing a Sunday. Somewhere in Joshua we each skipped a Sunday because of illness, but ran neck and neck through 1 and 2 Samuel and 1 and 2 Kings. The teacher finally decided to call it a draw and award each of us a watch.

That same afternoon I took my watch apart, but an Ingersoll is different from an Intertype, and when the mainspring came unwound and distributed itself all over the table, I gave up altogether. Here I had served the Lord conscientiously for two years, and here he was teaching me a lesson that I had not particularly asked for.

As some of my chums were attending the Methodist church, especially one of the girls who had struck my fancy, I started going there. A year's steady attendance at her church failed to impress her, however, so I drifted back to the Baptist flock.

In every home are events that are bigger than any of us. In our family, it was Christmas. Early in December the pace began to quicken at the *Guide* and post office, the former with the extra run of Christmas ads and the latter with Christmas cards and packages.

We had an annual deal with the Swanson pharmaceutical house, to which we gave the colorful name of "The Five Drops Company." "Five Drops," originally the name of their brand of liniment, was such a success that the company added Five Drops Cough Syrup, Five Drops Chewing Gum, Five Drops Laxative, and Five Drops Kidney Pills. In exchange for running their 1 x 2 ad a time or two, the firm shipped us, at Christmas time, a one-foot cube wooden box filled with samples. We opened this box with mounting excitement. The Five Drops Chewing Gum and the Five Drops Candies were the first to go. Even the Five Drops Liniment was useful, as everybody was always having cuts and bruises, and since the stuff was practically free, we slathered it on. Twelve months later, however, we would still have the kidney pills. As Father thought nothing should be wasted, he popped a kidney pill now and then as a general conditioner. The dosage for Five Drops Laxative was "two to seven"; Father, pondering this label on one needy occasion, decided to be conservative and try "three." The effect was total disaster. Seven, he said later, weakly, would have killed a horse.

Those were the days when our imperial home really became imperial. Nothing that happened anywhere was as important as what was happening at home. Don and I were fully alert to any packages that might be smuggled into the house. If we could find them, we secretly explored their contents and thus knew in advance most of the presents we would get for Christmas. That procedure eliminated a lot of needless suspense. Father and Mother never scolded us for this intrusion, but as the years wore on they got shrewder and wiser. Either they did not take delivery of the items until Christmas Eve, or they left them with the McClellands or some other neighbor.

You can imagine that if Christmas Eve came with our having no information whatever about our presents, we went to bed in a state of high excitement. I simply could not sleep at all; Don did little better. We could hear the folks in the front room, shuffling things about, mumbling in low voices, all without revealing any negotiable knowledge. Next morning we would be awake long before there were signs of stirring in the parental bedroom. Finally we heard Father stir about, building a fire in the stove; then it was safe to ask if we could get up now, but generally there was further delay until the house was warm and both parents were dressed. When the summons came, we bounded out of bed, rushed to the front room, and surveyed the wonders of Christmas.

Christmas is mainly for kids, and we enjoyed ours to the utmost. Usually we got a mechanical toy: a steam engine one year that had a real boiler that would generate power; a sand crane another, which would dip its long arm into a sandbox, scoop up sand, swing around half a circle, lower its arm, and dump its load into another box, generously sprinkling the area in between. Usually there were a few books, often of a trashy kind that must have been sold by the pound, but we would devour them all, often before the end of the week. Invariably there were nuts, candies, and oranges.

On occasion we were told in advance that since business had been bad that year, Santa Claus would not be able to bring us a large Christmas. One year we got only four tops, along with a narrative from Father that often in *his* boyhood hard times broke into Christmas, so that he and his brothers and sisters got only an orange each. On still another occasion one of his brothers had been naughty, so all he found in his stocking was a chopped-off possum's tail; he was pretty sure to remember that Christmas. I felt sorry for him then, but I know now he got great mileage in the years ahead out of that poor possum, serving him up every Christmas season to *his* children as a grim warning to mind their elders and not misbehave.

One Christmas we got a set of carpenter tools fitted into a neat, wooden toolbox; the lot comprised a saw, a hammer, a screwdriver, and a brace and bit. My favorite retreat had always been the attic. It was completely unfinished, the ribs of the roof and the ribs of the ceiling completely exposed, but it had a nice dusty smell, and directly under the cupola was a cross beam on which I could sit in utter solitude and enjoy the quiet of isolation. To get to the attic I placed a chair alongside the bedroom door, stepped from the chair to the doorknob, from the doorknob to one of Father's shelves bracketed higher up the wall, and then up through a sliding trapdoor. I saw no reason for telling my parents about this hideaway, and it occurred to me that if I had a secret way out of the attic I could get out of the house without coming down by way of the bedroom.

The carpenter tools suggested a solution. With Don as co-conspirator, I climbed into the attic with the tool chest and began to saw away at the timbers supporting the roof. We had planned to saw a square hole through the roof big enough to climb through, and then hinge a lid, covered with shingles, to cover the hole. Sawing with a cheap saw took longer than we suspected. Father unexpectedly came home, heard the racket, investigated, and quickly exposed the whole scheme. He could hardly believe his eyes. I was charged with being the ringleader, and whaled. As Don, a mere accessory, was let off entirely, the agony of my own punishment was doubled. In retrospect, however, I find comfort in thinking that no boy on earth could have come up with a good, sound reason for sawing a hole in the roof of his house.

Don and I were so different in temperament that we often got into squabbles, which led to scuffling, which usually meant that something got broken, which promptly brought Mother to the scene to appraise the destruction and identify the miscreant, a procedure that was roughly equivalent to opening a can of worms. It pains me to relate that we scuffled just about twice a day, which caused Mother much more distress than mothers should have to bear. We grew up under what has been called the woodshed theory of raising kids. This theory holds that the mother, who is usually close at hand when the misdemeanor is committed, is to award a holding punishment, such as a whack on the bottom, but the primary punishment was to be awarded by the father when he got home from work. He took the offender to the woodshed, reviewed the moral code so that the reason for punishment would be understood, and then brought out the heavy artillery. Father's procedure was to take his pocketknife, cut off a pear limb, trim it neatly as he called court into session, and then give several good whacks across the backside. I do not ever recall his ever giving me my rights, as is done on television. Actually there was no appeal of any sort.

Father was far too imaginative to rely on a single form of punishment. An interesting variation was to offer the victim the opportunity to prepare his own pear branch, but an unwritten codicil held that if the proffered branch were not sturdy enough, Father had the privilege of replacing it.

Generally, however, Father relied on the lecture. As we took these standing while he sat in a rocker, they were an unfair test of strength and endurance. The lecture always lasted longer than we needed, especially since we felt we got the point with a minimum of amplification. I remember little of what they were about: the necessity for hard work, I suspect, and doing things promptly, and persevering in a task, and not annoying one's brother as he had just the one brother. Each of these maxims can be supported positively by scores of good examples, and negatively by thousands. Any boy who did not follow these precepts was sure to end up in the poorhouse. The lectures were probably not more than ten minutes long, but they seemed like hours. When I hear a member of the current parent generation say that children need a strong hand, because punishment gives them the feeling of being loved, I know at once that I am listening to one whose own childhood was not ennobled by any of those blessings. My generation of kids can tell it like it was.

Yet any son would give a great deal to have his father back and talk to him as two men of the same age. He would ask a thousand questions about people, places, incidents, pleasures, worries. That road you traveled, Father (and Mother, too), what was it like? How cold was the wind at your back? How hot was the sun on your face?

Another persistent memory is the row of huge maples that lined the Broadway and Third Street sides of our house. Gilman City's proud claim that she had more blocks of shaded sidewalk than any place her size would be difficult to refute. In fact, Sugar Creek was named because of the abundance of sugar maples that grew along its banks. Our first residents transplanted them by the scores to border each new street. By the time we came along they were tall and imposing but still climbable because of their smooth bark and their nicely spaced limbs, of a size to provide handholds and places for feet.

Every other spring city workers went up one street and down another, climbing the trees, and, with handsaws and long pruning hooks, trimmed the branches that interfered with telephone and light wires. Our yard was quickly filled with lush, sweet-smelling boughs, which Don and I rearranged to form houses and tunnels. Father was expert at making whistles, since in the spring the bark could be slipped off in one piece and the twig shaped and notched. Our fun lasted for days, until the sap dried and the leaves wilted; then the branches were collected for a tremendous evening bonfire in the street itself. In the autumn our front yard was ankle deep in red, purple, and golden leaves that we heaped in great piles and wrestled in. Sometimes we marveled at a particularly gorgeous leaf and took it inside to show the folks or even to school to add to the teacher's collection.

When I think of our imperial home I tend to forget the backhouse and the coal stove and the chicken yard, the pump and the dusty carpets, and instead remember the pumpkin pies and fruit salad, the watermelons, the visits from our relatives, the Christmases, the attic, the cupola atop the house and the vine-covered porch in front of it, the pear and cherry orchard at the south side, and, along the sidewalks, that score of huge maples. The house still stands today, and if you can, in your imagination, put back the cupola, fence in a chicken yard, restore the maples, paint the house yellow, and make a few other improvements such as tearing out the interior plumbing, you would capture a fair idea of the splendor in which a Missouri editor and his family lived in the years bordering the First World War.

11

The Purple and the Gold

The Gilman City school system had been in existence almost from the day that the town's founding fathers had staked out its streets in that young cornfield. Serving the town children and the graduates of nearby one-room schools, it soon was offering twelve years of instruction.

Although the school building was hardly a dozen years old when my classmates and I first enrolled, it was already crowded. Our two-story brick structure was centered on a two-acre plot of land. A cinder sidewalk went diagonally from the corner to the front door. Along part of the east side was the girls' necessary, a wooden structure with a sheltering board stockade five feet high along front and sides. What lay beyond the stockade, I never knew nor dreamed of asking. In the extreme southeast corner of the plot was the boys' privy, which we all got to know well. Behind its own protective stockade was an inner corridor with a packed cinder floor, and if we timed our visits properly, which we usually did, we could meet a pal for a short game of marbles, mumblety-peg, or craps. The corridor opened into a facility technically described as a six-holer. Mail-order catalogs spiked to the wall were the beginning and the end of the sanitary arrangements.

To avail oneself of these handsome privileges, as every American knows, one held up two fingers, a request that the teacher routinely granted. The petitioner than wrote his or her name on the board, so that everybody in the room would know who was "out." If a name were already on the board, one was normally expected to delay his or her request. The teacher could hardly ignore, of course, a frantic waving of two fingers whether a name was already on the board or not.

Along the south edge of the lot was a third wooden structure, really more of a shelter than a building. Here the school stored its supply of soft coal from Melbourne. Stalls and hitching posts were provided for the horses that the country girls and boys rode. Once I set type for an item in the *Guide* about the saddle girth breaking on Geraldine Springer's mount; she had been thrown off, the saddle fell on her, the horse stepped on the saddle, and she was scratched on her face and limbs. But she made it to school and back home again.

Sometimes the roads were so bad, with thick, deep, frozen ruts, that the country kids could not even take a horse. And some walked all the time. Once at a county-wide track meet sophomore Jasper Vanderpool was our entry in the mile run. The contestants had to run eight times around the track, and Jasper was so far out in front that he lapped the nearest competitor, a Bethany boy. I can still see his long-legged, slender figure galloping across the finish line. I was astonished because I did not even realize he was a distance runner. "When did you practice," I asked him, like a good newspaper reporter. "Oh, I always run to school," he answered. "I just dogtrot across the fields."

Between the outlying structures and the main building were our play areas. Swings and teeter-totters were located in the east area. The west side featured the basketball court, scene of the interscholastic boys' and girls' games. Our enrollment was entirely too small to support a football team, but parents explained that football was a rough, brutal sport anyway.

The north area was reserved for tag games, which started in the morning as soon as two or three pupils showed up. Later arrivals were welcome to join the game in progress. As most of us tried to get to school early enough to get in on a few minutes of the fun, tardiness was not a special problem. Eventually the big iron bell rang and we trooped inside, hot, sweaty, winded, and excited.

During the summer vacation clumps of grass had gradually taken over the deserted playgrounds, and scores of yellow jackets had dug their burrows in the soil, but after only a few days of our vigorous play the grass would be worn away, the yellow jackets would disappear, and the surface would be hard and smooth again. Barefooted kids know all about yellow jackets.

The building had four classrooms downstairs and four upstairs, plus tiny offices and storerooms.

In our science laboratory, classes were held in agriculture and physics.

The room inside the front door, on the right, past the superintendent's office, held grades one and two, for six and seven year olds, respectively. No preschool or kindergarten was provided for children under six; in fact the *Guide* ran a piece each summer urging parents to keep the "babies," under six, at home, playing with dolls and other toys; they were much too young to start learning to read and write. By contrast, most young adults nowadays can hardly remember learning to read and write, since the blocks and coloring books they played with at home taught them their letters easily and gradually. We hardly realize that reading and writing are complex skills, for centuries mastered only by scholars. When Charlemagne was the head of his vast empire he decided to learn to read and write, but after a few months concluded it was impossible and abandoned the project. Some of our first graders who did not have a chance to learn the alphabet until they started school and who were to live and die without ever hearing of Charlemagne would have understood his frustration.

Down the hall was the third and fourth grade room. The remaining four grades were on the left, two grades to a room. Each teacher managed twenty-five or thirty pupils. Each room had its own stove and coal bin in the corner; so one of the teacher's cool-weather responsibilities was to keep a fire going. The older boys

Front row from left to right: Loren Reid, Lola Dryer, Florence Dunn, Marie Clark, unknown, Christine Harrison, Ervin Thompson. *Second row from left to right*: Homer Real, Erma Scott, Earl Gooding, unknown, Bessie Ray, Flora Maye Dowell, Edith Oram. *Back row from left to right*: Superintendent Vogelgesang, Joe Osborn, Harmon Ward, Frank Maxwell.

Only ten members of this group of sophomores graduated as seniors. Many of our eighth-grade group did not enter high school. One reason for the attrition was that the limited curriculum of the school was unattractive to many pupils.

liked to help with coal-firing duties and sometimes, accidentally or otherwise, covered the red coals with a thick layer of coal dust from a corner of the bin. After a certain amount of smothering and smoking, the coal gas would suddenly ignite and blow the door open with a loud whoosh, filling the room with smoke and fine ash. All instruction had to be suspended while windows were opened to ventilate the room. We always enjoyed these interludes, especially if they flustered the teacher.

We had no library—only a small collection of books in each classroom, roughly graded according to the needs of the occupants. I suspect they were mainly waifs and strays that had been donated. We had no arts, crafts, or counseling. We had no band, no glee club. We did have a supply of songbooks, including *The One*

Girls' basketball team, Gilman City High School. *Left to right*: Opal West, Viola White, Vera Williams, Edith Oram, Florence Dunn, Iris Welden. Vera was captain, 1920. Florence was captain, 1921, and competed that spring in the declamatory contest at Maryville.

Hundred and One Best Songs, and sang them all: hymns, patriotic songs, war songs, and other favorites. We had no gym; no cafeteria. Most of us trotted home for lunch. Others brought lunch boxes or pails, with country ham or spareribs, pie or cake, biscuits and country butter—or maybe just corn bread and molasses. A feature of every box or pail was an aluminum drinking glass made of circular rings that would collapse into something only a little bigger than a typewriter ribbon spool.

Among the classrooms of the high school, on the second floor, were two that could open into a single study hall, which could also serve as an assembly room if two people sat in each seat and a few stood. Often high-school pupils were assembled at the end of the day for general announcements. At our first assembly we had a good look at the superintendent, the principal, and the other teachers. I best remember I. J. Vogelgesang, who came our sophomore year and held the post of superintendent nine years with distinction before he was lured to a larger school. "Professor" Vogelgesang, as he was called, was a sturdy German, a little chunkier than average, with a temper that ranged from the forceful to the volcanic. I have actually, on occasion, heard him roar. He had been hired in the first instance to maintain discipline, and, after that, if possible, to see that the pupils got an education. The ability to maintain order was essential because in the school were a few boys twenty years old or older who had been held back because they could not pass Latin, and who got restless having to repeat other courses along with the Latin. Basically, however, he was friendly. And he was a good teacher; I thought he made algebra exciting by demonstrating that as a mathematical tool it was so much more flexible than arithmetic.

After the necessary information had been given at assembly, one of the girls took her place at the piano, watching Mr. Vogelgesang for the signal to start playing the music for our march out of the room and down the stairs. He, of course, would not give the signal until we were nice and quiet. Sometimes he would threaten: "I'm not going to dismiss you until you have settled down —I can stay here as long as you can—all night if necessary." Charlemagne himself could never have commanded greater respect. As we never wanted to make an issue of the matter on his terms, we speedily settled down. In a moment he nodded his head imperially and we marched out in a predetermined order—seniors first. It was a proud and spirited moment. The grade school had been dismissed a few minutes earlier, the idea being to get small fry well out of the way and homeward bound to avoid friction between older and younger pupils.

As we had lived in Washington, D. C., during my sixth year, I did not start school until I was seven. By prearrangement, I began with second grade, the normal spot for seven year olds. On the first day I remember reading line after line, with awesome fluency. After a week, or maybe it was a month, I was promoted to third grade. Nobody warned me of this sudden shift, nor even asked my opinion; I simply showed up at school one morning, was taken by my second-grade teacher to the new domain next door, was casually introduced to the other teacher, and told to "sit there."

In thousands of American homes, parents have had to face the decision of whether to allow a child to skip a grade. In every situation the pros and cons are difficult to weigh. The argument for shifting is to keep the child occupied and challenged, otherwise he will be bored. The argument against shifting is that the child may lose something in social development because of being grouped with older children. Large schools with wide resources can offer other options, but in small schools the problem of shifting must be met head on.

Few of life's obstacles are as fearful to a child as the gap between second and third grade. Second grade is primary school; third grade is intermediate. Eight year olds are notably bigger and stronger than seven year olds and are highly aware of the difference. Primary kids play on swings and teeter-totters and at the end of the day are sent home first; intermediate kids play tag games and are sent home with the other grades. Few can equal the scorn with which one third grader can say to another third grader, "Don't behave like a little second grader."

Normally those who cross the gap travel in a convoy of classmates who have been at their side for two years. These two years have given them a chance to learn something about what goes on down the hall. A few have older brothers or sisters to give encouragement or at least information. But here I was making the crossing—not with my peers, not even by myself, but escorted by—let's face it—a teacher. So, though I had done no wrong, I was thrust into an alien country, where the other inhabitants were eight and nine. They stared, and what was worse, they whispered and smiled. I had learned that the new teacher's name was Ona Terry. She was fifty—no, forty—well, twenty. She looked kindly enough. Some teachers liked to be called by their first name—for example, Miss Ona—but I knew she went by her last; she was Miss Terry.

I was left unattended for half an hour, then the third-grade reading class was called up. In turn each third grader—huge creatures of formidable appearance—stood and read. On the playground they were ominous enough, but on their own territory they were intimidating. Most of them read smoothly but a few had to be helped over words much as you would pull a mule through a mudhole.

Had I had good sense I would have stumbled somewhat when my turn came, but at age seven I had spent five years in a printing office. The third-grade reader was set in large type; in fact, it looked a lot like the 12 point Century we had at the *Guide*.

The long-er words had hy-phens and the lines were doub-le spaced. Words were fre-quent-ly re-peat-ed. I read my passage briskly without prompting. Instead of being halted after having read the customary two or three sentences, I was cut loose and allowed to continue for three or four paragraphs.

Miss Terry just shook her head—I wondered why—but said nothing. I sat down and others continued the reading.

My performance attracted little attention from my classmates, since the ability to read is not high on the list of pupil values, but disaster of an unexpected sort lay just ahead. One morning Miss Terry stopped me at her desk as I entered the room, put her arm around me, and gave me a big hug and kiss. This utterly ruined my standing, since, although she sometimes kissed the girls, she had not kissed any of the other boys. At the midmorning recess I had to endure several well-selected, unanswerable, undeserved comments. I was almost glad when one day she fell down a stairwell and broke her arm, which put an end to the hugging. Just as I survived this ordeal, however, she invited me to spend a weekend with her at her farm home near Ridgeway, a small town to the north. Although the visit was pure delight, this additional show of favoritism renewed the razzing. On the whole, however, the transition to third grade had no ill effects.

In third grade our major task was to memorize the multiplication table. Each morning at breakfast I reviewed the day's number with Mother. One morning it was the twos: one times two is two, two times two is four. Next morning it was the threes. I remember I learned the fives with ease, since the answers galloped along at neat intervals: five, ten, fifteen, and so on. The eights and nines were difficult—and still are. The elevens were a breeze, since the answers were so predictable: twenty-two, thirty-three, fortyfour. But I was glad to stop with the twelves.

Nowadays students learn only through the tens, and, with the coming of hand-held computers, may not need to learn to multiply at all. Yet, I was amused when recently I saw, over the campus stamp window of one of our large state universities—an institution whose name I will not reveal, since it is close to my heart—a sign, posted by the clerk: $1 \times 13 = 13$. $2 \times 13 = 26$. $3 \times 13 = 39$. The universal use of hand computers may be further away than we think.

Gradually my third-grade classmates accepted me and we went to school together for nine years, by far the longest time I ever spent in a company of students. And Miss Terry, wherever you are, I want you to know that all of us remember so much of what you taught us. And I also want you to know that I got over entirely my dislike of being kissed by attractive and charming girls of any age.

On the last morning of the school year, we were each given a certificate attesting that we had passed and were promoted to the next grade. The kids had the grades tagged in order of difficulty. Everybody declared that third grade was *hard*—read that with feeling—even harder than fourth grade. I was grateful that I eventually passed both.

Fifth and sixth grades with Zoe Webb, an attractive Mount Moriah girl, went swiftly. I remember little except that on the last morning of sixth grade one boy failed, so that next fall, instead of marching onward with the rest of us, he had to trod another forlorn year with the lowly fifth graders who had caught up with him. I'll wager *he* remembers sixth grade.

Seventh and eighth grades were tagged as *very hard*. They determine whether you will *ever* get to high school. Many who finished eighth grade in a country school never continued further; those who did would get their high schooling with those of us who managed to finish. For most of us, however, the room in the southwest corner of the building was the scene of pleasant memories. First, there was the teacher, Mabel Norwood, who read twenty minutes every afternoon as soon as school convened. She picked stories that kept us in delightful suspense and read them charmingly as well: *The Lamplighter, Anne of Green Gables*, and *Hans Brinker, or the Silver Skates*. (When I became a teacher I often read aloud—a direct heritage from Mabel Norwood.)

The seventh-and-eighth-grade room had a library of perhaps thirty volumes. In Edgar Allan Poe's "The Gold Bug" I found an interest in codes that still persists. One day at school I spent four solid hours reading *Treasure Island* (except for recess, which I patronized, as always; there is no sense in being an utter damn fool). I was completely absorbed. Recitations from seventh-grade arithmetic, eighth-grade English, and seventh-grade history floated around me, washed back and forth through me, buzzed over and under me, and all the time I was transported to a spot three thousand miles away ("Them that die'll be the lucky ones! . . . Ned Gunn? Dead or alive, who minds Ned Gunn?"). Miss Norwood sagely perceived that I did not need to know, just then, those other things and left me under the spell of R. L. S.

Geography fascinated me beyond all telling. Though the flag had forty-eight stars, New Mexico and Arizona having just been admitted, our map of the United States still had empty spaces marked "Indian Territory" and "Dakota Territory," the book being slightly behind the times, say twenty years. It showed Austria-Hungary, Serbia, Montenegro, and the Ottoman Empire, and the great cities of Constantinople and St. Petersburg. On the other side of the world were the Chinese Republic, Siam, and Persia. Our text was not wholly archaic, however; it did not go back as far as the Holy Roman Empire. In a way this old book made us aware of the changes that happened in our own short lifetimes, and that conflagrations and upheavals mark each change of a name or erasing of a boundary.

At times my seatmate and I opened our books to one of the maps, and each made a list of ten names. We then traded lists, to see who would be the first to locate the other's ten items. Thus we became familiar with those glamorous places: Ceylon, Hong Kong, Vladivostok, Helsingfors, and places that still dance in my fancy, Trebizond and Zanzibar. We also discovered that the hardest names to spot were those printed in tiny, 5 point type, like Entebbe, or those that were letter spaced and spread out over a thousand miles, like DESERT OF GOBI. How delighted I was, eons later, when I flew over the Pacific, and, on the leg between Taipei and Hong Kong, saw the fat, rounded belly of the Chinese coast, exactly as it had appeared in my geography book.

The subject that gave eighth grade its rugged character, however, was arithmetic. Nowadays I read that high-school seniors need special refresher courses to make sure that upon graduation they will be able to perform the simple calculations involved in holding a job and making a living. Even my generation wrestles with check stubs, but not because we were unexposed to the basic skills.

We did our best to warn others against permanently borrowing our textbooks.

Recently I dug up a copy of Milne's *Standard Arithmetic,* our eighth-grade text, used in thousands of schools, and was appalled to see the range of topics it covered. At one time we had to know not only liters, meters, and other units of the metric system but also grains, scruples, drams, pennyweights, quires, bales, gills, pecks, rods, and cords. We could shatter bushels into pecks or the other way around. We knew the mysteries of fractions: not only proper fractions, which have the smaller number on top, like 11/32, but improper fractions, which have the smaller number on the bottom, like 32/11. We could transform the latter into a mixed number, ending with something like 2 10/11. Given 3/8 of a dollar, we could give 1/4 of a dollar to a friend, and tell you what fraction of a dollar we had left; that transaction introduced us to the least common denominator. We could deal with the case of a man who owned 2/5 of a factory and sold 1/3 of his share for $3,500— and from that pennyweight of information, tell you what the whole factory was worth. We took in stride problems like that of the commission merchant who sold 35,000 bushels of wheat at 32 cents per bushel. He then invested the proceeds, along with $4,000 additional cash, in prints selling for 5 1/2 cents a yard. Knowing that his commission both for buying and selling was 2 percent, we could reveal how many yards of prints he bought.

We learned about square and cube root, percentages, and decimals. We could calculate the area of a circle or a cylinder. We studied profit and loss, commercial discounts, promissory notes, bank deposits, accounts and bills, brokerage, insurance premiums. When Milne trampled over an acre with his principles and examples, he left that acre well trampled. And Miss Norwood was not one to skip the hard parts; she took us through everything, problem by problem.

Over the years I keep remembering how bright this group was, both boys and girls. Our Friday afternoon ciphering matches, at times with pupils from another room as spectators, showed our ability as lightning calculators. I can still see half a dozen of my classmates at the board, writing three-digit figures as fast as Miss Norwood dictated them, the column getting longer and longer; then came the command, "Add!" and then the sounds of chalk tapping in and around the numbers.

A few weeks before the end of eighth grade, Miss Norwood resigned and her room was taken by Mrs. Ira Oliphant, the mayor's wife. Mrs. Oliphant had not taught for years but seemed glad to help out. Like Eleanor Roosevelt she was no beauty but also like Mrs. Roosevelt she had a warm concern for people and was truly interested in teaching us. She was entirely candid about what she did and did not know. One of her resources was Mr. Oliphant; she would say, in arithmetic class, that she could not get the right answer to the fourteenth problem, but Mr. Oliphant worked it out; or, in English class, "I wrote a set of test questions for you last night, but Mr. Oliphant said they were too hard, so I wrote a new set." She was a master of those difficult arts, probing and review-ing; symbolically speaking, she spent a good deal of time on our side of the desk. She praised honest effort, was excellent at com-menting on each morsel of improvement, and was highly per-ceptive in sensing the point at which a struggling pupil needed exposition or encouragement.

The notorious, dreaded, eighth-grade hurdle was to solve the famous 180 problems with which Milne's *Standard Arithmetic* ended.

These problems had a rural flavor, dealing with fencing a field, filling a silo, or sharing equitably a given portion of pie, dol-lars, or chickens. I remember struggling one evening with a prob-lem in wallpapering a room. The dimensions of the room were given, the challenge being to calculate the number of rolls of sid-ing, ceiling, and border that would be needed. The proper answer was given in the back of the book, but I couldn't hit it; I kept com-ing out with too much or too little siding or ceiling. Father took

The author, age fifteen.

over, but after a time sent me to bed; he sat up half the night, and when I woke up the next morning, I found he had solved it. Even Mr. Oliphant didn't get that one. On other days we showed up at school missing an answer despite our combined home resources, but on those occasions Mr. or Mrs. Oliphant would fortunately have hit upon the solution. Problem number 180 was especially feared. High-school students who had survived all 180 would say to us, "Have you come to No. 180 yet?" or "Wait until you hit No. 180." This was it: "Three men bought a grindstone 20 inches in diameter. How much of the diameter must each grind off so as to share the stone equally, making no allowance for the eye?" It was the queen bee of problems. Here is your grindstone, friend, brand new, 20 inches across; you may use it first, taking your one-third, and then pass it on to your partner. But if you grind off more than 3.68 inches, we will have your heart's blood.

With persistence and the aforesaid outside sources, we trudged through the whole 180.

Eventually came grammar school's final day. We appeared that last Friday morning for a brief session to receive report cards and also that thing of wonder, an eighth-grade diploma. I took mine at once to Bill Haines, had it framed, and hung it in the *Guide* office alongside the big picture of Billy Bryan. If ever you meet a senior citizen and he or she says, "All I had was an eighth-grade education," treat him—or her—with admiration and respect. At least as far as arithmetic is concerned, everything after eighth grade is downhill.

That glorious graduation day was the spring of 1918. The nation was geared for war. Our own world centered on the fact that now, as eighth-grade diploma holders, we could Go Out Into the World, or continue our education in high school, on the second floor, the very heart of the Purple and Gold. No one warned us that we would need to adjust, or work our way through a transition, or that we were now those Problem People called Teenagers. After all, since we had mastered the 180, we adjusted without fuss or feathers. We merely assembled on the top floor instead of the bottom floor. We coped with four teachers every year instead of one teacher every two years. Our group was larger, since we acquired a few graduates from nearby country schools, bearing names such as Haggarty, Hill, and Buckeye, yet the total high-school enroll-

WRITTEN EXERCISES. 367

172. How many shares of stock, at 113$\frac{1}{4}$, can a broker purchase for me with $ 22,675, brokerage $\frac{1}{8}\%$?

173. I am offered 6% stock at 84, and 5% stock at 72. Which investment is preferable, and how much ?

174. I am desirous of securing an income of 6$\frac{1}{2}\%$ or 7% on my investments. Can I do it by purchasing 5% stock at 75% ? What will be the rate of income ?

175. I have, as the net proceeds of a consignment of goods sold by me, $ 3816.48, which the consignor desires me to remit by draft at 2 months. If the rates of exchange are $\frac{3}{4}\%$ premium, and the rate of interest 6%, what will be the face of the draft ? (Allow days of grace.)

176. A man bought a horse and a carriage, paying twice as much for the horse as for the carriage. He sold them both for $ 662, receiving 15% more for the horse, and 8% more for the carriage than they cost him. What did they each cost him ?

177. A man sold 500 acres of land, receiving in payment $\frac{2}{3}$ of the value in cash, and the rest in a note due in 3 months without interest. He immediately discounted the note at a bank at 6%, paying $ 57.50 discount. What was the price of the land per acre ? (Allow days of grace.)

178. How many slates will be required to cover a roof, each side of which is 34 feet 9 inches long and 16 feet wide, allowing 4 slates to cover a square foot; and what will they cost at the rate of $ 4.75 per C ?

179. An article was sold at a price which was $\frac{1}{4}$ above cost. If the cost had been $\frac{1}{4}$ of what it really was and the selling price had remained the same, the gain would have been $ 6.75. How much did the article cost ?

180. Three men bought a grindstone 20 inches in diameter. How much of the diameter must each grind off so as to share the stone equally, making no allowance for the eye ?

A page from Milne's *Standard Arithmetic*, p. 367, showing the last group of the 180 "General Review Exercises." (Answers, given in the back of the book, reveal the solution to No. 180: to share the stone equally the three owners need to grind off 3.68, 4.78, and 11.54 inches, respectively.)

ment was between fifty and sixty. We had no elective courses; each of us, every year, took Latin, English, history, and mathematics or science.

Ethel Sloan, our principal and also our history teacher, had ninety-five hours of college education, which was a lot. I remember her as a fine teacher of English history. I also remember that she wore only two dresses: one blue, the other brown. She started with the blue dress and wore it day after day until even we became weary of the sight; then, about the middle of October, she shifted to the brown. Frost came, leaves fell, snow altered the landscape, Angles, Saxons, and Danes were replaced by the Normans, but the brown dress endured. Then one day the blue dress returned, and we were delighted to see it; with it we studied the Williamses and the Henrys, explored the Renaissance and Reformation, but in our class no Reformation, no Age of Enlightenment; day after day the same blue dress. But after the Glorious Revolution came the brown dress, which now looked glorious; and so it went during the year. Even so, we gained early in life an appreciation of our British heritage.

Miss Sloan's thrift was forced by the low salaries paid our teachers. Six hundred dollars spread over twelve months was a meager sum even in those days. Out of that sum our teachers had not only to meet living expenses, but somehow to finance summer school at Maryville or elsewhere.

Our teaching was sharply geared to the textbook. Teachers started at the beginning of the book and took things chapter by chapter, without much rearranging or skipping, and with no supplementary reading. At times the procedure got mechanical: we read ten assigned pages about New England poets, writing full notes on slips of paper; at recitation time we were allowed to refer to our notes though we were not allowed to peek at the text itself. Or we took turns reading aloud from "The Legend of Sleepy Hollow"; one student would read a paragraph, another student another. Our instruction had a rugged thoroughness about it.

Unfortunately the dropout rate was frightful. Of every ten who toddled to first grade, one was graduated from high school; and of ten who were graduated from high school, one got a college degree. Many good minds were not intrigued by Latin or medieval history.

Of our high-school teachers, Lois Graham, a physician's daughter, was the loveliest. She thoroughly captivated us. She was a shapely brunet, an authentic beauty, with a melodious voice. She taught English and, probably not too eagerly, Latin. She also coached our debate team and trained us for declamation contests. She had attended the famous Cumnock School of Elocution at Northwestern, at a time when Cumnock, along with Emerson College in Boston, were the top schools in the nation at which to study elocution. She persuaded us to abandon the vulgar characteristics of our small-town, midwestern speech and soften our *r*'s and broaden our *a*'s. We tried to say "fahmuh" for *farmer* and "ahnt" for *aunt* and "hahlf pahst" for *half past*, just to win her smile. Because of Miss Lois's instruction, I can point with pride to the fact that my cultural roots in my professional field of speech communication go directly back to the best of the late nineteenth-century tradition. Though the notion that the people of a large country like the United States should speak one uniform dialect soon wore itself out, it was interesting to be exposed to it.

Miss Lois had two or three boyfriends on the string who wrote her regularly and ardently. We were keenly interested in her romances. As she used their letters as bookmarks in her copy of Cicero's *Orations*, we bounded to her desk whenever she left the room, posted a watch, pilfered one of the bookmarks, and read it aloud. Since as a printer I had had a vast experience in reading all kinds of handwriting, I was one of those who drew the assignment of reading her mail, in my best, newly acquired, eastern diction. Despite this mischief, you must believe that we loved her dearly and not only gladly but eagerly obeyed every command she laid on us.

Miss Lois taught only one year in the Gilman City system. She was one of that vast army of young women who teach school a year or so and then turn their attention to husband, children, and home. These young women bring enormous energy, enthusiasm, and affection to their teaching, which help to compensate for their lack of classroom experience. If a pupil is exposed to a mix of young teachers and old teachers, with the corresponding "new methods" and "time-tested procedures," he or she has a fair chance to get a proper education.

I do not believe any of our teachers had a college degree. Each summer they did extra study at Maryville State Normal College, in order to upgrade their teaching certificates. Since to us they already seemed to know everything a teacher needed to know, we could not imagine what summer school had to offer them. Moreover, they got the powerful support of parents in their discipline of their charges. If a pupil got a paddling at school and complained, he got a second paddling at home. Thus we learned to apply ourselves.

When I said our school had no guidance or counseling, I was not entirely correct. Mr. W. P. Broadbeck, a tall, well built, graying, sepulchral sort of man who had probably been a preacher in other days, taught seventh-hour sophomore Latin. One day after class he stopped me for a conference after the other students had left and told me he had noticed I looked underweight, pale, and did not have good posture. I could have told him that I could play baseball from after breakfast to suppertime, but I accepted his comment as coming from Mount Olympus itself; whereupon, to my amazement, he reached underneath his desk and pulled out a pair of Indian clubs.

An Indian club is an astonishing thing with which to be suddenly confronted in a Latin class. He proceeded to demonstrate an amazing variety of exercises. Taking one pin in each great hand and putting it in a whirling motion, he extended his arms to the side, to the front, behind his back, and overhead, continually spinning the clubs. He gave quite a demonstration of physical fitness. He then insisted that I go through the routine, with many interruptions for refinements. After what seemed like a long session, he set me free. On the whole it was better than being kissed by Miss Terry, but I never elected to explore the artistry of Indian clubs again. Of course, if Miss Lois had kept me after school and had shown me her Indian clubs, I would have developed enormous enthusiasm. She would have demonstrated the exercise as a fine art, not as a remedial process. She would have added that boys with agile hands and long fingers would be very good with Indian clubs. Good teachers know that pupils learn better if you use an approach that captures interest and if you find ways of praising instead of criticizing.

For all Mr. Broadbeck's interest in physical fitness, however, he found it impossible to maintain discipline. On one disastrous occasion the older boys shoved him down the banister of the stairway so that he slid the whole distance from the second floor to the first. As everybody remembers, it was even more important for a teacher to maintain discipline than to teach the subject. This incident shattered his influence. He himself was none too happy about his situation, and the unexpected death of his father no doubt confirmed his decision to seek another line of work.

I should have shown more appreciation than I did for his concern about me. Other than the superintendent, he was the only male teacher I ever had in all my grade and high-school years. In college and graduate school the situation was reversed; those domains belonged almost exclusively to males.

One afternoon Mr. Vogelgesang informed us at the closing of an assembly that we were scheduled to be inspected to determine whether we would be continued on the official Missouri list as a first-class high school. As we had enjoyed first-class status five years, we did not want to lose it. To be on the list meant that we could enter college without taking a lot of examinations. Almost no one expected to attend college, but it was a nice dream anyway.

Next day the teachers told us what was involved in an inspection. The inspector would come to the building, visit many classes, and might even quiz us personally. Miss Lois, for example, warned us that if the school were dropped from the list, and it was because of the poor performance of the students in English III, we would be the ones to blame. From this moment on, she continued, we must pay strict attention. We must each be sure we understood what was being discussed, because, when the inspector stepped into our room, she might question us not only on that day's assignment but also on anything we had discussed previously. We saw she was using his visit to get the maximum amount of work out of us. We also saw that a chance to recite on something previously discussed gave us an additional opportunity to make good. But we did begin to feel a personal responsibility for keeping the Purple and Gold a first-class school.

The day came when the inspector arrived. He could hardly have been in the building two minutes before word was flashed down the corridors from room to room, "He's here." English III had just assembled when the door opened and a slender figure of average height, a man about middle age, entered. He did not wear a uniform nor display a badge, but then he did not need to. He gave us a look and nodded to Miss Lois, who waved her hand graciously to a seat well forward and near the door. The occupants fled to an empty bench at the back of the row, and His Eminence made himself comfortable. Several students offered him their books, pointedly open at the critical page, and he regally accepted one.

Our concentration was intense. In seconds we heard Miss Lois asking a question, in her clear, bell-like voice, about Poe's great code and pirate story, "The Gold Bug." Several people dutifully waved their hands in the air, each inwardly praying that he or she would not be selected. Once the first question had been managed, we began to relax. The questions came rapidly and so did our answers. No one could hardly have improved on our insights and perceptions. After some minutes Miss Lois asked the inspector if he wanted to ask us questions. We were not prepared for this bold move. Nor was he. Around the room breathing stopped utterly. After a pause he said, "No, I guess not. The pupils seem well prepared." He rose, smiled ever so briefly at Miss Lois, left the room, and closed the door behind him. We started to breathe again.

Actually nothing that we did really fooled the inspector. He knew that as soon as he set foot inside the building every teacher of every room would be aware of his presence. He knew that teachers were not likely to ask questions that pupils could not answer. But he also knew that the teachers would get the discussion on as high a plane as possible. He knew that discipline would be ideal while he was in the room and that alertness would be keen. But he could also see the major ingredients of a good school program; that our teachers were informed and articulate and the pupils a cross section of small-town America. We were learning the basic skills that one needed for farm, office, shop, or store. We had an idea of other times and other peoples. I write from the vantage point of having known three other high schools at close range. We desperately needed a wider variety of courses, but these would come.

One way or another, room by room and class by class, the school survived the visit. In due course we received the official word from Jefferson City that we had been continued on first-class status, with all units approved. That triumph called for a parade. Each of the four classes made a banner and also an extra large banner for the whole school that used a background of purple with an inscription in large, gold letters, "FIRST CLASS HIGH SCHOOL."

Our closing assembly that day was something special. We marched down the stairs to John Philip Sousa—nothing less would do. In front of the building each class grouped behind its own special banner. We swung on to the north-south thoroughfare known as Cook Street, and though we had no band we sang lustily and yelled the school cheers. The Purple and Gold was a first-class school when we entered it, and it was a first-class school when we left it. A few of us thought the inspector had made his decision when he visited our English III class.

12

Tom Paine and Col. Bob Ingersoll

In the spring of 1920, Superintendent Vogelgesang made the yearly announcement at the closing assembly that the annual declamation contest would be held in six weeks. He explained the usual divisions: dramatic, humorous, and oratorical. Each contestant was to memorize a ten-minute selection, to be presented at the Rex Theatre and to be judged by three judges. The winners would represent the school in the subregional contest at Trenton, and three winners would be selected there to go to the regional contest at Maryville.

I had occasionally recited pieces in grade school, and at home had skirmished with Don in living-room debates. Father's procedure was to devise a topic such as "Resolved, That the horse is more valuable than the cow," Don taking one side and I the other. Afterwards Father rendered a decision, usually and justly, I think, in favor of Don. A few days before the Vogelgesang announcement I had participated in an impromptu debate with Neal, his son; Lloyd Welden, who later became a teacher of speech; and Florence Dunn, daughter of Bob Dunn, one of our advertisers, on "Resolved, That country life is more prosperous and pleasant than city life." I had also heard a vast amount of speaking at the Gilman City picnic and at our lyceum and chautauqua. And I had heard previous contests, so I knew what they were: the Rex full of school kids and townspeople, the three divisions with four or five entrants in each division, the occasional side bet, the long pause while the judges prepared their ballots, the announcement of the winners with its thrill for a few and its agony for others.

In the first century and a half of the Republic's existence, speechmaking was a prime activity. Good speakers drew large crowds. The year 1920 was long before the prevalence of radio; televised sports were still in the distant future. The number one source of information was the newspaper, and the number two source an address by an informed citizen, such as an officeholder or even a candidate. When William Jennings Bryan spoke in Kansas City, a score of people from Gilman City took the O.K. to join the throngs in Convention Hall that had assembled to hear him. Some of my older relatives had heard Robert G. Ingersoll speak in Trenton. Their choice story was that once when Ingersoll had been scheduled to give a Sunday afternoon address, the city fathers, opposed to the idea of letting this notorious freethinker-agnostic have a public hearing, locked the door of the auditorium to shut out the crowd that had assembled. The explanation given was that the auditorium was unsafe, not having enough exits for so large an audience. A few of the men present went home and got axes, came back and chopped a couple of extra doorways in the building, declared that now it met fire safety standards, so Colonel Bob gave his address after all.

A St. Joe merchant, a Spickard attorney, a Mount Moriah minister, a Pattonsburg superintendent—anyone who had any kind of local reputation for speechmaking—could attract an audience. Father has described crowds of ten to fifteen thousand who went by train and team to hear a political debate. Often the people at the edge could not even hear the speaker, he recalled, but they stood quietly, hoping at least to pick up a phrase now and then. Afterwards, on the farms and in the towns, the debate would be a topic of conversation for days.

So that evening at home I was lying on the living-room floor, idly speculating about the superintendent's announcement. Mother was preparing supper. I said: "Mr. Vogelgesang told us today that there would be a declamation contest." Long pause. "I think I'll try out."

My memory is perfectly clear that at that precise second I had no intention whatever of trying out. Like many boys, I was just casting a fly into the pond to see what might happen. If Mother had said, "Oh, you're too young; you're just a sophomore; that's mainly a contest for seniors and juniors," I would have abandoned the idea. Or if she had said, "Why don't you wait a year or two," or, "You're not cut out to be a speaker," that would have been the end of it. Instead, Mother replied, "Why, son, that will be wonderful. You'll do real well and you'll win it." How marvelous mothers are! Of course, this particular mother knew her two boys had hung out the moon and the planets, or would someday soon.

More than that, when Father came home after his day in the *Guide* and the post office, she informed him that I was going to try out. I knew right then that I had passed the point of no return.

Unknown to most people, Father had cherished a lifelong dream of becoming an orator. He had always had admiration not only for Bryan, Ingersoll, Wilson, Daniel Webster, and that majestic lot, but even for lesser-known speakers like Governor Dockery, Judge Alexander, Sen. Daniel Vorhees, and Sen. Jim Reed. His voice choked so easily, however, and he was so petrified at the thought of facing an audience, that he never did attempt a speech. He could write an editorial that would tear the hide off its victim and was fearless in expressing his opinion on current issues, but he could not speak in a public forum. Accordingly, he wanted his sons to develop the talent that he did not have.

Father not only endorsed the idea of my trying out, but after our supper of fried rabbit, mashed potatoes, gravy, and biscuits, he acted on it. He knew the very orator: Ingersoll. And the very selection: "A Tribute to Thomas Paine." As a young man he had completely memorized this two-hour lecture. He still had the book, so he got it out and read aloud chunks of it.

Ingersoll had quoted a few of Paine's immortal lines: "These are the times that try men's souls. The summer soldier, and the sunshine patriot, will, in this crisis, shrink from the performance of his duty; but he that stands it now, deserves the love and thanks of man and woman." Moreover, Ingersoll had embellished Paine's words and deeds with his own magical language: "A few more years, a few more brave men, a few more rays of light, and mankind will venerate the memory of him who said, 'The world is my country, and to do good my religion.'" Even today hardly a campaign passes without some candidate declaring, "These are the times that try men's souls," or rebuking standpatters and sideliners and fence straddlers by calling them "summer soldiers" and "sunshine patriots."

In Father's generation the fact that Ingersoll was a freethinker meant, to all right-thinking, God-fearing people, that he was at that exact moment roasting in hell. Although Tom Paine was a revolutionary hero, he was also a freethinker, and was roasting right alongside Ingersoll. So when Father prepared to use a ten-minute excerpt from the tribute of one freethinker, Ingersoll, to another, Paine, he was contriving a selection that had "PG" written all over it, if not "R" or even "X." Most people would have declared the term *freethinker* to be too mild; they would have preferred "agnostic," "atheist," or even "heretic." As Father was aware of this attitude, his cutting mainly focussed on Paine's contribution to the Revolution, eliminating the references to religious beliefs.

After he had selected ten minutes' worth of Ingersoll's eloquence, he started me memorizing it. He read a few lines and I repeated them, until I had learned most of the cutting by heart. So much for casting a fly on a pond.

Miss Lois spent hours after school coaching the contestants. My practice period came between that of a girl who was reciting a sad story about Bobby Shaftoe, who had gone to sea, but who will come back and marry me, and that of a boy with a robust voice, whose selection by Webster about John Adams ended with the thunderous note, "It [the Declaration] is my living sentiment, and, by the blessing of God, it shall be my dying sentiment; independence now, and independence forever." I secretly had him tagged as the winner, since by contrast the quiet poetry of Col. Bob Ingersoll seemed a frail thing.

The Rex was jammed and packed the night of the contest. I was a skinny kid, still wearing knee breeches; the other boys, tall and striking, wore long trousers. My voice had not fully changed. In the humorous and dramatic events most of the contestants were girls, each dressed elaborately. After two hours, with the contest over, the audience buzzed as the judges reviewed their notes and prepared their ballots. Florence Dunn, my debate partner of the previous month, won first in the dramatic division and I won first in the oratorical. The two of us, with the winner of the humorous division, went to Trenton for the subregional contest. As Florence and I survived the Trenton judges, we had the rare opportunity of representing the Purple and Gold at the Maryville State Normal College, where would be chosen the best from the nineteen counties in that district.

Father and Don went with me to Maryville, a trip that Father especially enjoyed as he met many friends going back to the days when he had edited the *Nodaway Forum*. Maryville was also Don's birthplace. We could walk hardly ten steps down the main street before Father would meet someone he remembered, though a dozen years had elapsed since he had lived there. That evening contestants from all over northwest Missouri competed in the auditorium on the college campus. As our small delegation from Gilman City listened to the other contestants we knew we were up against strong competition but even so were disappointed when Florence placed third and I second.

At home, however, the reaction was entirely different. Gilman City had seldom done so well in a regional contest; year after year her representatives had been knocked out at the subregional level. Moreover, at Maryville our small town was competing with Bethany, Trenton, Maryville herself, and even mighty Central High of St. Joe. From that point of view, our achievement was substantial. To celebrate, the school organized a parade. The students put me in a chair and carried me, chair and all, to the depot to meet Florence, who had stayed behind for a brief visit; they put her in another chair and carried us through the town. Everybody wore purple and gold ribbons, and small groups hoisted banners announcing the victory. They stopped at strategic points and yelled and sang patriotic songs. To my utter amazement I had completely forgotten this momentous happening, but there it is in the *Bethany Clipper*: "After the parade, the hero and heroine were permitted to go home to dinner." This was the first time, it recorded with pride, if not with total accuracy, "that Gilman City had ever won anything in a contest."

Even so, Father was disappointed and wrote each judge a letter, pointedly inquiring into the reasons for such an inequitable decision. One judge candidly said her decision had been close, but she thought the winning boy was more mature. Father could find no fault with that. The second judge, the only qualified one in the lot according to Father's judgment, had placed me first. The third judge, however, wrote that Ingersoll was not a fit choice for a school contest, and "A Tribute to Thomas Paine" was a disgrace to decent people. She had ranked me last. Father carried on a lengthy contest with Judge Three, but the decision stood.

The next issue of the Great Moral and Religious Weekly revealed his full disappointment in the decision. He not only stated his own verdict but quoted the *Maryville Democrat-Forum*: "Many were of the opinion that the Gilman City boy should have had first place." Father was never a happy loser where his son was concerned, and I still cherish letters that he wrote during the next two years to judges that voted unwisely and incorrectly.

At the beginning of other contest years I needed to decide whether to stay with Tom Paine or switch to a less-controversial selection, such as Webster's "Reply to Hayne": "Liberty and Union, now and forever, one and inseparable." I decided to stick with Tom, and his scorn of the sunshine patriot who shrank from the performance of his duty. Out of a dozen contests I sometimes won, sometimes placed, sometimes showed; sometimes, as the boy said of his dog in the dog show, I got only horrible mention. After each contest, my expert and impartial panel, consisting of Father, Mother, Don, and the coach, discussed the judges' decision to determine whether their entry had been done right by. If they decided that he had been ill used, and that prejudice of Paine or Ingersoll was apparent, off would go a series of Father's letters to the judges.

Next year I was chosen, along with Esther Reilly, a senior, to represent the school in the state debate tournament on the question that compulsory arbitration between employer and employee is wise and feasible. Esther, who later was graduated from the state university, had had even less debate experience than I, but we bravely undertook to debate a question entirely outside of our experience. For information we relied on broken files of the *Literary Digest*, a bundle of material from the State Travelling Library at Jefferson City, and interviews with the better-read members of the community. We wrote our speeches, tried to imagine what arguments would be used against us and how they could be managed, and generally tried to familiarize ourselves with the pros and cons of compulsory arbitration. The question was, of course, the one chosen for use by high schools all over the nation. Experience had taught the national selection committee that the question must be a meaty one, with strong arguments on each side, as it would be studied by high-school youngsters throughout the country for the five or six months of the debate season.

Under the supervision of University of Missouri authorities, the state was divided into districts and regions. Pairings were announced, first on a county basis, and the winners of each round would be paired against one another. Each debate was a sudden-death event, though we did not use that phrase; a team that had lost once was out of the competition.

We drew Martinsville, a tiny town in the west central part of the county. Martinsville would approve compulsory arbitration; we would oppose it. The chips were down. We simply must not lose, least of all to Martinsville. Miss Lois was our coach; Mr. Vogelgesang undertook the logistical arrangements of determining place of meeting and selection of judges. The *Guide* carried a free ad to publicize the event.

The sparring began with our superintendent's blandly offering to host the debate provided that we could select all the judges. The Martinsville superintendent was a better bargainer than that; the offer to underwrite the expenses of providing entertainment was eagerly accepted, but he wanted to select the judges himself. For a while it seemed as if compulsory arbitration would be needed there and then. Eventually Martinsville gained the privilege of selecting one judge and of approving or disapproving our two. Martinsville selected someone from Eagleville, a neighboring town, someone we had never heard of; that seemed crafty. We selected an out-of-town judge who had formerly lived in Gilman City and another outsider who was related to a local family, all of which seemed eminently fair. We reserved the Rex, and although this large hall would tax the strength of my voice, we could somehow manage to have the judges seated well forward. Miss Lois determined to seat herself next to the Eagleville judge; she might have a chance to visit with him a little.

A few days before the debate, I had read an account of an experiment involving a man whose stomach had been opened by a gunshot wound. Every viewer of westerns knows that to be gut-shot is to invite a sure and painful death, but this victim escaped that ordeal and endured another. For a reason not clear, the attending surgeon, instead of promptly sewing him up, left the hole in his stomach open to observe the digestive process. The surgeon fed his interesting patient, for example, oatmeal, and then recorded the length of time the oatmeal was in the stomach. Roast beef, I recall, lay three hours and forty minutes in the stomach before being emptied into the small intestine. Roast pork was the most difficult of all: four hours and forty minutes. Other items were also listed.

I rushed the book into the superintendent's office. Like any German, he loved good food, and his wife was a superb cook. He immediately grasped the significance of what I showed him. Since as hosts we were obliged to provide the Martinsville debaters with supper, we would select a meal from the table of digestive times. Everybody knew that blood was siphoned from the brain after a heavy meal. Very well, we would stuff the visitors with proper foods, leading with roast pork. Mrs. V. would take it from there.

The great day arrived. At the supper table were the four debaters and their coaches. Two of our most bewitching classmates, fully briefed on the plan, waited on the table. They made sure that our guests had plenty of the main course and the supplements, including fried, browned potatoes and thick, rich gravy, all German style. Manipulation may be new in our consciousness today, but the practice is reasonably ancient. We ate sparingly. The visitors rose from the table goggle-eyed. The party had to hurry to get to the Rex on time.

The theatre was packed. The judges were comfortably seated on the fourth and fifth rows, Miss Lois with one of them in personal custody. The chairman introduced the speakers. The Martinsville boys spoke like veterans: Clarence Darrow and Eugene Debs could have done no better. We performed splendidly: Samuel Gompers and John L. Lewis would have been proud of us. Each debater was applauded wildly. When the debate was over, the audience buzzed excitedly. A contest could hardly be closer; the decision could truly go either way. On our side Esther and I felt we had countered every argument with something, we had used all the information we had, we had said all we had come to say.

Ushers collected the judges' ballots and carried them, like bank notes, to the chairman. The buzzing stopped as he opened the first envelope and extracted a white slip of paper. He put it on the lectern, to one side; ages later, it seemed, he located another slip, and finally the third; he added them to the pile. He still had his own little speech to make, thanking one and all, expressing his relief that *he* hadn't had to judge the debate, it was that close; and then came the skyrocket: by a vote of three to zero, the decision went to us. The applause was like thunder, cracking and crackling again and again.

We were bumped off in the next round by practically nobody, but no matter; we had seen the glory from the top of the mountain.

In the twenties, the selection of judges was a villainous business, and judging an occult art. If one contestant or one team is clearly superior to another, almost any critic can tell the difference, acting on intuition and mother wit if little else. Anyone can judge a horse race if one horse is a length ahead. The trouble comes when contestants are evenly matched. Today the emphasis in speech tournaments is placed on selecting trained judges, known to be professional and objective in their attitude.

I can think of no finer experience for a young person than to have training in speaking and debating. Everybody who wants to speak in public must serve an apprenticeship, and it is better to serve it while in school and college than to wait until one is elected or appointed to a position of responsibility. Nearly every outstanding speaker you can think of got his start in high school or college or the equivalent: Webster, Clay, Bryan, Douglass, Roosevelt, Martin Luther King, and many others. Lincoln had little formal education but started stump speaking at the high-school age. Wilson either debated or coached debate at each of the half dozen colleges and universities with which he was associated.

Grade school and high school are good places to get used to the idea of winning and losing. I was always highly elated when I won, and bitterly disappointed when I lost. To comfort me my teachers would say that one learns as much from losing as from winning, which is true, but to me it always seemed that there was nothing I could learn from losing that I could not learn just as readily from winning. Even today my heart goes out to the loser in an Olympic contest or other competition. Eventually, I suspect, we learn two lessons: first, it is an honor, looking over the competition, simply to be a contestant; and second, you can't win them all.

Everything considered, small-town pupils were exposed to a fair amount of classroom and public performance. As classes were small, everybody had a chance. Grade-school programs on Friday afternoons gave an opportunity to recite poems and other selections and to take part in short skits, before peers, plus a few visitors. In high school both junior and senior classes gave three-act plays at a local church or theatre. If the teacher had eight girls and six boys in a class, she looked through the play catalog, turned to the section marked "8f6m," ordered sample copies of promising titles under that heading, and read them with her own talent in mind, assured that she had a part for everybody. A junior class play was exactly that—a play in which every junior had a speaking role. High-school assembly programs also often featured debates, readings, skits, and an occasional mock trial. Tom Paine and Col. Bob Ingersoll would have had to admit that the small-town schools were doing all right.

13

The Great Picnic
and Other Spectacles

Mark Twain, born the year Halley's Comet streaked across the heavens, always took a personal interest in it and freely predicted his life span would end the year it returned. "It will be the greatest disappointment of my life if I don't go out with Halley's Comet. The Almighty has said, no doubt: 'Now here are these two unaccountable freaks; they came in together, they must go out together.'" And so they did, at the comet's peak display in 1910.

Similarly I always developed the keenest excitement about the annual Gilman City picnic, which was going full blast the day of my birth. I have long since survived it, but while it was around it occupied my devoted and absorbed attention each successive August, as did other spectacles that visited us more or less annually at other times of the year. On the two days of the picnic, business establishments closed as early in the day as they decently could, that is at 9:00 A.M., opening up again at 4:30 just long enough to let everybody get fresh supplies of everything. Even the post office had the special permission of the postmaster general in Washington to be open only from 11:00 A.M. to 3:00, just long enough to service the mail from the O.K.'s No. 1 and No. 2. The trains brought their hundreds, and wagons and buggies and automobiles brought other hundreds, so that five or six thousand people—think of it!—jammed this town whose normal population in those years was a tenth of that number. To appreciate this phenomenon, imagine five million people descending upon Kansas City. Many who came had attended every previous picnic; many could recall Gilman City's earliest days, with its board sidewalks and its collection of wood shacks; many could even recall seeing the first train that puffed over the brand-new tracks.

Father's description was seldom equalled and never surpassed: "Remember the Gilman City Picnic is loaf sugar piled a mile high and happiness a world circle with the rim knocked entirely off. If you don't come you will feel so blame bad you will want to go out behind the barn and hire a four year old mule to kick all the laziness and apathy out of your pants."

The heart and soul of the event was at the intersection of Main and Broadway, the very front yard of the post office, where the principal attraction, the merry-go-round, was erected.

Like Lincoln's friend who was fonder of gingerbread than anything else in the world and could never get enough of it, my friends and I never wearied of the merry-go-round. Early on Thursday of picnic week every dray wagon in town began the big job of hauling parts and pieces from boxcars on the O.K.'s siding to the chosen site. The hard core of merry-go-round mechanics hired local talent to help with the erection. Starting with the massive, central iron pole and its satellite cables, iron strips, wooden beams, and gears that made the merry-go-round revolve and its horses gallop, the crew, piece by piece, assembled all the parts into a magnificent whole, finishing by attaching oval medallions, brightly painted, emblazoned with gilt, on the outer border of the vast, overhead, circular canopy. August after August we watched this creation and knew where every rod and timber went. If we saw one of the new workers hesitate, we wanted to jump into the center of the show and say, "Oh, that beam goes right up there," but of course we never did. I haven't the slightest doubt but that if I had that old merry-go-round disassembled and stacked in my backyard today, I could figure the thing out and get it set up. The most painstaking job was to level it—an operation demanding careful attention; anybody could see that if you set it up on a slant, it would, when it really got rolling, fling its spirited steeds all over the landscape, and the riders along with them.

The merry-go-round was driven by a steam engine, presided over by a master mechanic who fired its boiler and operated the big lever that started and stopped the whole mechanism. He had the sole authority of beginning and ending the ride. When lines were long, the rides seemed short; but in the morning before full crowds had gathered, or late in the evening when traffic began to thin out, the rides were generously long. When we were riding we learned to keep an eye on him, hoping that as we made each new circuit and approached his station he would see fit to let us go around yet another time or two before reaching for the lever that would halt our wild gallop.

The music came sometimes from a steam calliope, sometimes from a mechanical organ. So the merry-go-round was indeed a movable feast—for the eye, for the ear, for those entrancing deep rhythms of muscle and movement, all the while the wind lifting your hair and fingering your hot scalp. An attendant had the exquisite pleasure of hopping on and off, even while the merry-go-round was in motion, and of making his way around the revolving platform, collecting tickets, weaving through the triplets of galloping horses and past the stationary seats where only babies and hopelessly ancient people rode. No matter how long the ride, it was never long enough; and no matter how imposing one's string of tickets, it disappeared far too soon. Whether you were on the merry-go-round or off it, you were always within hearing distance of its music and the cries and squeals and laughter of its riders. The poet who said disdainfully that life is only a merry-go-round never rode this jeweled wheel, this bit of earthly paradise, this enchanted whirl through space, that was entirely ours two full days of each year.

Concessions of all sorts lined Main Street and Broadway: booths, popcorn and peanut wagons, floss candy machines. Many were run by local merchants, who, though they closed their stores, dispensed eatables and souvenirs at stands and booths. Slick and Banty Thompson, for example, sold, from a stand, quarter pound hamburger or tenderloin sandwiches for a nickel, and for another nickel all the coffee you could drink. I remember the sad day when they had to raise the price of hamburgers to a dime—an increase of 100 percent—triple-digit inflation—but that was one of the lamentable casualties of the First World War.

As chairman of the concessions committee, Charley Hurst presided over this empire. Charley was one of the town's royalty. He sold real estate, knew a lot of practical law, loved kids and had four of his own, was the rural carrier on Route 3, and was active in civic affairs. I have already mentioned that for fifty years he was the town clerk. He was a hero of mine. His responsibilities were imposing. On the front counter of the target-shooting booth was an awesome display of .22-caliber repeating rifles. At the back, ten or twelve feet away, was an attractive array of targets:

white ducks that floated along from left to right, stationary bull's-eyes, glass balls that bubbled atop streams of water. Before the stand could open for business, Charley personally checked it out for safety by selecting a rifle, loading it, and firing point blank at the backstop, to make sure that it was, in fact, entirely bullet proof. For these and other courtesies and duties, he received loads of complimentary tickets to each of the important concessions. He must have had a fifty-foot roll of tickets to the merry-go-round, and if he, in turn, wanted to confer a royal favor on one of his friends, he would simply tear off a yard or two and offer them with a gracious gesture. For even a single foot of tickets I would have gladly pulled every dandelion in his yard, or scrubbed and polished the stripped-down, topless Ford in which he carried the mail.

In huge tents the ladies aid of the Baptist, Methodist, and Catholic churches served gargantuan luncheons for a quarter. For this sum you could have all you could eat of fried chicken, pork chops, spareribs, mashed potatoes and gravy, homemade bread or biscuits, string beans, wilted lettuce and other greens that had been delicately flavored with smoking hot bacon grease and vinegar, pickled beets, corn, slaw, fruit salad, pies and cakes. Occasionally you still find this kind of meal at a small, family-style restaurant on one of your travels—and if you do, you will call it the high point of your trip and will brag about it forever.

At other booths you could buy pennants, canes, souvenir hats, ice-cream cones, soft drinks, and that peerless delicacy, old Louisiana salt-water taffy. For a nickel or dime, one concessionaire would offer to guess your weight. If you were a man, he would feel your muscles, to ascertain the tone of your flesh; if you were a lady, he would eye you discreetly and base his judgment on other criteria. If you were a boy, he would brag on your promising biceps and predict that you would be another Jack Johnson. Having announced his estimate, he would invite you to step on the scales; if he missed by more than his advertised range, you won a prize.

At another stop you could hit an upright stub of a mechanism with a sledge hammer. Your blow would drive a chunk of metal on a slide up a high pole, and if you had struck hard enough, with just enough zip and zing at the end of your swing, the chunk would ring the bell at the top. That achievement would bring you a box of candy and, more important, the cheers of the bystanders.

Sometimes a big, muscular man would hit the stub with a blow that you would think would drive it into the ground a couple of yards, but the chunk would travel only halfway up the slide. Then a small, wiry fellow with limber arms and rubbery wrists would step up, shift his chaw of tobacco to the other cheek, grab the sledge, whip it through the air in a wide arc that seemed to start at the back of his heels, and the chunk would zip up the slide and ring the bell with, obviously, yards to spare. I cannot explain this strange happening, I can only report it.

There was no end of other things to do. You could have your fortune told; and you could see sideshows. You could see a South American boa constrictor so large that if it were the same size as its picture out front, it could wrap itself around the bandstand. Don tells about seeing it and watching in sheer terror as its keeper took it from its pit and draped it over the shoulders of the ten or a dozen customers standing in the front row. Among those shoulders, thus chosen and thus honored, were Don's. After hearing his story, I do not believe I elected to view that particular exhibit. I liked better the stand where you could throw baseballs at a target, three balls for a nickel, and if you hit the bull's-eye you carried away a Kewpie doll. This feat required not only complete accuracy but also a high degree of speed. Despite my familiarity with the Spaulding pamphlets on *How to Pitch* I never came away with a Kewpie.

The Augmented Gilman City Band, augmented, that is, by musicians from Routes 1, 2, and 3, played afternoon and evening concerts. I always went to see Ralph Eckles play either the piccolo or the flute. Always surprised that a grocer could play a musical instrument with professional skill, I asked him about it. He added to my amazement by explaining that the lip action for the two instruments was different, and that if you played too much piccolo it would set you back on your flute, and vice versa. The world is full of wonders.

I often thought that Father would have made a splendid chairman of the concessions committee; he could have fired a bullet into a backstop, and he could have well dispensed fifty feet, or even five hundred feet, of merry-go-round tickets. Instead, he was invariably the chairman of the speakers' committee. If this committee ever met, I never knew it. I always suspected that he was the committee. He carried on a personal correspondence with hot prospects like Senators Stone and Reed, with the governor, and with the judge; with big-city editors who had a reputation for speechmaking; in short, with anybody who was anybody. In June the committee would announce that it would bring a real headliner, like Bryan, to the picnic; by July it was settling for Thomas R. Marshall, who achieved immortality for a full thirty years with a single sentence—"What this country needs is a good five-cent cigar"—and by August it had actually signed the Honorable Thomas S. Ballew, the great Princeton journalist and orator, or the Honorable William S. Bogarth, distinguished mayor of Trenton. All of these were Democrats—Father seldom allowed a Republican to get on a Gilman City platform if he could help it. But whoever was selected was billed as a star attraction, and Father's account in the next issue of the Great Moral and Religious Weekly would be something that His Honor could cherish forever.

A great crowd, moreover, turned out for the speaking, held in the big tent erected two blocks away. After a morning of trotting to concessions and a big luncheon, people welcomed a folding chair in a shady tent and a chance to hear the mayor from our nearest metropolis. Besides, he might be a congressman someday —if he escaped hanging. After all, a Trenton boy and a Gallatin boy made it to the governor's mansion. Even so, I would have preferred Father to have had the inside track on concessions than on speechmaking.

Everybody had relatives in town. Residents and their visiting brothers and sisters and in-laws thronged from one concession to another, the men quick with their pocketbooks, eager to be the first to pay. Surely two boys can have no greater delight than to tour a row of concessions with their father and three uncles, each with an abundance of nickels and dimes and a generosity to match. And when you had transacted business at every booth and had crammed yourself with candy, popcorn, orange pop, and hot dogs, your day was still not over; the fabulous evening attractions still remained, especially the program on Saturday evening, the final hours of the picnic.

At 7 P.M., crowds assembled at the big tent, finding seats on benches, folding chairs, or blankets laid on the ground, for the last round of fun. First came the announcements, with prizes awarded to the winners of the Ladies' Nail-Driving Contest, or Husband-Calling Contest, or the Boys' Apple-Eating or Water-melon-Eating Contest. Next the Celebrated Lady Boxers and Wrestlers of Kansas City, Professor Lotto and His Sweet-Toned Harp and Guitar, the Mikado Trio of Japanese Jugglers, Princess Pauhi and her Hawaiian Songbirds, or similar troupes of entertainers, would put on their acts. The best, however, was saved to the last; outdoor fireworks by the famous Thearle-Duffield Company, with rockets and Roman candles and sparklers, all of the gaudiest kind, ending gloriously with the big display of shields and eagles and Old Glory, twinkling with red, white, and blue. Then the show was indeed over, and the crowds drifted home. Most of the booths and stands by then would have miraculously disappeared. The merry-go-round would still be cranking along, its few riders enjoying long rides, but by Sunday morning it would be again only a great iron pole and cables, with the beams, gears, horses, seats, and medallions heaped in piles, awaiting transportation to some other fair, picnic, or Old Settlers' Reunion.

Sunday morning, after tremendous breakfasts, visitors hitched up or cranked up and drove home, or congregated at the depot. By midafternoon all was quiet and still as a small town can be when business firms are closed and people pretty much in their homes. Monday morning brought final bits and pieces of cleanup; the temporary hitching racks that had been erected were removed and the big stock tanks that had been filled with iced drinking water were emptied and returned. Even though the streets had been heavily oiled, the dust continued to hover, so that Mother and other housewives would declare, only partly joking, that they wouldn't be able to hang out a wash for a week.

Just as kids born the last week in December note that their birthdays are smothered by Christmas, so mine were overshadowed by the picnic. Even so, it was such a glorious way to celebrate a birthday that I was seldom troubled. To us kids, however, the picnic marked the end of summer and fun, because in a few days school would start and it was back to Latin, history, English, and mathematics.

Before many weeks, however, other spectacles came along. We had, for instance, theatre. The season's bill would be headed by an *Uncle Tom's Cabin* show, with Uncle Tom, Simon Legree,

Little Eva, and a dozen fierce bloodhounds. The *Guide* force knew all about the performance, because the advance man had come to town weeks ahead, had hired a field where the company could pitch its tent, and had arranged for a proper distribution of posters and other local advertising. In exchange for a generous supply of tickets, the *Guide* printed a nice ad. For a reasonable sum the *Guide* also printed a supply of dodgers, and for an even more modest sum the editor guaranteed to find two reliable boys to tack them on telephone poles at strategic locations. These two reliable boys have been mentioned before in these pages. Unquestionably they have tacked as many bills, posters, sale announcements, reward-offered announcements, and candidates' cards on telephone poles as any two boys of your immediate acquaintance. The *Uncle Tom's Cabin* posters were always preprinted, with a blank space at the bottom to insert such important information as "Coming to Gilman City, Thursday and Friday, Two Nights Only, October 14 and 15," together with exciting facts about admission charges and hours of the performances.

Gilman City attracted the best of the Uncle Tom companies, as each one in fact billed itself as the "original and only *Uncle Tom's Cabin* company in existence." I still remember the stirring phrases from their publicity. They performed in monster waterproof tents, some of which seated twenty-five hundred people. They traveled in their own special train of Pullmans. Their combination Military Band and Operatic Orchestra gave public concerts twice daily. Their afternoon parade showed the stars in full costume and exhibited the savage bloodhounds in strong cages. Each company promised to give the play in its entirety. Each company was a household word wherever it had performed. Each company stood alone as King and Monarch of the Entertainment World.

You could hardly read the posters, with their lurid, wood-cut illustrations, without twitching. See the Ice-Choked Ohio River. See the Home of Phineas Fletcher. See the Legree's Red River Plantation. Hear the Jubilee Singers. Hear the Augmented Chorus. Hear the Plantation Melodies.

Since we had free tickets, we always attended both nights. The Little Evas we saw were probably in their forties, but behind the gas footlights and overhead lights that constituted the stage

lighting, they were unbelievably bewitching and totally undeserv-
ing of the fate that we knew awaited them. The scene in which
the bloodhounds chased Eliza across the ice was the high point
of a dramatic evening. Trouble was, it was always so brief, and the
lights would flicker so, that we never got a good look at either the
ice floes in the ice-choked Ohio or the dozen fierce bloodhounds.
I could never count more than three or four, and they seemed on
a mighty short leash, but I never doubted that I would have seen
a full pack if I had just been in the right seat.

At the intermission between the last two acts, Simon Legree
himself appeared in costume to announce the "concert" that would
be held immediately after the performance, featuring special musical and dramatic numbers, and for which tickets would now be
sold at only ten cents, the tenth part of a dollar, to all who wished
to stay. Members of the show will now pass among you, he would
announce, to serve those who wish tickets. Members of the show
will also now pass among you to sell popcorn and peanuts, for
only a thin dime. Members of the show will also now pass among
you to sell souvenir programs to those who have not yet bought
one and who would desire one. Our company has played in New
York, Chicago, and Kansas City, but we have never had a more
appreciative audience than we have had right here tonight in
Gilman City.

Most people stayed for the concert, munching popcorn and
inhaling floss candy until it wafted out of their ears. Road shows
invariably had these concerts, concocted from the odds and ends
of talent of cast and crew, and although I suspect the refreshments
were the best part, we were invariably among those who stayed.
I marvel at the boundless energy of my parents, who after a long
day of postmastering and editing could stay up for these late
shows, but they enjoyed them as much as Don and I. When the
curtain was rolled down for the last time, we slowly uncoiled from
our seats and joined the crowd that oozed down the aisles and across
the rows to the several exits that appeared at the sides and the
back of the tent. As we walked home, either by moonlight or in
pitch-black darkness, we recalled the glittering moments of the
evening. Eventually we reached our own front door. Mother felt
her way inside to where she had left the coal-oil lamp with a handy

match alongside it, and lit up, long enough for everybody to undress and hop in bed, and hurry along, boys, tomorrow is a school day.

Sometimes the event was a Dog and Pony Show, a genuine miniature circus. The ponies were gorgeous animals with their glistening harness, sparkling bridles, and gaudy plumes, attended by handsome men and women of dazzling beauty. The dogs could do everything but recite the multiplication table. Often children of the troupe were given parts in the show. We marveled at what it might be like to grow up in a world of dogs and ponies and travel from town to town in your own Pullman, baggage, and stock cars.

Or there would be occasional tent shows with a week's repertory of plays, so that we had night after night of theatre, barring only press night. We got well acquainted with the actors and actresses as they moved through different roles, play after play, despite their amazing changes of wigs, mustaches, and costumes. Alas, I cannot recall a single scene from a single play in a dozen years of seeing Gilman City's finest offerings. All in all, though I never got as many merry-go-round tickets as I yearned for, I was among the world's elect when it came to tent shows. I wonder if it is still true that the sons and daughters of newspaper editors still get free tickets to fairs, athletic contests, and such splendors.

Early in the winter, the most important advance man of all arrived: the representative of the annual chautauqua. Basically, the chautauqua was a series of programs lasting a week or ten days, usually scheduled for the warm days of midsummer. It offered a variety of morning, noon, and night programs, in a big tent at the edge of town, open to holders of season tickets and to others who paid single admission prices. The advance man worked with the local committee in selecting programs and especially in organizing ticket-selling campaigns. The principal gimmick was to persuade each merchant to buy a certain number of tickets, so that the committee would know how much it would have available for talent and other expenses. The *Guide* pushed the chautauqua vigorously in both editorials and news stories—or, to put it more accurately, in news stories that were editorially bolstered. Chautauquas were usually more successful in bigger towns like Gallatin and Bethany, but for a time Gilman City was part of this nationwide enterprise.

What were the programs? Speakers: good ones, like Billy Bryan or Bob Ingersoll, or senators, congressmen, or other statesmen; and on Sundays the best available pulpit orator. Other business or professional men made a part-time career of chautauqua speaking: Stanley L. Krebs, "The Business Man's Lecturer"; Brigadier General Eversham, "The Fighting Parson"; the Honorable David M. Proctor, a Kansas City attorney; the Honorable Charles M. Hay, once a candidate for the Senate. The darling of the circuit, of course, was Colonel Bryan. He had a standing offer to come for a flat $500 fee, or half the gate receipts at $1 a head, and the wise ones knew that the flat fee was the better deal for the local committee.

A popular event was the Swiss bell-ringing concert. Imagine six or eight men, women, and children, in native costume, standing behind a huge rack of bells of all sizes, each of a different musical note. The bells were rung singly and in combination by players darting from bell to bell, in wonderful cadence, playing all sorts of technically dazzling selections. The girls wore dirndl skirts, and the men, obviously mountain climbers as well as musicians, wore blouses and leather shorts.

A feature that has disappeared altogether was the Apache knife-throwing demonstration. The cast comprised two stalwart Indian braves, with a couple of lovely beyond words Indian maids; the props included a score of long, sharp knives, bigger than butcher knives. The men threw knives at exacting targets, hitting the bull's-eye every time. Then one of the lovely girls stood against a backboard, and one of the men, standing on the other side of the stage, threw knives at her, outlining her body with a dozen knives that often nipped a bit of her blouse or skirt, they were that close. But the climax came when one of the men blindfolded himself; the girl took her place against the backboard; no one in the tent breathed. We had all seen knife throwers many times, but then you never could tell. The girl stamped her foot so that the warrior could be certain of direction and distance; he said "Ugh!" like that, "Ugh!"; the girl stamped her foot again, and then a third time; the warrior hurled his knife and it struck the board, say between the girl's right arm and her right side. More stampings followed, and

Fowler & Clark's

FAMOUS

DOG

AND

PONY

S<u>HOW</u>S

Will Exhibit in

GILMAN CITY

AFTERNOON AND NIGHT

Thursday
MAY 13

1OO *Dogs and* *PONIES*

The Greatest Dog and
Pony Show on Earth

Free Street Parade
At 1:30 o'clock

Prices:

Adults and Children over
10 years of age   35c

Children under 10 years
except babies in arms   25c

We Guarantee to give you the
most pleasing
performance of Trained Animals
ever given in your city   Money
refunded to anyone not satisfied

Typical show ad, which was printed free in exchange for tickets. You could easily spend half an hour setting the one word *SHOWS*, with the big *S*'s at either end, the thin spaces between the letters, and finally in hunting up and cutting a piece of brass rule just long enough to underscore the "H O W."

(*Guide*, May 6, 1915)

more "Ughs!" and before long she would be enveloped in knives—around her body, around her arms, alongside her cheek, at the top of her head. Another brave stepped forward and pulled the knives out, each of which required tugging; the warrior snatched his blindfold off; then the girl stepped forward, smiled a brilliant smile that clearly said, "I enjoy this, I would really not want anything to be different," gesturing toward her companion; and the applause would be thunderous. You will never want to see anything more thrilling than a genuine Apache knife hurler do his blindfold act.

There were violinists, trumpet players, Bible singers, pianists. The programs were sometimes classical, sometimes popular. Ridgeway played Gilman City in a baseball game, thus allowing home talent to put itself on display. Minstrel shows were popular, by companies bearing names such as The Dixie Strutters. Some of the acts were staged outdoors: The Aronty Brothers, thrills galore from the top of a sixty foot pole; the Five Flying Fishers, trapeze artists; Frederick Dobell in the most daring high-wire act in the world. The chautauqua had it all.

The chautauqua was a social as well as a cultural event. Around the big tent were clusters of individual tents, since people left their homes and camped out to enjoy the atmosphere more fully. Inside the tents were pieces of furniture brought from home. The merchants set up their refreshment stands and the church ladies served their fabulous meals. Chautauqua's opportunities for relaxing and socializing plus the wide variety of its programs made it popular throughout the whole country; then it began to die out in small towns like Gilman City, though it persisted for a while in larger towns like Gallatin and Bethany and finally vanished altogether. It could not hold its own against radio, sound movies, and other forms of entertainment. While it lasted, we saturated ourselves with it. Because of Father's newspaper connections, we had standing invitations to attend the Gallatin and Bethany chautauquas and often did.

Lyceum was chautauqua's little brother. Each community promoted season-ticket sales, and from the projected income contracted for about half a dozen programs, held about two weeks apart during the late fall and early winter months. Our lyceum events were held at the Rex Theatre. As a lyceum series was less expensive than a chautauqua series, it tended to hang on a few years after chautauqua had been given up. The depression of the thirties practically killed it.

The most durable spectacles of all were the annual fairs. Though we did not undertake the long, hazardous drive to the Missouri State Fair at Sedalia, especially famous for its horse and mule shows and exhibits, we never missed the Pattonsburg Fair or the Gallatin Fair or the Bethany Fair, which so prospered that it became the Northwest Missouri Fair, thus taking in more territory than any of the others. As we got complimentary press tickets and box seats in the grandstands, we felt a moral obligation to pay our respects to all three fairs.

Each of these towns was about twenty miles distant, which is another way of saying that each was a challenging one-hour's drive in dry weather and half a day in wet. We got our Overland ready the day before, checking oil and gas—both needed inspection before a trip—filling her radiator (most cars would consume as much water as a team of horses), pumping her tires to the full sixty pounds front and seventy pounds rear, and making sure that tire-repair necessities such as extra tubes, blow-out boots, tube-patching materials, tire irons, and a pump, were in the compartment under the backseat. Also a chunk of firewood to put behind the rear wheel in case we stalled on a hill.

At these fairs Don and I especially enjoyed the Midway, that paradise of shills and barkers and marks and patsies, and though we had no interest in the girlie shows we did generally look in on the two-headed calf, the fat lady, the reptiles (hunted in the Amazon), and, of course, the ball-throwing stands where a single good throw would win a Kewpie doll. But the main reason for going to the fair was to see the Spectacular, whatever it was. One year it was Daredevil Wilson. Imagine a chute the size of a playground chute, only more perpendicular, not ninety degrees, which would be exactly perpendicular, but about seventy-five degrees; the downward end of this chute, instead of being more or less horizontal, would be tilted upward, so if one dived into the chute and hit it just right, he would plunge down it, hit the upward curve at the end of his plunge, and land on his feet. Imagine standing at the top of a ten foot platform, stationed over the chute, and diving headfirst so as to hit it correctly. If you dived too far out, you would land so close to the bottom that instead of being eased onto your feet you would flatten a considerable part of your frontal anatomy. And if you hit the upper edge of the chute you would crush your chest or snap your back or both. I suggest a height of ten feet because most boys and girls have dived from that height and know it is a distance to be treated with respect, even when diving into water. What Daredevil Wilson proposed to do was to hit the chute from a height of seventy feet.

For this occasion the Daredevil had erected a slender platform, high in the air. At the appointed hour he made his appearance, dressed in a gaudy uniform. He checked the guy wires with his assistant, closely inspected the chute, and probably also counted the house. Then while the Harrison County Concert Band played somber music, he slowly climbed the long ladder to the little platform, as high in the air as a six-story building. Once there, he made a little speech about why he had not enlisted in the war; while making this jump in recent years he had broken so many bones, which he itemized for us, that he could not pass the physical. After his talk he concentrated on the task at hand, beckoning to the assistant to take a tuck in this or that guy wire so the platform would be exactly positioned with respect to the chute. After a pause, punctuated by a roll of drums from the band, he slowly bent over and executed a straight, headfirst, hands pointed, feet together, dive. He hit the chute at the precise angle; there was a heavy thud and he landed on his feet; he took a bow and the stunt was over. His contract called for two jumps a day, and we heard he was paid the fantastic sum of $100 for each.

One year we hoped to see our first airplane, with Ruth Law at the controls; but she failed to show, so the sight of our first plane was delayed several months, when one was spotted lazily circling Gilman City, and the town turned out to see and marvel. Another year the Spectacular was the head-on crash of two locomotives in front of the grandstand. A few hundred feet of track had been laid, and an ancient locomotive put on either end. On the selected day, engineers and firemen got up a full head of steam in each, so the crowd could see the two locomotives smoking and glaring at each other and hear them panting. At a signal they started on their collision course, bells clanging and whistles screaming. Engineers and firemen leaped from their cabs after fully advancing the throttles, and the engines crashed midway, as advertised. Hollywood could not have improved on the performance except by having them meet head-on on a high bridge and tumble into a raging stream below.

Ten years later, when I was a Linotype operator in the Government Printing Office in Washington, trying to earn a little money to continue a college education, I often attended vaudeville shows at the Keith Theatre, and once more saw magicians, acrobats, bell ringers, singers, dog shows, knife throwers; Blackstone, Eddie Cantor, Gene Austin, Al Jolson, and others; and if I did not actually see the Great Wallendas, I saw other talented fliers on rings, stools, bars, and trapezes. To the nation's capital came the best the world had to offer, to perform in the splendor of plush and velvet against the background of the Keith's mighty Wurlitzer. Yet with little difficulty I could close my eyes and be back under the big tent, with the Swiss bell ringers, Uncle Tom and Little Eva, dogs and ponies, and the stirring music after the big show. And years later I saw the Chinese acrobats, certainly the final word in tumbling and balancing, but if I did not marvel as much as my companions it must have been because long ago I had seen Daredevil Wilson, accompanied by a roll of drums by the Harrison County Concert Band, aim headfirst for the edge of a chute seventy feet down, and make it. More than that, I have seen an American Indian, blindfolded, utterly surround an Indian girl with knives, hurled with killing force, the whole distance of the Rex stage. In the small towns we really lived it up.

"DARE DEVIL" WILSON
AT HARRISON COUNTY FAIR
SEPTEMBER 10-14, 1918

The above picture shows "Dare Devil" Wilson making his "Leap for Life" from the fifth story of the World-Herald building in Omaha, one day last week. The leap was eighty-three feet and it was presented as a free attraction for the Soldiers' Smileage Fund, and as a result of his daring act the silver coins flowed in a stream from the pockets of the immense crowd, falling on a large American flag spread in front of the building for the purpose.

Wilson's wife, a mite of a woman, and his four-year-old girl, stood on the sidewalk scarcely a half dozen feet from where he was to land. The little tot watched her father every moment until he jumped from the towering window. The wife did not look at him after he made ready for the leap.

"Dare Devil" Wilson will perform this "breath-catching" feat twice each day of the Harrison County Fair FREE.

Bethany Democrat, August 29, 1918

14

In a Small Town
You Entertain Yourself

During these years I set a thousand or more columns of type about social events, baseball games, and other ways in which the inhabitants of a small town entertained themselves the decade before there was any radio at all, much less television.

Gilman City was filled to the brim with organizations. At the top of the social heap were the fraternal orders: Eastern Star, Odd Fellows, Royal Neighbors, Knights of Pythias, Modern Woodmen, Masons, Elks—we had them all. Next were women's and couples' clubs, with names like I.H.C., W.P.F.A., and Bijou. After each meeting, the group's reporter wrote a full account, generally in longhand, brought it to the *Guide* office, and I deciphered and set it. The *Guide* did not bother with a copy editor; the operator did what he could on the wing, with spelling, punctuating, and paragraphing, even supplying proper headlines.

Clubs planned their evening in beautiful detail. Decorations were invariably elaborate. Washington's birthday, Valentine, Halloween, or Thanksgiving themes were carried out both in the colors and the ornaments. For an autumn party, the dining room might be draped and festooned with autumn leaves. So each meeting was an event, the preparations reflecting pride and affection. The fare could consist simply of candy, apples, popcorn, and grape juice, but more likely the host and hostess would serve an elaborate menu, described later in the write-up as a four-course supper. A typical group feasted on veal loaf, hot biscuits and butter, creamed peas, mashed potatoes, plain and stuffed olives, relish, baked apples, nuts, and ice cream. Another had creamed chicken, dressing, gravy, mashed potatoes, deviled eggs, plain and stuffed olives, cranberry jelly, strawberry preserves, hot rolls and butter, apricot ice cream, angel food cake, salted peanuts, and coffee. One could hardly entertain without plain and stuffed olives. I can imagine the hostess planning her menu and writing "plain and stuffed olives" firmly on the list. Or perhaps checking her preparations at the last minute, exclaim "My goodness! I forgot the olives!" and sending her young Jimmy after them. Jimmy could have got the olives at four different places in town—five if you count a certain non-advertiser. I doubt if you could find even two places in a modern small town where you could buy olives.

As soon as guests arrived, they were fed and provided with activities. Little was left to chance. They played rook, which later was replaced with auction bridge. Or they played a series of games, progressing from one to another, each involving a degree of skill: identifying smells while blindfolded, reading sections of advertisements and naming the advertiser, hunting treasures hidden around the house. Or the hostess rendered musical numbers on the guitar, or played records on the Edison. Everyone might be called upon to relate an adventure; or the party might be called a sunshine party, each one telling about a happy episode in his or her life. A debate might be featured: "Resolved, That chickens are more profitable than cows."

None of the festive spirit was lost in the *Guide*'s write-up. The menu was described as delicious, or bountiful, or, more frequently, dainty: "The hostess served dainty refreshments." A prize, often called "the favor," was awarded the winner at whatever game was played: "Mrs. John Oram won the favor." The blinking of the lights, reminding everybody that the city power would be turned off in ten minutes, broke up the party in a hurry, but not in so much of a hurry that the guests would not have time to vote something, or pronounce something, as: "All departing voted the Wards delightful entertainers," or "The guests left reluctantly, pronouncing Mrs. Honan a gracious hostess."

High-school basketball did not then provide much entertainment for townspeople, though we students followed girls' teams and boys' teams with equal zeal. Our outdoor dirt court limited practice time and shortened our season. West of the Hotel Harmon was a tennis court, constructed by a group of the younger business and professional men. They seemed willing for us to use it at off hours. If the chalk lines were obliterated, we scratched the boundaries with a pointed stick and were as happy as if we were playing on the center court at Wimbledon. At the other end of

Main Street, east of the Wetzler building, was a croquet court, maintained by the older men. Its carefully graded dirt surface was maintained in first-class condition. Any of us would have loved to play on it, but if we ventured onto it we were speedily and angrily chased off. Although we regarded the croquet players as an unfriendly lot we admired their skill and enjoyed watching them.

Baseball was a well-established institution. In fact, baseball had come to Gilman City the first year of its existence, just behind the churches and just ahead of the school. As soon as school was out, which is to say as soon as it got warm enough to go barefooted, the boys warmed up in a nearby pasture and the town team began to get organized for its season.

Every boy's ambition is to be a pitcher. The Spaulding Sporting Goods Company had issued a set of paperbacks: *How to Pitch, How to Play First Base,* and others. With money saved from delivering papers I was able to buy everything available about the art of pitching. My hero, Christy Mathewson, one of John J. McGraw's most illustrious Giants, had developed an effective pitch called the fadeaway, a kind of in-drop. The ball was grasped with the two main fingers on the seam and delivered overhand with a last-minute outward twist of the wrist. Improperly done, the delivery of the fadeaway would twist the arm off at the elbow. Properly done, the ball zinged toward the plate, breaking at the last instant, to a right-handed batter, down and in. In my mind Mathewson was the greatest pitcher that had ever lived. His peerless control was, and still is, outstanding. His personal life was saintly, and his departure from the scene by a serious illness, at a relatively young age, was a tragic blow to his thousands of admirers.

I sawed a heavy slab of wood as wide and high as the strike zone, nailed it to the garage door, measured the proper distance, and hurled away. In those days I believed I could do anything if I worked hard enough, and it was not difficult to dream that one day I would eclipse Mathewson's record of winning thirty-seven games in a season. I did not realize that baseball requires unusual physical strength; and at that time I weighed a mere eighty pounds. Curve pitching is strenuous, so all I got for my trouble was a sore arm.

On Saturday mornings I could hardly make it fast enough to

the pasture where a game would be on the make. We played with whatever number showed up; as few as four or five to a team, or as many as ten or a dozen. Everybody was welcome. If a boy arrived after a game had started, he would be waved to one team or the other. A team might have half a dozen outfielders. We had our own ground rules—a batter might hit a ball under a wagon in left field or under a cow in deep center and would be limited to a fixed number of bases. Except for a hurried lunch, we played all day.

Sunday afternoon was reserved for the town team game. Doc Quinlan, a man with a good baseball head, was manager. At times when I had visited Doc to get one or more teeth repaired he had given me a used baseball, a magnificent present. I re-sewed the seams with black, waxed thread—Father was a cobbler in his spare moments—and thus put the ball back into vigorous circulation. Quinlan scheduled games with Mount Moriah, Eagleville, Martinsville—all in the county—and, of course, Bethany.

One Sunday we received an unexpected shellacking from Bethany, a by-product being that a good deal of local money was siphoned off. For the next engagement, Quinlan and his confederates planned a full and satisfying revenge. Instead of the regular pitcher they engaged Ray Sanders, who had just been released by the Kansas City Blues, an American Association club. He had also pitched for the Pittsburgh Pirates, and was known as a good hitter. Good players from other teams were also acquired. About the only regular was my schoolmate Shorty McClelland, who played right field. Keeping in the dark all information about the revised lineup, Gilman City supporters quietly picked up all the Bethany money in sight, at attractive odds.

Bethany people suspected that Quinlan might engage the Lyle Brothers from St. Joe to fortify his lineup; a good choice, but Lyle was no Sanders.

On the Sunday afternoon appointed for Bethany's destruction, such a caravan of automobiles headed for the county seat that a good percentage of the spectators at the county fair bleachers were Gilman City folk in on the secret. The crowd was described as by far the largest of the season. Jasper Vanderpool, my schoolmate, recalls that Morley Hagerty, one of our townsmen, in the stands with a huge fistful of one dollar bills, waved them at the Bethany fans and found plenty of takers. After the preliminary practice on the field, the umpire called the game and announced the battery for Gilman City; not Lyle and Lyle but Sanders and another new name, Carrol. Immediately the crowd was in an uproar, with Bethany spectators threatening to call off the game. Since, however, Sanders had the proper release papers, the situation was entirely legal. Bethany's pitcher was G. J. Dippold, also a good hitting pitcher, who in real life taught vocational agriculture at the high school. In previous games, he had given us fits.

The Bethany spectators were sullen throughout the game. The wrangling broke out anew because from time to time a Bethany batter complained that Sanders was using a touch of emery on the ball. Dippold, no slouch of a pitcher, struck out eight, but Sanders, one way or another, struck out fourteen. Moreover, Sanders hit a home run with one man on base, and another single that scored a run. The final score was eight to five for Gilman City. Throughout the grandstand our fans collected their bets.

Next week Bethany demanded, and got, a reinterpretation of the rules and also a return match. This time Dippold faced Lyle and won eight to two. As Gilman City sportsmen sat on their wallets, they felt that, on balance, they had come out ahead.

Summer was a relaxed time for the *Guide* family. Once the paper had been distributed Thursday morning, we had much of the rest of the week off. Swimming was a great sport on a hot July or August afternoon, so while Mother tended the post office, Father and Don and I got out the Overland and drove to Tombstone Creek, a few miles east of town. We found a small pool at the base of a limestone cliff and spent hours swimming and diving.

The pool was just a few yards from the O.K. tracks, so when Father could not go with us, Don and I gathered other boys and walked down the tracks to Tombstone, or to a nearby hole that I had named, for an obvious reason, Old Dead Hen hole. As an afternoon, westbound freight steamed along daily about five, we timed our swimming trips so that we could finish and wait along the right-of-way minutes before the O.K. was scheduled to pass. As at this point the train had to climb a grade, it had to slow down enough so we could each grab a ladder on a near boxcar and hang on. As the oldest boy, obviously responsible for the welfare of the others, I waited until everybody else, especially Don, had got a safe hold before I myself grabbed a ladder. On one occasion, look-

ing ahead along the side of the train as it passed slowly by, I failed
to see Don, so, thinking he had missed his grip, I let the whole
train go by so he would have someone either to pick him up or to
walk home with. The cars passed one after another, the brakeman
in the caboose giving me a chummy wave, but Don was nowhere
to be seen. As I trudged the three miles homeward I had a good
many reflections about kid brothers. He had, of course, hopped
the train skillfully and had swung out of sight between two cars,
not realizing that I had not seen him. Neither of us thought it would
be helpful to report the incident at the evening supper table.

No American holiday has changed as much as Halloween. For
us it was not trick or treat, it was tricks, period. My size fry was
allowed out for a couple of hours after dark, but our mischief was
nominal: removing unattached articles, writing with soap on windows, ticktacking houses by holding the opened side of a tomato
can against the side of the house, and then stroking a rosined string
that had been poked through a nail hole punched in the bottom
and fastened with a knot. The resulting noise was supposed to
suggest to anyone on the inside that, that particular wall was about
to fall in. For the Big Boys, however, All Saints' Eve was a night-
long enterprise. Upsetting loosely anchored outhouses and fastening a sheep to the roof of the school building were only starters.

One morning, in the middle of Main Street, between the banks
at the west end of the block and the pump at the other, early risers
after Halloween saw a strange sight: a neat row of ten privies. To
remove these from their normal locations, haul them downtown,
and set them in a row, their fronts facing Eckles and McClary,
Doherty's Drugstore, the Gilman Bank, and other establishments,
and their backs facing Robertson and Beckman, the Rex Theatre,
the Gilman Mercantile Company, and Haines's Furniture and Undertaking, was a major achievement. The creative feature, however, lay in the fact that hanging over the front of each privy
entrance, was a neat sign, also borrowed for the occasion: "Charles
M. Hurst, Real Estate"; "Ira O. Oliphant, Insurance"; "W. B. Parker, Optometrist and Elgineer"; "P. L. Gardner, M.D."; and others.
The owners of the shingles had as much fun as anybody, Jim
Crump boasting that his "Blacksmithing and Horseshoeing" sign
was attached to a magnificent three-holer, whereas "Dr. M. J.
Quinlan, Dentist" adorned a mere two-holer. That bit of irony,

of course, had not been accidental; it was part of the master plan of the artists and engineers who conceived the deed.

Crowds gathered on Main Street to see the sights. Many pronounced it one of the most successful Halloweens ever. By noon the owners of the various shingles had bolted them back over the original doorways. The owners of the privies hauled them back to their original sites. They did not think any of it was very funny.

There was, of course, the usual fun with girls. Saturday night the boys from Coffey came to town to date our local girls. The visitors loafed in Slick's Cafe and sparred with the local guys until the time came for everybody to collect his date. Gilman City boys also roamed to nearby towns to court their favorites. Often these acquaintances began when girls' and boys' basketball teams played out-of-town games, since, after the final whistle, various introductions were sought. Actually, however, when it came time to settle down, many of the boys married girls they had gone to school with. Any graduating class had a fair share of cousins.

For the most part, girls gave me a bad time. The princesses I worshipped, and fell in love with, and would have served forever and ever, lent their smiles and charms to the bigger boys. The girls would not have been flattered, however, if they knew that what I really enjoyed was to go roller-skating in the evenings. We had a lot of sidewalks, in excellent shape, and a half a dozen of us would collect and skate as late as our folks permitted. In the wintertime we had a choice of two or three ponds where we could go ice-skating; the procedure was to build a bonfire at the edge of the pond, scrape off the snow, and try all sorts of plain and fancy skating. Occasionally we had such a heavy sleet storm that we could skate from home to school, across yards and down the sidewalks. When snow covered the ground, we got out our sleds and hitch-hiked rides from the farmers who drove their sleighs into town. We also hitched to the rear axles of cars, but the wheels tended to throw snow and ice into our faces. Years later I had a chance to go skiing in the Bavarian Alps, but I doubt if I enjoyed it any more than I did being pulled down Main Street behind a sleigh, the horses clop-clopping along briskly, the bells ringing as if to make up for lost time.

Nobody can realize all his dreams, however, and one of my frustrations was wanting a bicycle and never having one. Occasionally I could borrow a ride on another boy's bicycle, but one ride simply whetted my appetite for more. I studied the bicycle pages in the Sears and Monkey Ward catalogs; I ordered catalogs from bicycle companies, my favorite being the Ranger, then the prince of bicycles. Finally I got one, but never rode it much, and went away to college, not knowing or caring what had happened to the Ranger. By then I discovered that girls were much more interesting than roller skates or bicycles. So the girls won out after all.

I do not want to give the impression that everybody gave parties, played card games, or participated in or even attended sports events. Some opposed card playing on principle; others thought Sunday ball games or even movies were improper. My schoolmates who lived in the country usually had to go home right after school to do their chores, so their opportunities to develop athletic or social skills were limited. Their parents, and a good many townspeople as well, worked early and late and thus had little time or energy for amusements, limiting their entertaining to family, relatives, and neighbors.

Mother was among those who had little desire to learn games or plan parties. Her long hours at the *Guide* and post office did not give her much free time. She was keenly interested in our outdoor activities and enjoyed the baseball games as much as any of us but took a dim view of lodge or club activities. Though she herself could be a gracious hostess, her entertaining was limited to relatives or to visiting politicians or newspaper editors.

In the end, however, Mother paid a price for her absence from parties. When the family moved to Iowa, she was slightly less involved for a time in newspaper duties, and not at all in post-office duties, so when her boys left for college, she longed for the social activity that she had missed in Missouri. When I happened to mention casually in a letter that I was learning to play bridge, she immediately wrote that when I came home for the Thanksgiving break I was to teach her the game.

On the first morning of the holiday she proudly displayed her possessions. She had bought a folding bridge table with a red plaid top; four matching, folding, steel chairs with red cushioned seats; a double deck of cards, a score pad, and a pencil. She had confided her needs to one of our advertisers, who not only sold her the full quota of equipment, but stuff of the finest quality. Obviously you can play a better game of bridge if you have a red plaid table and matching chairs. We sat across from one another and she said, "Now son, show me how to play bridge."

I dealt four hands of thirteen cards and told her to pick up her cards and arrange them by suits. Her agile fingers, so skilled in feeding a high-speed press and operating a Linotype keyboard, sorting mail, quilting, playing the piano, skinning a rabbit, and a hundred other things, gathered the cards fumblingly, some of them slipping away and falling on the tabletop. I helped her corral them, suddenly realizing that she had never before managed a deck of cards. Never had it occurred to me that some little dexterity is involved in shuffling, dealing, picking up the cards, and unfurling them almost instantly so that only the critical corner of each card is exposed. When she got the cards steadily anchored in her two hands she asked, "Now what was it you said about suits?" I pulled a card from my hand and explained, "This is a heart; group all the hearts you have, in order of rank." Even this needed clarifying, so I pulled my chair alongside hers and explained the subtle meanings of A, K, Q, and the values of the suits.

That was all we accomplished in the first lesson, and we got little further in the sessions that followed. I taught her a simple game of solitaire, so she would get used to handling and recognizing cards. But her yearning for bridge speedily vanished. She never brought up the subject again. Eventually cards and scoring pad disappeared, though the table and chairs were around a long time. As I said, they were of first-class quality.

Mother had missed out on pitch and rook, and when bridge came along, it was too much. What she lacked in card skills, however, she more than made up with the food and the boundless affection. When I returned to school I did not fail to thank her for the dainty refreshments, nor did I omit voting her a gracious hostess, pronouncing the first holiday away from school entirely wonderful and memorable.

That experience confirmed me in the belief that as one grows up one should learn a few selected vices as well as the required virtues. It is advisable to be well balanced in these respects.

Social historians who write about the generation just ahead of mine elaborately describe the ways in which pioneer Americans created their own amusements: the impromptu wrestling, running, and jumping contests of the men, the competition in arts and crafts of the women. We, too, had the double fun of being both spectators and performers. We were as emotionally involved when rooting for Gilman City versus a small town ten or fifteen miles away as we were decades later when rooting for the Big 8 or the National League. We got as excited about outrunning a competitor or solving a hostess's treasure hunt as we did later watching the world series. Once you have seen two of the *Guide*'s most distinguished advertisers, each devoting his supreme energy to the rolling of a potato, with his nose, toward a finish line, surrounded by a living room full of screaming partisans, you have plumbed the depth of human competitive instincts. In a small town, you entertain yourself. We never missed the Super Bowl.

15

These Few, Long Remembered

The *Guide* had a staff of country correspondents who, in return for paper, envelopes, and postage, reported the doings at Blue Ridge, Melbourne, and other nearby communities. Occasionally it also published letters, political comments, and poems, contributed by subscribers. The most popular of this group was E. W. McClelland, the town's leading poultry dealer, known to everybody as "Mac."

Mac's first poultry establishment had been just across the street from our home, in a wooden shack with a little office in front and a dirt-floored storage area in the back for crates of poultry and cases of eggs. He also bought scrap copper, zinc, and lead. In the winter he did a lively business in muskrat, skunk, and other furs brought in by local trappers, and in rabbits, freshly shot by local hunters. In this respect, Mac was a practitioner in the first Missouri enterprise—the hunting, trapping, and merchandising of fur-bearing animals. On the way home I often stopped to see his latest batch of furs and at one time knew the market price on, for example, narrow-stripe and broad-stripe skunks. On his front sidewalk, especially when a heavy snow brought the hunters out, was a heap of more-or-less freshly killed rabbits that readily sold at a nickel apiece. On occasion he shipped whole carloads of rabbits to the Kansas City market. After a few years, Mac moved into the large brick building at the corner of Main and Broadway, catty-corner from the post office.

Mac frequently visited the *Guide*, sometimes to bring a contribution for the paper, sometimes just to visit. And as he and his wife and his son, Shorty, lived next door to us, I was often in his home. For many months Shorty, two years older than I, was my constant companion. No two boys could have been more different. I was thin and wiry; he was chunky, strong, and powerful. We loved to wrestle, though our bouts generally ended by his getting me flat on my back and pinning my arms and legs to the ground.

Holding me helpless, he then entered into long conversations. He insisted that he was stronger than I was and could throw me anytime he liked. I countered, once, by maintaining that I was smarter than he was, which was not a useful tactic.

Shorty was enterprising, resourceful, and venturesome, all qualities I prized and envied. We walked up and down back alleys picking up choice bits of zinc, copper, and brass, which could be sold to his father, especially during the war, at a few cents a pound. Mason-jar caps, for example, were zinc; we broke out the glass and sold the metal. Once we stumbled into an empty house where a sale had just been held. Someone had purchased an incubator but had unwisely neglected to take it home, so we ripped out the copper tubing and sold it for fifty-seven cents—a fine contribution to the national supply of war metals. When the purchaser called for his incubator, he must have been furious to see that it had been disembowelled, and if he reads this and gets in touch with me, I will refund the entire fifty-seven cents. We also collected the tin tags that came with Climax and Horseshoe chewing tobacco, worth half a cent each. A good afternoon's scrounging would net quite a few pennies.

Shorty and I built ourselves a house out of chicken coops from his father's establishment and thus had a cozy hideaway. One day I brought a deck of cards and taught him to play pitch, one of the best of the two-handed card games. He had good card sense and usually won. Later he graduated to poker, started playing with other groups, and I suspect won more than he lost. In a sense, I was a wicked influence on him.

In another sense he was a wicked influence on me. He thought we should learn to smoke, so we got a nickel bag of the cheapest tobacco available—a hideous brand called "Corn Cake" that was about four times as cheap as the cowboy favorite, "Bull Durham." As men generally rolled their own those days, we should also have got a packet of Riz la Croix cigarette papers, but, lacking those, we used mail-order catalog paper and fashioned cigarettes six inches long and half an inch thick, securing the edges with a paste made of flour and water. In moments we were both deathly sick, but after repeated efforts we became staunchly hardened to this vice and spent many hours playing pitch and smoking Corn Cake.

Late one afternoon I thought it would be interesting to teach

Don to smoke, so I rigged a cigarette and we smoked it together. In a few moments he turned green. About that time Mother called us to supper, but after only a short time at the table he ran to the backyard and vomited violently. Father and Mother wondered what the trouble was, but I did not think it would be a good idea to tell them. While they debated whether to call Dr. Gardner, I retreated to the smokehouse and prayed God not to take Don, at least not just yet. Meanwhile the folks decided that for now they would just send Don to bed. Don, whose loyalty could never be questioned, obeyed uncomplainingly; perhaps he even felt like going to bed.

From Corn Cake, Shorty and I mainlined to Bull Durham, protecting our breath by eating onion sandwiches after each smoking orgy so that our folks would not discover our wicked ways. Eventually, however, Mother, who had grown up with five brothers, did find out and gave me as severe a lecture as a boy ever received. She ended with these immortal words: "Son, if I ever smell onion on your breath again, or tobacco smoke, or if I ever catch you smoking, or hear of you smoking, or even suspect that you are smoking, I am going to buy a pipe, and I am going to sit in the front window of the post office, so that when people come to get their mail, they will see your mother smoking."

I did not have the slightest doubt but that she would carry out her threat. Nor could I bear to be disgraced by having my mother smoke in public. I not only stopped smoking then and there, but lost all desire to smoke. The little chicken-coop house also lost its fascination.

Shorty's enterprise led to all sorts of adventures. He was strong and athletic enough to play outfield on the town team. He dropped out of school and the next thing I heard he was with a troupe of actors, seeing a great deal of the country as the troupe went from town to town. After a few seasons, he came back to Gilman City, married a lovely girl, worked with Mac in the family store, and eventually established a business of his own.

Spending hours with Shorty pinning me flat on my back convinced me that I had to learn to wrestle properly. Like foot racing and broad jumping, wrestling was then a popular pastime. Gilman City had excellent wrestlers, among them Charley Neff, manager of the Farmers Telephone Company. I have mentioned him before as one of the leading citizens. Charley used to throw his sons and nephews regularly, even after they became full grown. Every year, however, the matches got closer, especially with one nephew, and Charley finally saw that he would have to end his career as a wrestler. This nephew was so persistent, however, that Charley agreed to wrestle him just once more, if it could be understood that this would be the last time. The match was long and grueling, but Charley's experience prevailed over the young man's ruggedness, and Charley was always proud to say that he had quit while he was still ahead.

As I avidly read the newspapers and magazines that the *Guide* received on exchange, I had frequently seen ads by Charles Atlas, promising to make one strong and powerful, and by Farmer Burns and Frank Gotch, offering a correspondence course in wrestling. Burns and Gotch were famous titleholders. Farmer Burns argued that if a man could wrestle he could defeat anybody, and, in fact, had once challenged a famous heavyweight boxer to a match, and had succeeded in pinning him to the mat.

The Farmer had a set of neck muscles so powerful that when he contracted them, tendons stood out half an inch all around his neck. To display its strength, he once submitted himself to being hanged on a gallows. Standing on the trapdoor, he allowed the noose to be fastened around his neck, his hands tied behind his back. When he signaled, his associate sprang the trap. His muscled body fell the standard distance, his neck receiving a jerk that would have removed the head of an ordinary man, but he emerged from the ordeal unharmed.

These credentials were impressive. Farmer Burns was the man for me. And when one day a teammate, whom I will call Musko, elbowed me from second base and announced that he was going to play that position, I decided I needed to teach the imposter a lesson. The time had come to enroll with the Farmer, so I mailed the seven dollars the coupon called for.

In a few days the booklets arrived. Essentially the regimen consisted of calisthenics and other conditioning exercises, but it also illustrated basic pins and holds, as well as balance and weight distribution. As Don was also fascinated with the course, we practiced diligently, and learned a good deal about the manly art of self-defense.

Genuine "Bull" Durham and Riz La + paper won—or maybe lost—the West. Almost anybody would say Bull Durham was better than smoking corn silks or even Corn Cake. (*Guide*, May 12, 1920)

Some weeks later when I took my turn at the plate, Musko grabbed the bat, pushed me to one side, and declared that it was his turn. He was basically a good-natured kid who acted more out of mischief than anything else, but the incident struck me as a transparent outrage that called for a strong response. I snatched the bat back and threw it to one side. He was so astonished at this sudden turning of the worm that he did not know quite what to do. I grabbed his hands, pulled him toward me, quickly fell on my back, pulling him down over me but with my foot on his stomach and, still holding his hands, threw him over my head, flat on his back. We both jumped up and he came at me again. I grabbed his left hand in both hands, wheeled and put my right shoulder on his left armpit, and threw him over my shoulder so that he landed heavily on the ground (Burns and Gotch, Lesson 5, Plate 14). Don and I had practiced these maneuvers many times. Musko and I got up again and now I was secretly terrified. I had not yet got as far as Lesson 6, and here he was still on his feet, fully aroused. I had nothing left but moral indignation, plus boundless experience with Shorty McClelland. For a moment the situation was tense. Suddenly, unexpectedly, Musko grinned and said, "Don't get sore, I was only kidding, everybody knows it is your bat," and we got along fine.

One of my grade-school chums was Tom Dorney, great nephew of the John Dorney who had owned the land on which Gilman City was built.

Tom's left arm ended just above the elbow but with that stub plus a husky right arm he participated as an equal in our sports. In our baseball games he could bat as well as anybody. When fielding he wore his glove on his right hand, but after making a catch would stick the gloved hand bearing the ball under his stub, and extract the ball and make the throw with amazing speed and dexterity. I used to practice that move but found it was not easy to avoid fumbling the ball or dropping the glove, or both. Tom was so agile I almost wished my left arm was like his. I am not the only one who has harbored these kinds of thoughts. When the famous three-fingered pitcher, Mordecai Brown, used to mow down the top of a batting order, the defeated manager would puzzle over the probable advantages of having three fingers and threaten to chop a couple of fingers off the hand of his own star hurler.

In a scuffle, Tom could more than hold his own. Unless the opponent were unusually strong and agile, he would soon find himself firmly held by Tom's right arm and feel that short left punching into his face or neck. Tom was so good natured and full of fun, however, that he had many friends.

As Tom was such a late bloomer scholastically that he ran into academic difficulties, his family enrolled him in a Kansas parochial school. There and later at St. Benedict's College he made a good record as a student. He also excelled at football, playing left end and winning all-state, hall of fame, and most valuable player awards. To me the amazing fact was that he probably never saw a football until after he left Missouri. Obviously he developed mental alertness and qualities of leadership that overcame any other disadvantages.

After graduating, Tom taught and coached for twenty years and then administered a sports program for parochial grade-school youngsters. He ran for sheriff of Wyandotte, third largest county in Kansas, missing election by only fifty votes.

I am not sure that Father kept abreast of Tom's career, but he would have cherished Tom's achievements. Father's poem, "The Perfect Man," argued that a man's strength lay not in his physical endowment but in his character.

Gilman City's range of economic distinctions covered a broad band—not ranging all the way from "millionaire" to "slum dweller" but at least from "well off" to "poor." At the low end of the scale, I recall seeing the occasional man or woman pulling a wagon along the O.K. tracks, picking up chunks of coal that had fallen off the cars. Nobody begrudged them these gleanings. The menfolk mainly did odd jobs of hauling, digging, moving, and other unskilled chores, and the women took in what washing or ironing they could or helped with housecleaning. Occasionally there were gifts of Christmas food, but generally the poor families seemed to be looked after by immediate neighbors instead of by organized community effort.

Well-off members of the town were visible to us boys chiefly because of their automobiles: the Markeys had a Marmon, the Orams went in for Buicks and at least one glamorous Stanley Steamer, and so on. As the source of prosperity was land, the farmers who grew crops and bred livestock and the townspeople who

acquired farms to rent seemed better off than most others. Even
farming, however, had frightful reversals, so that a "well-off" person might end up "poor." Bugs, droughts, floods, mortgages, and
shifty markets could be ruinous. I remember Billy Welden and
the time he bought a brand-new Buick. He owned several hundred
well-improved acres and steadily acquired more. A collapse of the
market, however, finally caused him to lose almost everything he
possessed. In his last years he once observed that people who used
to address him as "Mr. Welden" called him, after his financial disaster, "old Uncle Billy."

We did not think of ourselves as having a criminal element,
but in 1913 Main Street was visited by a series of baffling burglaries. The city fathers had hired Foxy Lawrence to patrol the
streets at night but his duties were mainly to check the doors to
make sure that no one had made a forcible entrance. One midnight he had knocked on our front door at home to inform Father
that he had found the *Guide* unlocked. Father hurriedly dressed
and went with him to see if anything was amiss, but everything
seemed in order and he concluded that one of his sons, who will
not be named, had failed to snap the lock. For Foxy, that was a
busy night.

Then came a burglary of Dan Lierley's grocery and dry-goods
store. Dan, a broad-shouldered, dark-haired, dark-eyed, sturdy
man, with a heavy mustache and a booming, resonant voice, was
one of the fine businessmen and citizens of the community; no
kinder, better, bigger-hearted man ever lived. His store was on
the north side of Main Street, between the hotel and the Citizens
Bank building. Father called on him regularly and occasionally
sold him an ad. Once Father bought a suit, taking it out in advertising, a deal that pleased both parties since no hard money
changed hands. I knew him as well as an eight-year-old kid can
know an adult by casual meetings on the street or occasional pur-
chases in the store.

The burglars did not make a vast haul, but Dan could ill-afford
any loss. Foxy had not heard them, but it was obvious to him and
everyone else that they had simply waited until he passed the
store on one of his nightly rounds and had then broken in. His
movements would be easily traced since he was carrying his lan-
tern. The Chillicothe bloodhounds were sent for, and although

they made a great show of pawing and sniffing, they picked up no clue and the case remained unsolved. Some evidence indicated that the burglars had come and left by buggy.

In the next six months burglars hit the place twice, the last time also breaking into Slick's Cafe, probably to enjoy leftover hamburgers and tenderloins along with a bowl of chili. Perhaps they even helped themselves to ice cream and stirred up a malted milk. Again, they escaped without leaving a clue.

Dan was terribly worried about the repeated break-ins and confessed his concern to Father, who, of course, related the situation to Mother in the evening, with old pitcher-ears, me, listening in. By now Dan's losses totalled $600 or $700. After the third burglary, he revealed to Father that he had mounted a shotgun at the end of the grocery counter, facing the front door, with a cord tied across the aisle, threaded through a series of staples, and fastened to the trigger, so that anyone who struck the cord would discharge the gun. Even though this was an age when most people had a weapon at home and had just passed the age when young men carried revolvers wherever they went, Father was disturbed by the plan and tried to dissuade his friend from carrying it out. "As sure as anything," he warned, "some morning when you open the store you will forget about the gun and hit the cord yourself." "No, Dudley," Dan replied, "that gun is always on my mind. I couldn't possibly forget it. I am even going to open up the store myself instead of asking the clerk to do it." Father, when solemn, could look more solemn than anyone I ever knew, and I remember the expression on his face when he repeated Dan's words: "No, Dudley, that gun is always on my mind."

Then came a Tuesday morning when Mr. Lierley, as I always addressed him, opened the door of his store at 6:30, unthinkingly walked into the cord and received the full blast of the shotgun in the fleshy part of his thigh, shattering skin, muscles, and ligaments. He crawled to the telephone to reach Central, but the switchboard was not yet open. He dragged himself to the street, blood gushing from the wound, and yelled for help, but no one heard him. Father, accidentally, was among the few who found him later, lying in the street, amazingly still conscious. They carried him to the hotel and summoned a physician, who dressed his wound.

As nothing more could be done for him locally, he was taken

to a Kansas City hospital on the two o'clock train but died the following night. His body was returned to Gilman City on the noon train. Billy Haines with a host of sorrowing friends was there to receive the casket. After the funeral Dan's body was carried up the hill to the Masonic cemetery where he was laid to rest.

A thousand people who heard of the accident, reported in newspapers all over the state, recalled the biblical warning that a man who digs a pit for his neighbor shall fall therein. Among the readers of the *Guide* must have been one or two people who read of the incident with a particular and personal horror, leading him or them to abandon the career of crime. At any rate the burglaries stopped altogether.

Sometimes Don accompanied my chums and me when we went on swimming or moviegoing expeditions. And sometimes I played with him and the younger fry. One of these was Lewis Dunn, age seven, six months older than Don, the youngest son of Bill Dunn and wife, owners of the town's largest store.

Behind the Dunn home was a huge grape arbor, built of timber uprights with horizontal wood crosspieces. The whole structure was as eminently climbable as the stockyard fences and in season supported such a wealth of grapes that it was an ecstatic pleasure to climb over it, pausing now and then to pluck a few ripe, purple grapes, suck the pulp through your teeth, and blow out the seeds and skin. In addition, Lewis and his brother, Theophilus, had nailed a couple of wood-slat levers atop the arbor, so you could straddle one of the high beams, grab a lever, move it forward or backward, and pretend that you were at the throttle of a locomotive. Other kids played with us from time to time, one of them being the fair, chunky, Hugh Charles Burrell, age four, son of Charles R. Burrell, cashier of the Gilman Bank, and his wife, Eva. Both boys were sweet, gentle, lovable members of two of the town's best-liked families.

On a Saturday noon in August, Lewis and Hugh Charles were playing quietly at the Burrell home, as they had done many times. As the afternoon wore on, the boys shifted their base of operations to a huge barn behind the house. That morning the barn had been filled with hay, fragrant but dry. A team of mules was also in the barn, tethered to their stalls.

After a time, neighbors passing by saw smoke coming from

the barn and yelled "Fire!" The blaze leaped with incredible speed and soon the roof was ablaze. Soon a large crowd gathered, particularly as the business district, hardly two blocks away, had been jammed with Saturday traders. Mrs. Burrell feared that the two boys were in the barn but nobody knew for certain. Before long two or three hundred people had gathered to help wherever they could, though no one could do much since the fire, fed by the loft full of hay, spread rapidly. The alarm flashed through the crowd that at least two little boys were in the barn. The mules could be heard, screaming with terror.

Over the years, the vivid and tormenting memory has haunted me of Lewis's brother, Theophilus, five or six years older than I, running frantically from person to person, at the edge of that vast crowd, crying, "Have you seen Lewis?" to which I could only shake my head, as did everybody else. Others began worrying about the possibility of their children also being in the barn. I hurried to the post office and found that Father had returned to see if Don were with Mother, and when we found that Don was not there, we added our alarm to that of the others. Just at that moment Don, unhurried as always, strolled through the back door. Then the three of us returned to the blazing barn, leaving Mother in charge of the post office.

Meanwhile a quiet, slender man, of incredible courage, had entered the blazing inferno to see if he could pull out the boys. That was Jake Tedlock, we learned immediately, and now everybody knew three people were in the flaming structure. The suspense, the fear, the agony mounted. The mules continued their screaming. Some of the members of the bucket brigade who were closest to the barn had to draw back from their outposts. Emerson Young was one who suffered from heat exhaustion or something close to it.

Finally Jake staggered out of the barn, almost completely overcome by the heat and smoke. Somewhat incoherently he said that he had been able to grab one of the boys, but the mules, crazed and terrified, had broken loose. One of them had kicked and trampled him and had temporarily knocked him out; but for that, he said, he could have rescued the boy. Jake was taken away for medical attention. Although he was feverish through the night and at times irrational, he slowly recovered.

I cannot forget the bravery of the people who fought the fire, staying on the job longer than they should have, and especially the immense courage of Jake Tedlock, whom I never really knew. In later years when as a young reporter I covered fires of residences and business buildings and felt again the tremendous blast of the heat and smelled the choking fumes of smoke and ash and watched the firemen calmly perform heroics, I could recall that once Jake Tedlock had entered just such a structure, had almost accomplished his mission despite the kicks of a half-crazed team of mules, and had, just barely, survived.

Not until late could the bodies be recovered, clasped in each other's arms. Minta Haines gave them their last earthly attention, telling the folks in my presence that she had done the best she could, considering the circumstances. The double services at the Baptist Church drew the largest crowd that had ever attended a funeral in our part of the county. Scores came on the train from Coffey, Bethany, Gallatin, Trenton, and elsewhere. The huge overflow stood quietly outside the church. The two white caskets were profusely covered with flowers, a white dove on a floral pillow at the head of each.

Everybody said that the Reverend Mr. Paschal Meeks preached his finest sermon on the theme, "Is it Well With the Child." Father, writing the obituary, tinted his prose with the dawn of tomorrow. "Mighty and mysterious are Thy ways, O God! Unto Thy hands we consign these heavily afflicted parents. . . . We have a hope that somehow Thou wilt find a way to redeem the darkness; to banish the ghosts of grief within these doors and replace them with the angels of Hope and Love."

Father and Mother well knew, as did many sets of parents, that only the finger of God had kept the tragedy from touching still others.

Remorse struck many in the community with bitter intensity. My own little thought at the time was that if I had been with the boys I would have seen the danger sooner than they had. I was an experienced player-with-fire. On the other hand—but that thought was too terrible to hold. The parents of the two boys relived the events of the day a hundred different ways, and even though each remorseful statement was sympathetically received by understanding friends, it had to persist until it utterly wore itself out.

A further loss to the community was still to come, as both the Dunns and the Burrells began to feel that they could no longer live close to these crushing memories. Bill Dunn was an imaginative and resourceful merchant, a pillar on Main Street, with a personal acquaintance that extended over two counties. Mrs. Dunn and the children were universally loved. Before long they announced that they had sold their big store and were going to live on a farm in Calloway County. Charley Burrell was a highly respected and competent banker; both he and Mrs. Burrell came from old-line, Sugar Creek families. They moved to Kansas City, Charley becoming a state and later a national bank examiner. He died at about the age of fifty-five; Bill at about the same time.

Tragedy strikes a small town with special bitterness. It is not like reading about a grim accident in a faraway place. It is not even like being touched by a human disaster that happened to a fellow citizen in a large city. Everybody knew the Lierleys, the Dunns, the Burrells, and their many relatives; everybody also knew that each person met in a store or on the street, or seen at the funeral, knew them also. There were no mere onlookers; everybody was caught up in a personal way by the same chain of events. As grief matures an individual, grief that is felt and shared matures a community.

The town shook itself and went about its business, but with a new feeling of closeness. The world had to move on. Next week came the Gilman City picnic, with its merry-go-round, its speakers and lady nail drivers, its Flying Quintette and its renowned Trenton Concert Band, its hot dogs and its shooting gallery, its bountiful supply of fresh, pure drinking water for one and all, its crowd of four or five thousand people tramping up and down its heavily oiled streets. And in a few days I celebrated my ninth birthday.

On my last trip to Gilman City I talked with former schoolmates about these events and these people. We found we shared a pool of memories. Everyone recalled the shooting of Dan Lierley—and everyone remembered where he or she was on that Saturday afternoon when Lewis and Hugh Charles lost their lives. Tom moved to Kansas City, Kansas. Shorty, after returning to Gilman City and going into business, died at the age of forty-four; he collapsed while playing croquet. It seemed ironic that his venturesome life should have ended on the town court. Undoubtedly, there were countless moments when all of these friends and acquaintances were within a few hundred yards of one another, since in a small town residents are seldom widely separated. Each of the people I have mentioned still holds a place in the thoughts of Gilman City people. I know because I have talked to Gilman Citians and former Gilman Citians. These few, long remembered. . . .

16

The Automobile Comes to Stay

The kids I grew up with—that remarkable generation born between the turn of the century and the First World War—readily remember when their families bought their first automobile. Our fathers, and occasionally our mothers, had had to learn to master the horseless carriage after they were fully grown adults. But our sons and daughters learned to drive as soon as they could reach the pedals with the tips of their toes. And as soon as they finished their schooling and got jobs, they acquired their own cars, so, as it happened, their children, and their children's children, were born into families that were already fully powered.

Ask the senior citizens of your acquaintance, therefore, if they recall when the automobile first entered their parents' homes, and then reach for a chair, for the answer will be lovingly detailed. If, however, you ask *their* children, the answer will likely be, "Well, actually, I don't remember a time when father and mother did not have a car." And, actually, each of them was probably driven home from the hospital, wrapped in a pink or blue blanket, cradled and snuggled in Mother's arms, in the family automobile. Of course, there are thousands of exceptions, but America is a land of millions, and one inescapable fact of American existence is her long-standing love affair with the automobile.

My generation lived at a time when the horse was on the way out and the automobile was on the way in. Father and Mother held out as long as anybody, but when they finally bought a car—an Overland—in 1916, they signaled the whole world that the automobile had come to stay. Once they caved in, the horse was doomed.

The horse died hard, however. Originally Gilman City had had two livery stables, one at each end of Main Street, but a garage had replaced one of them about the time I was in third grade. The remaining one smelled a little like the Gilman Mill, since its upper loft was full of hay and its bins were filled with grain, but at the same time it had its own penetrating aroma—compounded out of the huge piles of manure that graced both the inside of the structure and the immediate exterior. Given a proper day when a gentle wind blew from the northeast, anyone standing in front of the post office, a long block away, would not need to ask where to go to hire a team. Even when the noon train rolled in and its clouds of smoke coiled over the stable on their way to the post office, one could still locate the stable despite the overriding bouquet of soot and ash.

The typical livery stable was a frame structure, twenty-five or thirty feet wide and fifty to eighty feet long, with a row of stalls on either side and a wide center aisle, the primary depository for the manure cleaned out each day and the storage area for the display of buggies available for hire. Pegs were inserted in the studding on either side of the building on which hung collars and sets of harness. Toward the front the proprietor had partitioned a small office holding a battered desk and chair, and a receptacle that we irreverently called a gobboon—in such a place, an unnecessary refinement.

One could rent a livery team for $3 a day, but everybody knew that a livery horse ranked at the very bottom of horse kind, and was hardly a horse at all. Mother could describe with the scorn of a connoisseur the sad-looking teams hired by young men who had called on the young ladies of her neighborhood.

In addition to the stable, Gilman City had several blocks of hitching line, a few scattered hitching posts, and a good many hitching rings cemented into the sidewalks. The stables, the hitching racks, and the traffic that moved up and down the streets meant that horse manure was well distributed, along with horseflies, houseflies, blue-bottle flies by the tens of thousands. Anyone walking down a street on a summer day had to keep both hands in motion, brushing off the flies; kids, being sticky and juicy, were doubly pestered.

As the number of horses began to decrease, and the number of cars to increase, the city fathers found themselves passing strange ordinances. To hitch an animal to a railing, fence, or tree, without the permission of the owner, became an offense. A man is likely to overlook the niceties when he needs to park his conveyance in a hurry, whether it is a team or a car. A law was enacted concerning speed limits: twelve miles an hour in the business district and fifteen miles an hour elsewhere. Another ordinance required every car to have a horn, at least two headlights and a tail-light, and a workable muffler; and since each car was also equipped with a cutout to bypass the muffler, signs were erected at the city limits: "Close Your Cutout." As the early mufflers were so inefficient that they noticeably reduced the power of the motor, drivers opened their cutouts as soon as they were out of town, partly to enjoy the increased speed but mainly to relish the mighty roar of their four-cylinder engines.

The basic automobile as everybody knows was the Ford touring car, complete with a top that could be raised or lowered, available for $400 or less. The self-starter was first introduced as an option. There was no door next to the person who sat beside the driver; no ignition key, just a lever; no dials or gauges; the lights were powered by magneto, so the slower the engine speed, the dimmer the light. In other words, when you slowed down at night to confront a road hazard, your lights dimmed so you couldn't properly see it. The gasoline tank was under the front seat. To find out how much gas you had, you got out of the car, removed the cushion, unscrewed the cap of the tank, and used the measuring stick that you kept handy for that purpose—a twig, a ruler, or a piece of yardstick. For Fords, you could buy a special stick calibrated in gallons. Human beings learned the hard way not to light a match to see how much gas was in the tank.

Companies grew prosperous selling extra equipment for the Ford. You certainly wanted a horn; you might want to install battery-operated or Prest-o-Lite gas headlights; you needed tire irons and other tire-changing and tire-repairing equipment; you wanted side curtains to attach during a rain; you were certain to need tire chains. Later you found yourself carrying extra spark plugs, and even spark-plug cleaning materials; and a whole set of basic tools like a wrench and pliers, plus a screwdriver to use to short out one cylinder at a time to determine which spark plug was not firing. Optional equipment gave each Ford such an individual identity that every boy knew which Ford belonged to whom.

Of course, there were other makes. Dr. Oyler, one of our veterinarians, drove a Brush, whose chain-driven rear wheels made a whirring sound as he whizzed by. Don recalls seeing the Brush bogged in a mudhole near the intersection of Main and Broadway. The Markeys had a white locomobile with a sporty leather strap wrapped around the hood and later acquired a new Marmon that looked, Father said, like a long, gray steamboat. Bill Oram, a well-to-do farmer, had a Buick, a prince of a car, but when farm prices advanced at the onset of the war, he traded it for a Stanley Steamer. It had a range of twenty-five miles or less; when the supply of steam ran out, the driver refilled the boiler with water, lit the Prest-o-Lite fire, and waited until he had a fresh head of steam. The town had a Chalmers, an Overland or two, and a Saxon, which boasted that each of its major components was built by a specialist: ignition by Bosch, engine by Continental, and so on. We also saw Maxwells, Dodges, air-cooled Franklins, Chevrolets, and, as the phrase goes, other kinds too numerous to mention. By 1918 the *Guide* was also advertising Fordson tractors.

As the purchase of a car was highly newsworthy, the *Guide* chronicled each new owner: the Ford Motor Company delivered four new Fords this week; Ben DeWitt is the proud owner of a new Krit; Billy Welden has been driving a spanking new Buick on our streets recently. People often drove by the office in their automobiles and took the editor and his family for a ride. Once a new Buick came to town and no ride ensued; whereupon Father wrote a front-page piece that Buick owners were stuck-up and too stingy to give the poor editor a ride, but that he didn't really care, he wouldn't be as stuck-up as a Buick owner for anything, and much preferred to walk anyway. That bit of tomfoolery hit the mail on Thursday morning, and before the week was out he had had rides in three Buicks, two Dodges, a Winton, and a Stanley Steamer. Father's description of his ride in the Stanley, with its whispery stream of power, left the impression that there was no real difference between riding it along the county-line road and riding a chariot along the Milky Way with Gabriel. When Charley Hurst stripped a Ford one-seater to a race-type streaker and painted it fire-engine red, Father promptly dubbed it a hella-to-scoot and said it could overtake a wild turkey on the wing.

Because Father had enjoyed so many rides in so many fine automobiles, he could not bring himself to buy a mere Ford when the fever finally gripped him. From a carpenter and shrewd trader, Ben DeWitt, who years before had sold us that secondhand Olds

Ford Cars

The Universal Car

"Will the Ford Motor Co. refund from $40 to $60 to retail buyers of Ford cars between Aug. 1, 1914 and Aug. 1, 1915?"

This question has been asked us hundreds of times in the 1915 season.

On a personal visit to Mr. Henry Ford, the most wonderful automobile manufacturer of the day, an aggressive agent recently queried Mr. Ford and then published this interview:

"Mr. Ford," I suggested, "is there anything I can say to our people with regard to the Ford Motor Company's 300,000 car rebate plan?"

"We shall sell the 300,000," was the quiet reply, "and in 11 months—a full month ahead of August 1st."

I then said to Mr. Ford: "If I could make a definite refund statement we would increase our local sales 500 cars."

"You may say," was Mr. Ford's deliberate and significant reply to this, "you may say that we shall pay back to each purchaser of a Ford car between August 1, 1914; and August 1, 1915, barring the unforseen, the sum of $50. You may say that I authorized you to make this statement."

What more can We say?

On May 3rd we have just seven cars on hand. The factory is 50,000 to 75,000 cars behind on their orders, we are not sure when we can get more cars. Other towns surrounding us are OUT OF CARS NOW.

First come, first served.

WILLIAMS' GARGE

GILMAN CITY,   MISSOURI

What's new about rebates? (*Guide*, May 6, 1915)

More than three thousand different makes of cars and trucks were manufactured in the United States. Although the K-R-I-T company was in business only three years, it had a dealership in Gilman City.

(*Guide*, August 14, 1913)

engine for the Great Moral and Religious Weekly, Father bought, for $400, an Overland, Model 69T, year about 1914 or 1915. The car had long sat idle in Ben's garage, but he successfully persuaded Father that this careful storage simply proved it had been well taken care of and was practically as good as new. For the same money Father could have bought a brand-new Model T but he was impressed with the idea of having a big car. Since he did not have a garage, Ben offered to build him one, for an extra $134.75, as it turned out to be, plus lumber.

Father's friends immediately showed him how badly he had been suckered. The Overland needed paint. Its old-style lights operated from a tank strapped to the running board. Other leather straps ran from the top corners to the front springs; no modern car had its top guyed down with leather straps.

Father invested an additional $50.00 to have a house painter and decorator paint it black with white wheel spokes. When the job was finished it looked as if a house painter had done it, but we thought it was lovely. Father himself removed the leather straps and wired the top to the windshield frame. He bolted a black toolbox to the running board. He installed electric head-lights, operated from a battery bolted to the other running board. The battery would have to be recharged periodically at the garage, but one did not use lights much anyway.

The Overland 69T had its steering wheel on the right side, since in the early days manufacturers had simply followed the practice of buggies and stage coaches. Then came a time when some steering wheels were on the right and some on the left. By the time we got the Overland the industry had pretty much determined that the driver should sit on the left. Father could do nothing about the steering wheel, however.

The "T" in the "69T" stood for "touring car"; open, not closed; with a top but no sidewalls. In fair weather we could ride even with the top down. In rainy weather we hoisted the top and, around the inside, buttoned fabric side curtains, with small isinglass windows. As this job took some minutes, one could easily get drenched if he waited until rain actually started to fall before digging out the side curtains.

The hood was opened, not from the front, but from either side. The four cylinders of the engine were impressively large. Atop each

The Overland Model 69T, $985 F.O.B. Toledo. Steering wheel on the right-hand side. "You want to mention the name with pride, not apology. You ask no odds of anybody, or of any car—no matter what its price—if yours is an Overland."

That's the way the factory described her. To us she was—Old Betsy. (From an ad in the *Guide*, May 1, 1913) one was a spark plug, and alongside the spark plug was a small petcock. In freezing weather the procedure was to open each petcock, pour a few spoonfuls of raw gasoline into the cylinder, and then close the petcock; this priming of the engine was supposed to make it start easier, and sometimes it did. The 69T had no starter, no generator, no air cleaner, no oil pump, no water pump, no heater, and, of course, no mechanism for wiping or washing the windshield. Most cars, in fact, lacked these refinements.

Mounted on the wooden dashboard was a speedometer, useful not so much for indicating the speed, which was determined by the condition of the road, but for recording mileage. Everybody took pride in noting the length of a trip, since the automobile was making it possible to travel greater distances than ever. The steering wheel was made of wood, with metal spokes. A lever to advance or retard the spark was under it at the left, and another to increase or decrease speed was at the right. Since we had acquired a battery, we also installed a horn, and its switch was fastened to the steering wheel. The cord from switch to horn was taped to the steering column.

An ignition lever was also mounted on the dashboard, but the ignition key was still to come. Auto thievery was practically unknown. I doubt if the *Guide*, in all the years we had it, ever ran a story about a local car theft. Nor did we worry about people stealing tools, lap robes or other clothing, or spare tires. Cars did not have trunks, except as owners bought a trunk as a special attachment and fastened it to the rear of the car with brackets. When, in the mid-twenties, the trunk became popular, Detroit decided to include it as a built-in rear compartment, large enough to hold two suitcases upright; but this compartment was still called a "trunk."

We promptly named the car "Old Betsy," Mother undertaking to learn to drive her. Ben showed her how to adjust the gas and spark for cranking, where the two pedals were and what they did, how the gearshift lever worked, and then took her once around the block. That, he said, is all there is to it. The way to learn is simply to start driving.

Not too far from where we lived, a mother showed her daughter how to run the family car and took her for a practice ride down the lane and back. The daughter took the car out for a short spin and promptly wrecked it. Well, we reflected, she was just unlucky.

Later, we learned that the mother herself had learned to drive only the day before. Even so, I have met scores whose instruction was equally casual. You were supposed to be cautious and prudent until you got the hang of it.

We decided to take our maiden voyage to Jamesport, reached by a winding, hilly, challenging road. On a Sunday afternoon Mother took the driver's seat, adjusted herself as carefully as if she were sitting down to the Intertype, and, under our apprehensive scrutiny, put the gearshift lever in neutral, released the hand brake, and adjusted ignition, spark, and gas levers exactly as Ben had advised. The engine started at first cranking, and Mother advanced the spark and calmed down the gas as she had been instructed. She depressed the clutch, put the gear in reverse, let out the clutch, and the car bounded backwards, so suddenly that she was outside the garage before she realized it. This maneuver killed the engine, but we got it restarted.

The new garage that Ben had built was located fifty feet from the street. To get to the street we had to back through the orchard, a maneuver not overly difficult but one that still required some care. And as everyone knows, driving in reverse is a fine art in itself. Soon Mother was aiming the car so much too far to one side that she threatened to take out a pear tree. Father was beside himself. "Stop it, stop it, Josie, goddammit, stop it!" he explained, and once more she killed the engine. Mother's backing out was a series of weaves, first to one side of the orchard and then the other, with Father steadily yelling directions at her, some of them exactly wrong. Neighbors gathered to watch the best free show since Daredevil Wilson. Finally she made it to the street. But no fruit tree was ever safe when Mother backed out.

The first few miles of the trip were uneventful, but soon we came to the series of steep, winding, curving hills that everyone dreaded. Occasionally Mother killed the engine on a hill, but with plenty of advice and help from her passengers she made it to the top. On the return trip, merrily rolling along at good speed, she turned a sharp corner and unexpectedly met another car head-on at a narrow culvert. With lightning reflexes, honed by years of working around nervous horses during her girlhood days, she yanked the car to the extreme right of the culvert so that both cars could barely clear it. I still remember looking down at the rocky bottom of the creek some yards below us. Eventually we reached the level roads of the Bancroft prairie and Mother's trials were over. She should have received the Congressional Medal of Honor and Father a Purple Heart. When next day Father told Ben that we had gone to Jamesport on our first trip, his face turned a pale, sidewalk gray. He had never dreamed that we would start on such a high level of adventure.

Of course I was wild to learn, though I was hardly twelve, and before long was going for rides under Father's sponsorship. There was nothing casual about my instructional sessions. Each lesson was preceded by a talk on safe driving. I heard Father's lecture so often that I could have picked it up at any point and delivered it through to the end. Years later, as I taught my own children to drive and they sought permission to take the car out on their own, I would ask, "Do you want to take the car under Plan A or Plan B?" The first time I offered them such a choice, they naturally asked me to explain each plan. "Plan A," I replied, "is accompanied by a short, but highly informative, lecture on safe driving. Under Plan B you get the car without a lecture." As they seemed invariably to elect Plan B, I never got to give the lecture at all.

With or without Father's stream of cautions, I looked forward to the driving sessions and he did also. After the weekly issue of the *Guide* was published, on the warm, pleasant afternoons after school, we drove south to the county line, turned left, and went a mile or two in each direction around a big square, eventually returning to the county-line road. The road was smooth and level, the kind of contour that had brought the O.K. to that region in the first place. Although the turns were usually right angled, often they were steeply banked so you could take them at fair speed. Old Betsy performed beautifully at twenty or twenty-five miles an hour, and even at thirty, but at greater speeds the vibration warned you to keep to thirty or below. Usually we traveled at fifteen but occasionally we let it out to twenty. If we overtook a buggy or wagon, we followed the procedure of slowing down and especially of avoiding honking, so as not to frighten the horses. The older teams were not bothered, but young teams were occasionally so disturbed by the appearance of an automobile that the driver had to keep a firm hold of the reins and shout encouraging words. We also needed to be on the lookout for cows and chickens; sometimes we had to come to a dead stop until these trespassers got themselves sorted out.

Eventually we moved into hilly country. Everybody who drove in those days became a master at downshifting. Many hills could just barely be climbed, even in low. We carried a chunk of firewood in the back so in case of a stall Father could hop out, put the chunk behind a rear wheel, which would keep Old Betsy tethered until I could adjust the spark and gas levers, crank the engine, and start the climb again. I roared to the summit, leaving Father behind with the chunk. Once he saw that I was safely at the top, he hobbled up the hill, carrying the chunk, to rejoin me.

With the sole exception of the Bethany business district, every street, alley, and highway in the county was a dirt road. The way to Jamesport, Pattonsburg, Gallatin, or for that matter St. Joe or Kansas City, was over a dirt surface. When winter weather came, most people drained the radiators of their cars and stored them until spring. We have a letter from Charley Hurst, dated February 1935, relating that he had got his car out only twice since November; and when, on the second trip, he ran into a ditch near Trenton and had to be pulled out, he decided he had had enough of winter driving. And Charley, a veteran mail carrier, was not one to be easily intimidated by driving conditions. When spring arrived, however, and the rains ceased, the roads were nicely graded with a rounded crown in the center, the side drainage was reestablished and the ruts were smoothed over by a road drag. The Missouri road drag was in fact one of the country's prime inventions, like the metal-tipped plow. In those days people boasted, "You just can't beat a good dirt road," a claim that persisted even after graveled roads were commonplace.

Even during the better seasons, however, we were entirely at the mercy of the weather. On the day of a trip we anxiously scanned the heavens, appraising each cloud, speculating whether we could get somewhere and back without encountering rain. A big event was when Grandfather and Grandmother Tarwater, and our uncles, aunts, and cousins on both Father's side and Mother's side would drive from Gallatin or Winston, twenty miles away, normally an hour and a half ride, to spend a Sunday with us. We would have a great dinner in our front yard, consisting of the stuff they brought, like fried chicken and green beans and corn on the cob and watermelon, and stuff Mother made, such as fruit salad and pumpkin or apple pie, and we would have a noon meal fit for threshers. After dinner, however, if there were clouds in the sky, the visitors would begin to worry about the homeward journey. "I don't like the look of those clouds, Brick," Lon would say, and Brick, a mail carrier, who had to contend with the weather every-day and decide whether to use auto or buggy, would be reassuring or doubtful, as the case would be. If the verdict was unfavorable, everybody would start loading immediately and the four-car car-avan would start for home. What might be a fifteen-mile-an-hour trip on dry roads would be a three- or four-mile-an-hour trip slog-ging through mud.

Roads mainly followed the old section lines, so everything moved at right angles except when the lay of the land called for curves or bends. Often you had to cross a bridge before you could start up a steep hill, and as the approach to the bridge was gen-erally rough, you could not get a running start for the hill. No roads were marked, so if you did not know the road to Trenton, for example, you would ask an expert like Bill Middleton, our mail carrier, for directions. He would draw a map with notations such as "red barn, turn left" or "go east past three cemeteries until you come to a schoolhouse and turn right." Bill's sketches were our Rand McNally. Occasionally you would also find a sign stuck on a pole or fence, lettered by a farmer who had been irritated by countless inquiries from lost drivers, decorated with an arrow and information such as "TRENTON 5 MI." These were always cheer-ing to see, especially at night when you had gone miles without meeting anybody. Gradually the important roads were marked by colored bands painted on telephone poles. A combination of blue and white horizontal stripes meant the Jefferson Highway, a north-south artery that ran from Minneapolis to New Orleans. Other parts of the Midwest were proud of the east-west White Pole road and the Lincoln Highway, marked with red, white, and blue bands. A reward of traveling came after one had driven many doubtful miles in a mystified state of mind and all at once saw a striped pole ahead of him that guided him past a corner and as-sured him that his previous guesses had been right after all. Lack-ing such a marker, one frequently stopped at crossroads and

studied the ruts to see which seemed to be the main road. As the
telephone company gradually replaced the striped poles that had
broken off or fallen over with new poles that had no stripes, the
marked poles, over the years, became fewer and fewer.

Even on a good road you sometimes came to a genuine mudhole where you had a choice of ruts. If you inquired if it were
passable you might be told, "Passable? It's not even jackassable."
Some ruts were so deep, it was claimed, that voices could be heard
from below. Still, one rut was probably navigable if only you could
figure out which one. The fainthearted would back off several
yards and wait for the next car to come along, hoping that its
driver had previously sounded and charted the spot. If, however,
the next car were a Ford, a remarkably high-slung auto, and it suc-

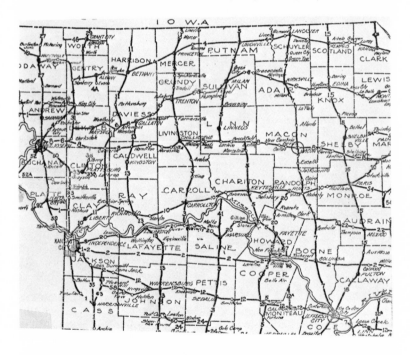

In the twenties, some of mid-America's roads were dirt, some were
gravel, and some were hard surfaced. Missouri's Kansas City-St. Louis road,
now Interstate 70, formerly U.S. 40, is shown here as No. 2. Even so, Missouri
highway officials say, today's roads, except for straightening, widening, and
leveling, follow, in general, the courses of the older routes.

Thousands of old-time drivers still alive would classify this road as pretty fair.

Ready for a joyride, December 1912.

cessfully weaved all the way across, you still had no assurance that your car, if a different make, would do as well. Eventually you had to make a decision, and when you did, your passengers debarked; you climbed behind the wheel, took a deep breath, revved your motor, and plunged full speed toward the selected rut. With luck your car would twist and struggle and snort and you found yourself safe on the other shore. Without luck you would sink to your hubcaps and even your axles would be partly buried. The nearby farmer would have already heard the noise and would have started to hitch his team. When you knocked at his door and appealed for help, he was ready. One of the great sights of those years was to see two powerful horses hitched to the front part of the frame, dig in with their feet, muscles taut, and, after a mighty heave, pull the auto out of the swamp and drag it safely to dry land. Last time I saw this display of brute force I was glad to hand over three dollars and proceed on my way.

By and by you picked up a variety of advertising signs by Trenton merchants, some provided by the manufacturers of nationally advertised products for their dealers, and the road would

Road repairs were routine in the early days of the automobile.

be better marked so you could proceed confidently. Finally you came to a sign, "Trenton—City Limits—Speed Limits 12 Mi. Per Hr. Close Your Cutout." At the same time you might pick up a little brick pavement. You might also wonder why you had undertaken this drive when you could have got there by train.

Every trip was an adventure. Once we counted eight cars stopped alongside the road: one with a broken wheel, one with stripped gears, six with tire trouble. If two cars sideswiped on a narrow road, both drivers climbed from the wreckage unhurt but swearing a blue streak. Neither had any insurance. People sometimes walked away whole and sound from a head-on collision or from colliding with a telephone pole and ruefully surveyed smashed radiators and bent fenders. You were prepared to vulcanize tubes or repair casings on the road. If you made a round trip without a flat, you boasted of it: "We went all the way to Pattonsburg and back without any trouble."

All drivers learned to make a variety of repairs and adjustments. As spark plugs were mounted atop the cylinders, you could get at them easily with a crescent wrench or even a pipe wrench. Grease cups were installed at strategic points; at regular intervals you gave each one a hearty twist until you saw fresh, yellow goo emerging from around the joint. Father often tinkered with the timing. The trick was to advance the spark as much as possible to get the best combustion, without advancing it so much that when you tried to crank the engine it backfired. A good backfire would break an arm. If a kid at school had an arm in a sling, and generally at least one kid did have an arm in a sling, you knew what had happened.

Just for fun I once decided to take the wheels off the car. Father appeared when I had the two back wheels off and caught me busily trying to remove the rear axle as well. "Son," he exclaimed, "what in the hell are you trying to do?" At that exact moment an answer such as "I'm taking the wheels off the car" seemed insane. I offered to reverse the operation, a proposition that he immediately accepted, since he was not an expert on wheels. He withdrew and in an hour or so all was sound and whole again. Given a few simple wrenches, a screwdriver or two and a pair of pliers, almost anyone could make any repair.

Today the principal driving skills are entering, exiting, and changing lanes on a crowded superhighway. Where a modern driver is now at a disadvantage is in being confronted with ice and snow. On any kind of slippery road, however, the drivers of my generation come into their own. When I am on an icy surface I feel that I am once again a skinny, blond-haired kid, downshifting up the Blue Ridge hill, on a muddy road, avoiding the steep ditches on either side, selecting the best of the ruts, hearing Father's cries, "Watch it, son, watch it!" and gradually ascending to the majesty and the glory that awaits the driver at the top.

People so loved their cars that they demanded better and better roads. Just before the First World War, highway associations began to spring up through the Midwest. The Interstate Trail, linking Des Moines (and north of that, Minneapolis), St. Joseph, and Kansas City, passed through Eagleville and Bethany. Unfortunately, it missed Gilman City by several miles. Communities along the Interstate took pride in it, giving extra attention to grading and trail marking. Eventually it became federal Highway 69. Missouri had seven major routes at that time, two famous ones being 63 from Des Moines to Jefferson City to Memphis, and 40, which crossed the country from Baltimore to San Francisco, entering Missouri at St. Louis and leaving at Kansas City. Both of these great arteries missed Gilman City. In fact, most roads missed Gilman City. If you were to lay a ruler across northwest Missouri and center it on Gilman City, though you pivot it as carefully as you can, you will find your ruler will not align anything with anything. That situation was fatal.

The State Highway Commission, moreover, started making actual traffic counts. The commission put a small table alongside a road and stationed two men at it, who tallied the cars that went by, classifying them by types and states. These surveys showed that little traffic went through Gilman City. Once the town hoped to have Highway 13 from Bethany to Gallatin, and on to Arkansas, routed through it. Gilman City people pointed out that its route would save the state the expense of building a costly bridge over Grand River, but the commission wanted the shortest possible route and was not impressed. Again, it was a vain fight, as one can tell by looking at the map, so even the battle for Highway 13 was lost.

Then, just as we left Missouri in 1921 came the statewide vote

on a $60 million bond issue to "Lift Missouri Out of the Mud."
When the bond issue passed, Missouri started its program of building six thousand miles of hard-surfaced roads. A community could
decide whether it wanted a certain number of miles of pavement
eighteen-feet wide, or twice as many miles nine feet wide. Most
opted for the single-strip, nine-foot pavement, so they could double their mileage. If the paved half was on your side, you had the
right-of-way, and the oncoming vehicle turned off onto the dirt
side. Even if the roads were muddy, turning off was no great inconvenience since as soon as the cars had passed, the offside car
could turn back onto the paved strip. Under this program the
through roads were hard surfaced first, so it was a dozen years or
more before the small towns, served only by county roads, got
their share of state money.

As Missouri got more hard-surfaced roads, more people
bought automobiles, and traffic increased. Suddenly a lot of people
saw the opportunity of providing goods and services to tourists.
Enterprising farmers set up refreshment stands along the busier
roads, selling sandwiches and soft drinks. Later they added a pump
and sold Standard Oil products. Bethany, Gallatin, and even Gilman City built tourist camps to accommodate drivers overnight.
These were rough cabins equipped with the bare necessities of
cots and mattresses and a central facility for toilet and showers.

Bus lines were organized, a bus line being, for example, an
eight-passenger Studebaker plying on a regular schedule between
Bethany and Albany, or Bethany and St. Joseph. For seventy cents
one could go from Bethany to Princeton, stopping at Cainsville
along the way. Eventually came bus lines to Kansas City and St.
Joseph. Distances were greater then than now. From Bethany to
Kansas City was, then, 134 miles; now it is 92, a marvel as great
as if Bethany had been picked up bodily and moved 42 miles to
the southwest. One day came the announcement that the mighty
Pickwick organization was planning to enter Missouri with its
nationwide bus system.

The O.K. and other railroads also felt the pressure, as people
traveled more and more by car and bus. The loss of passenger
traffic was, however, not so disastrous as the slow but steady ero-
sion of freight traffic. The early trucks, with their solid rubber
tires, did not appear to be formidable competitors, but their num-

bers increased and they nibbled steadily away at the railroads' short-haul business. Trucks and cars also displaced teams. A State Highway Commission check noted that in a sixteen-hour period almost a thousand cars passed the intersection of two nearby highways, but only eight horse-drawn vehicles.

The changes wrought by the automobile affected various people in various ways. One day the manager of the Hotel Harmon realized that he had not had to use any of his third-floor guest rooms for some weeks. The West End Livery Stable was sold and turned into a garage. Another new garage was called an "Auto Livery." Many residents, in fact, began to remake their barns into garages.

In the *Guide*, we stopped capitalizing Automobile. Finally we stopped printing news like "Mr. and Mrs. W. H. Oram motored to Trenton Friday" or "Mr. and Mrs. E. W. McClelland motored to Milan Thursday to spend the day with her parents." These items became entirely too commonplace. Weeks began to pass without Don and me printing a single stud bill. The automobile had come to stay.

People who lived in Gilman City before and during the First World War era did not buy automobiles for purely economic reasons. Nobody lived more than a few minutes' walk from the depot, post office, stores, school, or a church. Even those who lived within a five-mile circle could reach Main Street by team in an hour or less. Moreover, the natural obstacles to driving cars were formidable. Heavy spring or fall rains could easily knock out scores of bridges over the county's streams. Winter weather brought snowdrifts, frozen ruts, and, later, bottomless mudholes. Anyone could get to most county-seat towns by train over two or three different routes. Anyone could list several valid arguments against buying a car.

Yet family after family pushed these reasons aside and invested several months' wages in the purchase of an automobile. The word *joyriding* leaped into the language to describe the afternoon tour of two or three hours either to a neighboring town or around the countryside. You might drive to Bethany, for example, do nothing more than buy ice-cream cones all around and then return home. But next day you would tell your friends about your adventure, bragging about tire trouble or other repairs that you made along the way, about climbing a hill in second that ordinarily called for low, or even about making the trip without killing the engine.

National advertisers finally got the message that dreams and aspirations as well as hard, firm reasons entered into the purchase of a car. One of the innumerable makes that has long since vanished was the Jordan, a fairly expensive automobile. I do not recall that any local family owned one, but I do remember seeing one parked on Broadway one afternoon and that several of us gathered around it and passed our learned judgments on its capabilities. The Jordan company came out with a sporty model that it called the "Playboy," put a price tag of more than two thousand dollars on it, and advertised it in appealing language as being especially built for the laughing, brown-faced, western girl who was waiting for her boy to return from somewhere in France. A Jordan ad became famous among experts as one of the greatest ads ever written. Its headline was "Somewhere West of Laramie" and its text went on to say that "somewhere west of Laramie there's a bronco-busting, steer-roping girl who knows what I'm talking about.... The Playboy was built for her.... Step into the Playboy when the hour grows dull with things gone dead and stale. Then start for the land of real living with the spirit of the lass who rides, lean and rangy, into the red horizon of a Wyoming twilight." With no mention of the Jordan's engineering refinements, the company sold thousands.

A lot of Gilman City people who drove automobiles those years also knew what the man was talking about. Their Jordan was a humbler sort—like a Ford, Buick, Chevy, Marmon, Winton, Saxon, Brush—and even like our Old Betsy. But, like the steer-roping girl in the ad, we liked to go joyriding when the hour grew dull with things gone dead and stale, along a dirt road that we shared with chickens, dogs, and skittish teams, stirring up the red and purple and yellow leaves of an autumn afternoon, into the beckoning horizon of a Missouri sunset.

Not long ago I asked a class of 250 students, the youngest the age of my oldest granddaughter, "How many of you are licensed automobile drivers? Hold up your hands." The hands in the air

Somewhere West of Laramie

SOMEWHERE west of Laramie there's a broncho-busting, steer-roping girl who knows what I'm talking about. She can tell what a sassy pony, that's a cross between greased lightning and the place where it hits, can do with eleven hundred pounds of steel and action when he's going high, wide and handsome.

The truth is—the Playboy was built for her.

Built for the lass whose face is brown with the sun when the day is done of revel and romp and race.

She loves the cross of the wild and the tame.

There's a savor of links about that car—of laughter and lilt and light—a hint of old loves—and saddle and quirt. It's a brawny thing—yet a graceful thing for the sweep o' the Avenue.

Step into the Playboy when the hour grows dull with things gone dead and stale.

Then start for the land of real living with the spirit of the lass who rides, lean and rangy, into the red horizon of a Wyoming twilight.

JORDAN

JORDAN

JORDAN MOTOR CAR COMPANY, Inc., Cleveland, Ohio

One of the most famous ads ever written, stressing not the practical reasons for buying a car, but an entirely different approach.

were as thick as stalks in a cornfield. Then I asked, "How many of you can harness a team?" A few hands sprang to life, their owners grinning from ear to ear.

I reflected that nowhere in this wide world except in the United States did such a high percentage of young people know how to drive automobiles. I also reflected that if the same questions had been asked my father's generation of young men and women, the responses would have been reversed. My generation would have shown by far the greatest proportion of people who could do either. We were the ones who saw the working horse and mule leave the scene and the automobile and tractor come to stay.

17

Pollution Started Right Here

Pollution was first identified and described, not by the modern generation, but by the residents of thousands of small towns, well on the distant side of the First World War. Long before the Sierra Club was founded, we had problems with air, water, dust, and, in fact, the whole environment. If the surgeon general had put his mind to it, he would have determined that living in a small town was dangerous to the health.

At its beginning, Gilman City had no sidewalks except plank walks on Main Street. To get to one's home, one walked alongside the street. Occasionally extra planks were laid across bad ruts or mudholes. Dirt streets mean heavy mud in rainy seasons and thick dust in dry seasons. In wet weather mudholes were created that a wise buggy driver would prefer to detour rather than to challenge head-on. In dry weather any passing team or automobile would kick up a heavy cloud of dust. By the time I was in school, cement sidewalks were everywhere but the roads were still dirt, oiled in the summertime to reduce the dust. Mudholes were still available but mainly on the side streets.

When I write "cloud of dust," I am really calling upon an honored cliché. Our dust was 10 to 40 percent horse manure particulate, plus other ingredients, such as the cinder ash belched into the atmosphere by the O.K.

The stockyards also added their share to the general pollution. The principal occupants were horses, mules, cattle, and hogs (we were not a great sheep-raising community) brought from nearby farms for shipment to Kansas City—less frequently to St. Joseph and Chicago. Farmers hauled the animals in wagons, deposited them in the pens overnight or longer for watering and feeding, and then drove them up the chutes into stockcars. The atmosphere of the stockyards was authoritative and penetrating; if a stranger had had to inquire, "Where are the stockyards?" he would have been set down as a supreme idiot. When the wind was from the northwest, a trained nose could tell whether the stockyard mix was principally horses, mules, cattle, or hogs, and the owner of a truly sensitive and artistic nose claimed he could identify the breed—Holstein, Duroc Jersey, Poland China. Actually most residents hardly noticed the odor, showing the remarkable facility with which human beings adapt.

I have often wondered why people who lived next to a nice, clean corn oil or oleo plant, or even steel mill, with its hot, sterilized smoke, would complain about pollution. Gilman City in its best days could look Gary, Indiana, or East St. Louis right in the eye, without flinching, and brag about its superior product.

As soon as the spring sun warmed the soil, we started going barefooted. We waded through dust and played in dust. The standard summer costume for boys included B.V.D.s, overalls, and blouse, the latter a no-tailed shirt that generally revealed a sample of the underlying skin. What girls wore, other than a cotton dress, I can only speculate. In every home the evening, go-to-bed ritual included a foot-washing outdoors under the pump. We washed only under compulsion supported by supervision. If mothers did not check, the operation would be skimped or hurried. In our home as Don slept at one end of the bed and I at the other—an arrangement that was believed to lessen squabbling—we cozied up to each other's feet in a way that would shock a child care expert.

Our backyard, like everyone else's, was fenced, to accommodate a flock of chickens. If someone's chickens broke out and roamed over the neighborhood, the marshal could be summoned. He did what he could short of actually filing charges to keep peace among neighbors. If the situation got out of hand, he asked Father to print a warning in the *Guide*. Many residents also had a barn to keep a cow or horse; they were stabled in the barn although pastured at the edge of town. Chickens disposed of the kitchen garbage, and rats got whatever grain the farm animals missed. On the whole it was a comfortable ecological system.

Sanitary facilities were also outdoors. Thousands of people are still alive who can describe the ordeal of getting up in the middle of a winter night in an unheated bedroom. After serious contemplation of the advantages of getting up and getting the trip over with versus those of lying quietly in a warm bed and suffering a little longer, one finally had to face the inevitable. The adventure involved slipping into shoes, grabbing a coat, and trudging over a snowy path to the family backhouse; and, finally, exposing one's bare bottom to the icy wind that whistled through the opening. One did not actually sit on the hole—at least not often—one hunkered over it. Back in bed, one huddled in a tight ball until one's chilled body was thawed out—unless the process were speeded by snuggling against the bedmate just enough to feel the glow but not enough to awaken the sleeper, which would ruin everything. Anyone who has romantic memories of the family privy is probably thinking of spring or autumn, not winter.

Hot days brought chiggers and flies. Our front-yard grass was not thick and nourishing enough to support chiggers, but a fishing expedition, a rabbit hunt, or especially a berrying foray, would attract a bodyful. Soda water, turpentine, or saltwater soothed the itch, but still better was a styptic pencil, as the alum tended to shrink the swollen area. A caustic pencil was even more effective as it would burn the bite out although it would also remove some of the hide if liberally applied. A well-fed chigger, working overtime, would make you willing to give up some hide, however, just to slow him down.

Flies were less manageable. Nourished by chicken yards, hitching racks, stockyards, and farms at the edge of town, flies swarmed everywhere. Although most houses had screening, a few flies drifted in every time a door was opened, and soon the rooms would be a-buzz. Physiology texts showed vivid pictures of flies coming directly from stable to table; dotted lines indicated the path of flight. For a long time I thought flies flew on dotted lines.

We used various devices to control them: fly swatters, tanglefoot sticky paper, and daisy fly killers, a poison dispensing device. But where we killed flies by the hundreds, nature hatched them by the millions. Flies were a prime nuisance to grocers, butchers, and restaurant operators. Meat, poultry, and butter on display had to be kept continually covered. Patrons eating in a restaurant got accustomed to seeing their waitress stop serving to swat a few flies. Every vaudeville entertainer had a joke about the fly in the soup. At times man himself seemed to be the endangered species.

We bought our milk from Uncle Joe Bogue and his wife, who lived at the edge of town and kept a Jersey herd. Uncle Joe was a

Harrison County native who had moved to Gilman City when it was only three years old. In his younger days, he had served as mayor but was now semiretired. He and Mrs. Bogue were fastidious in their handling of milk, but the only form of refrigeration was with pond ice. The notion of tuberculin-tested cattle was just beginning to become prevalent. I shudder to think what a modern lab would report on Gilman City's raw milk, but we drank gallons of it. I eat a candy bar and find it contains hydrogenated coconut oil, sorbitol, lecithin, and propyl gallate. Uncle Joe's milk had its own mysteries, but nothing you couldn't spell.

In the center of the intersection on Main and Broadway, the city maintained a town pump, with a large tank nearby for watering teams. The top of the well cannot be said to have been entirely sealed, so it got some of the surface drainage. Business firms and thirsty shoppers relied on this well for drinking water. At home we had a drilled well, a foot or so wide, lined with ceramic tile and covered with a wooden platform on which the long-handled pump was bolted. The intake was submerged deep in the well, so that surface contamination would not be pumped up. This simple bit of design did wonders for sanitation. As an additional precaution, Father had the well cleaned every other year. I remember observing the process on one occasion. The workman hauled up a dead rat and other additives, but as he seemed to take these gleanings as a matter of course, I was not particularly disturbed. Father's comment that it was a good idea to clean a well every year or so whether it needed it or not seemed to cover the situation. I realize now I have lived the whole cycle, from dead rat to propyl gallate. Today it is considered admirable to be friendly to animal life, as witness any movie about deepest Africa, and that is what we did as a matter of course.

When uncles, aunts, and cousins came to visit us, they would inevitably, about the second day, come down with a diarrhoea that resulted in a steady procession of patrons to the backhouse. They would observe, matter of factly, "We're not used to your water yet," and inevitably, in a day or so, their digestive functions would be restored to normal. If not, Father would be prepared to dispense Five Drops pills. Or we would visit relatives at their country homes and have the same experience. Everybody docilely endured this minor inconvenience.

Periodically I came down with a complaint accompanied by fever and stomach upset, an illness that no one could diagnose. Dr. Magraw or Dr. Gardner would prescribe a round of calomel, to stimulate the inner workings, followed by a round of Epsom salts, to purge the system of the calomel. Calomel, a tiny white tablet, was administered in a series of half a dozen, taken two hours apart, along with the caution that during the dosage one must not eat anything sour, like pickles or lemons, or he would *salivate*, a word that meant, we were told, that our teeth would drop out. In about five days I would recover, having survived both the ailment and the treatment, but would be weak for a long time afterwards. When the family moved to Iowa, I ceased having these attacks altogether, and in the years that followed I was as well as anybody. The family verdict was that I outgrew this childhood idiosyncrasy.

Other effects of pollution were more subtle and dangerous. A baby could usually get through its first summer, living primarily on mother's milk, but the second year it might be carried off by colic or "summer complaint." The transition to man-made or man-handled food was too great a hazard for its tiny system. The milk, the water, the flies, the dust, the food spoiled either from lack of refrigeration or contaminated by ice, one way or another, singly or in combination, got to it. Every parent worried about the second summer and was profoundly grateful to get the baby through it. And if it survived the second summer, it still faced hazards. The older residents of northwest Missouri knew that Governor Dockery and his wife had had seven children, and that all had died in infancy. Well, not quite in infancy; Aunt Grace remembers a little girl who made it all the way to seven. The physician could not do much for diphtheria, scarlet fever, smallpox, and typhoid except give the child good care and hope that it would pull through. Three of my uncles and aunts never lived to be old enough to enter school because of these and other dread diseases. Children in small towns were exposed to the worst there was, short of cholera, yellow fever, and the plague. I did not get my first smallpox vaccination until I was twelve, my first diphtheria shot was administered at sixteen, and my first typhoid inoculation came when I went to army camp, at twenty-one.

Castor oil, calomel, and salts were the physician's all-purpose, tentative, stand-by remedies; he could administer any of these and await further developments. The patient, meanwhile, would be fully occupied. Gilman City was pretty much calomel-and-salts territory. Gallatin and Winston, however, were deep in castor-oil territory. When on a visit to my Aunt Mit's I came down with a stomach ailment, she, in consultation with Uncle Jim, prescribed castor oil. Only a brave boy could take this oily, slick, disagreeable-tasting concoction without flinching. Aunt Mit, Father's oldest sister, had therefore worked out her own system, developed after years of rearing her own brood. To mask the taste, she prescribed a tablespoonful of Uncle Jim's corn whiskey, and to cut the greasy effect, a teaspoonful of coffee grounds. I can see her now, with each of these ingredients lined up on the kitchen table for speedy access, along with a glass of cool water that had come, Uncle Jim said with attempted cheer, from the northwest corner of the well. White-faced, tense, and dewy-eyed, I faced my ordeal with true courage. In rapid succession I forced down the castor oil, fighting to hold back the convulsions; then I swallowed the spoonful of fiery whiskey, which made me choke and gasp; after breathing was restored I rolled the coffee grounds around the inside of my mouth, which brought on violent coughing; and finally I flushed out the remnants of all these remedies with gulps of the water that had caused the trouble in the first place.

Many families kept a bottle of whiskey on the premises to use for just such medicinal purposes. At twenty-five cents a jug it was cheap, powerful, and dependable. Other remedies were also available. Turpentine was freely sloshed on cuts and bruises; its sting would make you forget your other worries. Once while visiting I snagged my bare foot on a sharp rock. The gash, a good inch long, would today get hospital attention and three or four stitches. Grandmother, however, washed it out, made a poultice of bread, milk, and a touch of soda, and applied the mixture to the wound with a bandage made from a freshly laundered cotton rag. The bread and milk were soothing to the foot and kept the gash soft and moist. Besides, the soda, as she explained, drew out the infection. As she was right on every count, I escaped lockjaw, gangrene, and blood poisoning, and today have only a faint scar to remind me of the incident. Cold packs were good to control fevers. If all the nice, cold towels that Mother has laid on my burning forehead were laid end to end, they would reach from our house to the *Guide* office.

Cut Out and Save   No. 5

How to Wean Baby Successfully

Never Wean Your Child During the Hot Summer Months

Try to nurse baby all summer.
Even part mother's milk may save his life.
Ten bottle-fed babies die to one that is breast fed.

At nine months, give one bottle of cow's milk to replace one
breast feeding. The proper proportions are:
6 oz. milk,
2 oz. water,
1 level teaspoonful sugar.

After two weeks, replace another breast feeding with cow's milk
of the same proportions.

Wait two weeks and replace a third feeding.

Keep on nursing the other two feedings for a month and then
wean entirely.

If the mother has plenty of milk up to eleven months, it is not
necessary to give a bottle at all.

At eleven months a child can drink milk from a cup.

As the child learns to eat more, a drink of milk with his cereal
can be substituted for a breast feeding, and he can gradually be
weaned, without use of a bottle.

Boil all-milk (and chill rapidly) all hot months.
All milk should be kept on ice.
If the baby is constipated, don't give him medicine.
Use a soap stick suppository. Medicine upsets his stomach.

To keep well, a child's bowels should move once a day.

Time spent training baby to a regular hour will save many a
doctor's bill.

Compiled under direction Children's Bureau U. S. Department of Labor.
Missouri Woman's Committee, Council of National Defense.

The country weekly published free a great deal of what might be called
"public-service" material. This advice should help mothers get their babies
through the dangerous summer months. (*Guide,* January 1, 1919)

The drugstore had a remedy for everything—sour stomach, loss of sleep, and worms.

I have often wondered if the parents of large families had a nagging fear, seldom put in words, that sooner or later they were destined to lose a youngster. Father, in fact, had been told by well-meaning neighbors, with reference to me, "You'll never raise that child." This advice put a fine edge to Father's and Mother's apprehension whenever "that child" came down with an ailment. It was certainly true that death often struck suddenly and unexpectedly. When someone fell ill, the family promptly summoned the doctor, who arrived with his black bag, looked at tongue, throat, and ears, felt and prod, took the temperature, and asked questions. In the back of everyone's mind was the unspoken worry: "Is it one of the serious things?" Finally he would say, "I do not believe it is one of the serious things," and, to the general relief, would prescribe a simple remedy of, say, castor oil, since, when in doubt, it was generally wise to "clean out the system." A few decades earlier it would have been generally wise to let a panful of blood. Not for many years would the black bag contain sulfa derivatives or antibiotics.

One day Father learned a new way of cleaning out the system with a concoction of figs, raisins, and senna tea. Senna is a powerful, Old World, purgative. Mother prepared the recipe and served it at supper as a kind of dessert. A sauce made of stewed figs and raisins, with a little sugar, is delicious, and the small amount of senna could not be tasted. We each gobbled a saucerful and asked for another. Needless to say we each made several outdoor trips that night, joking about the turn of events as we passed one another in the dark. We had no further interest in senna tea, and I relay the recipe only with the sober warning: "Use only as directed."

Drs. Magraw and Gardner were the two of Gilman City's three physicians that we called on—think of the small towns today that have no medical service at all—and they were readily available. Either could ordinarily be at the bedside in minutes. They were calm, tough, and radiated all the hope that was to be had. Out-of-town physicians also occasionally visited the town, holding clinics at the hotel, following an ad in the *Guide*. Dr. W. J. Croziero billed himself as a Spanish specialist in chronic and female diseases. He could cure your disease without asking embarrassing questions. If you are sick and neglect to care for yourself there is but one sure, positive, certain end—*death.* The United Doctors of St. Joseph employed the latest bacterial, serum, and electric discoveries. Hundreds of testimonial letters are on file, some from this community. They never mutilate the human body with the knife. Sentences like these illustrate the tone of their ads. Yet even with all this local and imported talent people would quietly suffer for years from an ailment that today could be cured. Each of my parents was crippled by a condition that today would present no problem.

Only the most independent papers followed a policy of not accepting patent-medicine ads. We advertised Lichty's Celery Nerve Compound. Castoria, for infants and children—they cry for it. Scott's Emulsion. Dr. King's New Life Laxative Pills. One-Minute Cough Cure allays inflammation, clears the head, soothes and strengthens the mucous membrane, relieves lung troubles. Rocky Mountain Tea brings attractiveness to listless, unlovable girls, making them handsome, marriageable women.

On the Intertype, I set testimonials by the dozen. One read: "I suffered from chronic diarrhoea for thirty years. After taking several bottles of Chamberlain's Colic, Cholera, and Diarrhoea Remedy, I was entirely cured." Eat your heart out, Kaopectate.

Frequently the community would be shocked by a strange and terrible and now almost archaic word—*quarantine.* One would be strolling down the middle of a street, kicking his toes in the hot dust, perhaps dodging a Buick, Brush, or Winton, and spot, nailed to a front door, the dreaded yellow card with "QUARANTINE" in large letters, followed by the name of one of the fearful killers: typhoid, smallpox, diphtheria, or scarlet fever.

Quarantine meant that the family would have to decide who would remain isolated with the stricken person, who would live elsewhere and make the family living. All that physician and relatives could do was to sustain the patient, supply hot or cold packs, change the bedding, and provide a few sips of soup or water. Neighbors left supplies on the doorstep. Physicians showed courage even in entering the place.

When one of our good advertisers, Charley McClary, the grocer, was stricken with typhoid, he lay abed for weeks. The news that trickled from the house, and that was reported in the *Guide,* was that he was doing "as well as can be expected." As days went on and he became weaker and weaker, he was still reported as doing "as well as can be expected." The community awaited what was called the "climax"—the peak moment of his sufferings, at which point he would take a dramatic turn one way or the other.

In Charley's case, the fever broke at the climax, and the family sighed with relief. He fell into a deep sleep, the sweetest and most sustained he had had for weeks. At this point, experience said, he must not be allowed to sleep for more than an hour or two at a time; if he were not then awakened, he would never awake. The bone-tired, weary body must not be allowed to give up; it must be poked and stirred at intervals. Mose LaMastres, the tailor, had volunteered to watch during this critical period. Wearied by his long vigil, he had fallen into a doze, and when he awakened, he realized that he had allowed Charley to sleep much too long. Mose was a powerfully built man, but his shaking, jouncing, and poking were not drastic enough to arouse the patient. Finally, desperately, he lifted the foot of the bed high in the air and let it crash to the floor; *that* did the business, and Charley asked, sleepily and feebly, "What's going on?" Mose was vastly relieved that he had roused the desperately ill, completely exhausted man from what might have been a terminal sleep. Eventually Charley recovered completely and was back at the store, looking like a skeleton, having been ill nearly two months. Not everybody was so fortunate.

Smallpox was also a vicious ailment. Over the years a rumor had persisted that once the whole town had been quarantined. A young man with smallpox had gone to a dance, had danced with several young ladies, had chewed tobacco from the plugs of several young men, and thus had thrown not only Gilman City but half the county into quarantine. People tended to conceal the disease, if they could, just to avoid quarantine, thus aggravating the situation.

Just before the outbreak of the First World War, a fresh epidemic of smallpox hit the community and half a dozen quarantine signs appeared. Don and I were taken out of school and told that either we must be vaccinated or else not leave the front yard. Vaccination itself was a serious ordeal; the vaccine had impurities of its own and was administered in such doses that the scar itself, bigger than half a dollar, would persist forever. Nor did it always work; the vaccination itself might bring on the disease.

Father and Mother thought it unwise to force vaccination upon us. In their memories lingered stories of parents who had done so, with disastrous results. After a few days of solitary confinement, we agreed to submit to vaccination and showed up at Dr. Gardner's office to face this unknown ordeal. He simply made a few scratches, rubbed in a few drops of liquid, and applied a bandage. The scratched places, however, turned into huge sores that were incredibly slow to heal. Scabs formed and were knocked off in play; celluloid shields like tiny tents were improvised and taped over the sores, but even the shields would be knocked off and the sore re-injured. The alternative, however, was frightful; those who came down with the disease developed huge sores all over their bodies, and if they survived were left with pockmarks. Half a dozen of my schoolmates, boys and girls alike, had heavily pocked faces. Even so, they were lucky to be alive.

The doctors developed a strategy for placing the vaccination. A right-handed boy was shot in the left upper arm; if one arm had to be partly immobilized, it should not be his better arm. Girls were shot in the side of the thigh, since in later life they would want to wear sleeveless dresses and would not care to display a scar on the arm. The doctors, however, could not foresee everything. If today you see a shapely grandmother of a certain age on the beach, you can see a smallpox vaccination scar just below her bikini.

We also endured the non-quarantinable ailments. Mumps was almost welcome; if one child had mumps, others would be exposed so they could get over the disease while they were still young. Measles and chicken pox were in the same category. Lockjaw sometimes followed wounds to bare feet or to hands that had been punctured by rusty nails; it was practically incurable and is today a serious ailment. One farmer punctured his thumb on a barbed-wire fence. Infection, or as we called it, blood poisoning, set in; his arm and shoulder swelled up; in a few days he was gone. In the summer came the mad dog scares. If, on a swimming expedition or hunting trip we saw a dog acting strangely, we gave it a wide berth. If the scare got bad, farmers got out their shotguns and thinned the stray dog population.

Some years later, after we had moved to an Iowa county-seat town, Father persuaded Don and me to visit a physician and get inoculated against the diverse ailments that up to then we had somehow missed. We went to a general practitioner whose training was so far advanced that he operated his own two-story hospital, and who routinely did surgery of the kinds that we had always associated with St. Joseph and Kansas City. He was so amused to see two grown boys who had not had their infant shots that he shot Don in the belly and me in the back. For two days I could hardly sit and Don could hardly stand. The adult members of the family and of the printing office were highly amused but Don and I did not find it humorous.

In retrospect I did more business with our two dentists than with our physicians. As a boy addicted to the candy habit, and enough pennies and nickels from delivering papers to support it, I nearly always had cavities and could not bring myself to do anything about them until a tooth began to ache. Then, driven by pain, I confided in Mother, who got in touch with Doc Quinlan, whom I have introduced before as manager of the town baseball team.

M. J. Quinlan, one of Gilman City's first resident dentists, was a graduate of the University of Illinois dental school. He was small, slender, red haired, blue eyed, and enjoyed a good professional reputation both in our community and in nearby Coffey, where he also maintained an office. He had an unfailing sense of humor and usually had one or more gags going with Father and with other friends. He had the habit, however, of occasionally taking a nip from the bottle, which alarmed Mother, who had learned about the effects of drinking both from people she had grown up with and from printers who had occasionally worked for us. She waited until he came to the post office to get his mail and then engaged him in conversation; if he passed her scrutiny, she made an appointment for me that same afternoon.

Dr. Quinlan had an upstairs office in the middle of the block on South Main Street. The reception room, uncarpeted, had two or three chairs. Through the doorway leading to his office proper one could see the chair—not nearly so fancy as those in the barbershops, but still large and substantial. Alongside it on the right was a cabinet for burrs, a collection of forceps, and hand tools for exploring, prying, and shaping. Near the cabinet was an upright pillar with a flexible cable terminating in a receptacle into which different shapes and styles of burrs could be inserted. A series of wheels and small belts connected the drilling mechanism to a foot treadle. Part of the dentist's skill involved supplying the foot power that kept the burr rotating at an even tempo and at the same time manipulating the burr to grind out the decayed parts of the tooth. I knew about foot power since both of our job presses could be operated by pedals.

In the cities one could then occasionally see the sign, "Painless Dentistry." The use of local anesthetics had not yet come to Gilman City. On one trip I sat waiting in Doc's outer office, watching him treat the older brother of one of my friends. I heard the verdict that the tooth had to come out. As there was no way to numb the agony, the tooth had to be pulled by brute force. Doc gave his patient a swallow of something, perhaps whiskey, applied his forceps to the tooth, and twisted, tugged, and pulled with his entire strength. Utterly horrified but strangely fascinated, I crept to the doorway to view the operation at point-blank range. The patient moaned and grimaced; the blood so drained from his face that he was as white as a dentist's coat. Finally the tooth emerged, Doc holding it high to be viewed; in my memory it looms as being an inch square, with roots another inch long. Only those with small, literate minds will question these dimensions. The color returned to the patient's cheeks, but slowly. He paid off, probably a dollar, and, weak kneed, left the office.

When I climbed into the chair, I was also white faced and weak kneed. I knew the routine well, since I had been there so often before. I learned to tell by the feel, as he explored each tooth with his probe, how many cavities there would be in addition to the one that had brought me, since, if there were a cavity, I could feel the sharp-pointed explorer tool catch on its edges. If it were sensitive, I knew the cavity was a big one. Nearly always there were four or five. Wisely, Doc's strategy was to grind out the big cavities first. Skillfully he skirted the edges where the pain was not so acute, but where decayed matter had to be removed; then he would make a pass over the deep part, which would lift me off the seat; not intimidated, he kept on until he had done a fair proportion of the total job.

A patient can do so little when a dentist is burrowing into a tooth. If it is a lower, he can slink into the chair, but the burr pursues him. If it is an upper, he can tilt his head back further and further, but never so far that he can escape the burr. I know now that the burrs of that day dulled easily and that the pain was aggravated by heat and friction, but after each minute of drilling I could only think to myself, "Well, that much is done, I won't have to go through that bit again." The next go-round would be briefer, but still painful. Then he would announce, "One more will do it," and so would finish. Eventually all four or five cavities were reamed out.

The finishing procedures were more endurable. He rolled balls of cotton to keep tongue and lips away from the sites where his bulldozer had been, mixed a hod of silver amalgam, sometimes lining the bottom of the cavities with a layer of cement to act as insulation, and then one by one plugged the holes. Finally came the last touches of his scraper, a test for occlusion, and the job was done. Doc ran a small professional card in the *Guide*, and I suspect his advertising bill just about balanced his bill for services. I staggered home by way of Slick's Cafe, got half a dozen Brazil nougats, and tried to recover my strength. You would think that after a session with the dentist I would leave candy alone. All things considered, however, I was lucky to get through high school without having any teeth pulled.

Our generation of Americans ran a hazardous obstacle course just to make it to school age. Life expectancy, today more than seventy years, was then only thirty-five. Of a hundred boy and girl babies born at the turn of the century, fifteen or twenty died at childbirth or of infantile disorders. Of the children remaining, another ten or fifteen succumbed to the diseases associated with food, water supply, and living conditions. After all, we had had only minimal support from vaccinations and inoculations during our growing years. A few others were carried off by heart failure or were killed in automobile accidents. The rest of our lot, the hardy and lucky survivors, are still going strong.

18

Making Sugar Creek Safe For Democracy

During its first two decades, the new town in Sugar Creek Township had many patriotic occasions, especially on Decoration Day when the veterans put on their uniforms and medals and participated in a Main Street ceremony followed by a parade to the cemetery. After short speeches came the rifle salute to the dead and the always-moving, ever-stirring taps. I was greatly impressed that in the parade were men who had actually fought in the wars we had studied in school.

Once I had read a piece in the *St. Joseph News-Press* about the death of a Mexican War veteran; he had fought in a conflict that had taken place sixty-five years previously. Although we had no veterans of that war, we had a score or more who had fought on one side or the other of the Civil War. Our small part of the Grand Army of the Republic contained veterans who had served with Grant, McClellan, and Frémont. One of our Confederate veterans had proudly served with Stonewall Jackson. Many old-timers had seen Lincoln on his visits to the front, and a few had heard him speak.

Some of those who participated in the Decoration Day celebrations of 1915 and 1916 must have been aware that America's long era of peace was seriously threatened by the bitter conflict across the ocean. Certainly the presidential campaign of 1916 was followed with intense interest. Wilson, running on the slogan, "He'll keep us out of war," was highly persuasive. In Charles Evans Hughes, however, he had a strong opponent. Both sides waged a vigorous campaign, with scores of meetings and speeches throughout the country. The candidates did not need to invent an issue; the issue was already at hand, expressed in words like *intervention, neutrality, war, peace.*

save

1-wheat
use more corn

2-meat
use more fish & beans

3-fats
use just enough

4-sugar *use syrups*

and serve
the cause of freedom
U.S. FOOD ADMINISTRATION

Country newspapers printed free ads during the First World War—and still others were paid for by advertisers. (*Guide*, February 28, June 20, 1918)

Halt the Hun

Provide the boys with the things they need to make short work of him.

Guns, clothes, aircraft, food, munitions and the ships to get over with. These are the things the boys need, and they cost money ---hunks of it.

June 28th
National War Savings Day

Make a pledge to buy War Savings Stamps

The more quickly our soldiers have all the things they need, the more quickly the ships will be bringing our boys back to us.

E. W. McClelland Produce Co.

The *Guide* family had a personal interest in the outcome of the campaign, since Father could not continue as Wilson's representative in Gilman City unless Wilson himself were reelected. A Republican incumbent in the White House would spell the end of the Reid family's having a postmaster and an assistant postmaster. Father, a long-time admirer of Bryan, noted that Bryan, whose support had helped Wilson win the nomination in 1912, had embarrassed the Democratic high command by offering to campaign in 1916. Although the party leaders were afraid his brand of oratory would be ineffective, they could hardly refuse outright the services of a man who for so long had been the leader of the party. Finally they decided to send him to California, where he would do the least damage, since Wilson would probably lose the state anyway.

After supper on election day, a crowd gathered at the O.K. depot to hear the telegraph dispatches as they trickled in. The early returns that came over the wire were cheered by one group of partisans or the other. As the evening wore on the Republicans cheered more and more and the Democrats less and less. Hughes had apparently captured New York, New Jersey, and Pennsylvania, and as his electoral lead piled up it seemed obvious by midnight that he would win by a close vote, even though Wilson was leading in other parts of the country. California had not yet reported—a snow in the Sierras had held up the final tabulation—but the four of us walked home, discouraged and gloomy. It had been nice to have a Democratic president after so many years of Republican rule, so it was doubly sad to feel that the Democrats were now to go down the drain after such a short time in power. Father, however, pulled himself together and assured us that even though we had lost this election, we would win the next one. This eleven-year-old citizen-in-being went to bed with that comforting thought.

Not until late next morning did dispatches begin to come through that Wilson had carried California, and with that the election. A Democrat would be at the helm to see us safely through this period of world tension, and also four more years of postmastering. Father was convinced that Wilson had carried California because Bryan had been sent there. Having heard Bryan speak two or three times, I would need a lot of evidence to be convinced otherwise.

Five months after the election, however, the nation was at war. The daily papers carried the big headlines—about submarine warfare, armed neutrality, the war in France, the draft, the mobilization of the country's resources. The *Guide* carried the smaller stories—about Curly Higgins, for instance, the son of one of our leading real estate and insurance families, who was the first to sign up, and later about the scores of other Harrison and Daviess County boys who were drafted or who enlisted, and about the different kinds of war activities that women were engaged in.

Mother checked carefully on the comings and goings of our soldier boys during her twice-daily visits to the depot, reporting their assignments, transfers, and promotions. Each week I set up two or three letters written to folks back home. Fathers and mothers brought these precious pages to us for printing, with instructions to save and return. Many of these must still be in existence, pierced by the copy hook of the machine and bearing my inky fingerprints. Place names like Camp Dodge, Camp Funston, Fort Sill, and Jefferson Barracks began to invade our small-town insularity. Letters told about getting up early in the morning and having hot biscuits for breakfast, about drill, about the free sack of Bull Durham every week along with other gifts from the Salvation Army and the Red Cross. And they told about the flu, which reached epidemic proportions. Occasionally they recorded a promotion to corporal or even to sergeant.

Later came the letters headed "Somewhere in France" that were read the most eagerly. Most soldiers had landed at a place they called "La Harve." They noted that French farmers used oxen, not horses; that if farmers did use a team of two or four horses, they hitched them in front of one another. They marveled at the scenery and noted spots that looked like good places to hunt quail. They were surprised that the houses were made of stone, not wood. They were amused by the size of French boxcars, so small that they would hold only eight horses, or forty men. They saw hay being cut with a scythe: "A Frenchman wouldn't know what a mower looked like." A different set of place names began to appear: Argonne Forest, Château-Thierry, Ypres, Alsace-Lorraine. Any war is an unforgettable course in geography.

Under the administration of George Creel, a national propaganda ministry supplied the *Guide* and other newspapers with reams of prepared copy on war aims and purposes, liberty loan drives, rationing, and other phases of the struggle. Creel also organized the famous Four-Minute Men, consisting of citizens who prepared themselves to give four-minute talks at churches, school assemblies, service clubs, and elsewhere. Even at school older students prepared and delivered four-minute speeches. Occasionally a soldier came home on furlough from camp and talked to the school assembly about his experiences. Invariably he said something about airplanes, the most impressive way in which this war was different from others.

Father bought an assortment of cuts—castings or engravings used to print pictures—so that we had a supply of flags, shields, eagles, and stars. The upper corners of the *Guide's* front page now carried a picture of the flag. We turned out ration coupons entitling the holder to scarce commodities. One form was to be signed by housewives who could buy extra sugar provided they agreed to use it for canning. Although sugar was a scarce commodity, it did not occur to anyone to fudge or cheat. Slick's Cafe had a big sign back of the counter: "Use Less Sugar. Stir Like Hell. We Don't Mind the Noise." Other forms that we printed entitled customers to buy wheat flour, also scarce, provided they also bought a fourth of that amount in the form of cornmeal, oatmeal, or barley flour. People began to try spoon corn bread, fried cornmeal mush, cornmeal fish cakes. Rabbits, formerly a nickel, went to a dime apiece, but families continued to eat a lot of rabbit.

We continually printed stories about buying Liberty Bonds. Bond-selling drives were held over the country: Douglas Fairbanks, Mary Pickford, Charlie Chaplin, and others spoke at the big ones. We did not have any of the famous names, but when the O.K. pulled the "Liberty Train" into the station, with its exhibit of rifles, uniforms, gas masks, machine guns, and other war materials, local people made speeches and sold bonds to the huge crowd.

At school, pupils brought in their pennies and bought Thrift Stamps at twenty-five cents each; sixteen of these or four dollars worth could be traded for a War Savings Stamp that could be redeemed at its face value of five dollars in five years. Don, learning the art of hand composition, worked hours setting up a patriotic dialogue, supplied from Washington, that went like this:

Q. Should I continue to buy Thrift Stamps?

A. Yes. Ask for a new Thrift Card and begin again.

Q. Do Thrift Stamps bear interest?

A. No.

Q. Why does the United States borrow this money?

A. To pay the expense of the war.

Eventually Don set up a whole column of Qs and As and beamed with pride when they appeared in print.

Mose LaMastres, the tailor who had looked after Charley McClary, organized a Home Guard for men ranging in age from eighteen to fifty, who drilled evenings on Main Street. The O.K. offered to let anyone who wished start a Victory Garden along its right-of-way, and many did. In the cities, women worked in factories and shipyards; Rosie the Riveter became a symbol for the liberated female. In Sugar Creek, women had always been busy and kept on doing what they always had done. The various social clubs, however, began to play less rook and auction and began to knit socks and sweaters and roll bandages. The soldier boys overseas loved the heavy woolen socks, although the story was circulated of one who put on a fresh pair just as he headed for a long stay in the damp trenches. On the march he felt a foreign object in the toe of one sock but could not stop to investigate, nor could he in the long, frantic days that followed. When finally he had a chance to remove his sock and relieve his sore, rubbed toe, he found a wad of paper, on which some one had written in a girlish hand: "Soldier boy, I love you." Our women firmly denied that any of them had put notes in socks.

Certain things even twelve- and thirteen-year-old kids could do. Shorty and I patrolled the back alleys and thus got copper, brass, zinc, and lead for the nation's smelters. We gathered peach stones, which were collected by the ton throughout the country and used for making charcoal for gas masks. Coconut shells were also good, but coconuts were seldom seen in Gilman City, and we would hardly have recognized one even if we had seen it.

The term *slacker* came into the vocabulary, to be applied to those who dragged their feet. Several publications were barred from the mails because of inflammatory statements. Generally these were Socialist, Anarchist, and Women's Peace Party organs.

WANTED!
200 War Horses

4 to 9 years old, and must be sound and in good flesh. Will also buy good **Eastern Horses** and good, fat **Mules,** 15 to 16 hands, 4 to 8 years old; must be fat. Show us your good stock. We are on the ground floor and can pay as much as anybody in the business. We'll be at

Coffey, Wednesday, Feb. 3
Gilman City, Thursday, Feb. 4

SHOW THEM TO US

A. O. Fisher & Son

The First World War could not have been won without Missouri's horses and mules. (*Guide*, January 28, 1915)

So we had our patriotism but we had our prejudices as well. Germans were particularly subject to abuse. A German family living on our own countryside had its barn painted yellow. The study of German in schools suddenly became not only unpopular but also unpatriotic. This particular prejudice did not hit us, as we had only Latin. Nor were we sophisticated enough to ban Wagner, Bach, and Mozart, as happened in the big cities. Long ago Teddy Roosevelt had warned us about speaking of Irish-Americans, German-Americans, Italian-Americans. There should be no hyphenated citizens, he declared; they are all Americans. We had not yet learned that unity must provide the strength that makes distinctions possible.

To save paper, Father eliminated the four-page, ready-printed, supplement shipped each week from Kansas City, with its syndicated serial story, national news, and other kinds of boiler-plate. He printed only the basic four pages of local news and ads. He had never been a ready-print fan anyway, and even after the war was over never reinstated it.

As postmaster, Father joined the war effort by buying a big flag and paying $6.55 out of his own pocket to erect a sixteen-foot pole atop the post-office building. During the next four years, he began and ended each day by raising and lowering the flag. The volume of mail not only greatly increased but its character changed. The mailing of packages to soldiers in camp and overseas doubled, as did the mail of letters to and from the men in the forces. Rural route carriers hauled far more mail than they ever had. First-class postage, which for ages had been two cents, went to three cents. Mother encouraged patrons to save paper by using one three cent stamp instead of three ones. No danger now of the post office ever sinking to fourth-class status. From her station at the front window, Mother sold Thrift Stamps and War Savings Stamps and handed out cards and booklets for keeping them and a good deal of related literature as well.

The flu was an even greater enemy than submarines and bullets. Before it had run its course, half a million Americans had died, compared to the three hundred thousand battle casualties. Throughout the world twenty million people died.

Father felt that he and Mother were in an especially exposed position, since everybody showed up at the post office, bringing who knows what kind of germs and contamination. But he learned that formaldehyde fumes would sterilize a building—formaldehyde had long been used to disinfect homes after quarantine—so every midmorning, as soon as the early rush was over, he heated a big coal scoop in the stove until it was red hot, poured formaldehyde on it, and carried it through the post office—front lobby and back room. As the fumes were strong enough to rip one's eyeballs out, patrons who visited the office immediately after one of Father's treatments transacted their business speedily and rushed out with tears streaming down their cheeks. The fumes would persist in strength for most of the day. Yet folks appreciated this cautionary measure, and I think a lot of them dropped in just to get well fumigated. And as it turned out, none of us got the flu.

Actually the epidemic for the most part bypassed the community, though several farm people, middle aged and vigorous, were carried away. One of my schoolmates, however—Frank Maxwell—red headed, freckle faced, skinny, wiry, and muscular—was stricken and missed school for I do not know how many weeks. On the day he returned, we gathered around him, staring in open amazement. His long siege had stripped him of whatever extra flesh he had had. His face was as pale as the teacher's chalk; even his freckles were bleached. He had been drained not only of his energy and vigor but also of his sense of mischief and deviltry.

Though his recovery was slow, by the end of the school year he was as active as ever. Fate had saved him for something else. Many years ago, quite by chance, I read that he had been killed in an automobile accident at the age of about forty-five. The news was compressed in a three-line local, but I paused to recall that Frank Maxwell was, to me, a symbol of the disastrous flu epidemic that had claimed so many American lives and also to reflect that if we had still been running the *Guide*, Father would have written not three lines but half a column or more about Frank, and I would have set it up on the Intertype.

In the windows of homes and business establishments, flags with blue stars appeared to show that the family had a son or the business firm an employee in the service. Then came the times when the blue star would be replaced by a gold star; tragedies like this struck the whole community. Curly Higgins was one of the gold stars. Ironically, his death had come in 1919, months after the armistice. He was then a dispatch bearer, attached to the general staff; one night he was shot and robbed of his money, guns, and valuables. The depot platform was crowded the day his body arrived from overseas. Later Bill Haines, with considerable difficulty, opened the metal coffin, to make sure the body was Curly's. All in all we had four gold stars; this was part of Sugar Creek's contribution to make the world safe for democracy.

What with the formaldehyde and the Four-Minute Men, the ration coupons and the War Savings Stamps, the copper and zinc scraps and the peach pits, the shipments of livestock and agricultural products that went out over the O.K., and with that great Missourian, General Pershing, at the head of the expeditionary forces and that other great Missourian, Woodrow Wilson, at the head of the civilian effort (you suddenly stopped reading? remember, Wilson's signature was on Father's post-office commission, and his picture was in the post-office lobby, so he was at least an honorary Missourian), Kaiser Bill suddenly found himself with nowhere to go.

On November 10 we learned from the depot telegrapher and the morning dailies that an armistice had been signed; these headlines were later struck down as rumors, but next day came the fact. On the evening of November 11 the whole town gathered on Main Street and built a tremendous bonfire. The flames leaped so high they almost burned out the overhead streetlight, but nobody would have cared. We just stood around and whooped and hollered—men, women, boys, girls—we felt so exultant. Suddenly the men began throwing their hats into the fire, Father among them. I asked him later why he had done that, and he said he knew that would happen, that men had always tossed their hats into the fire at great celebrations, so he had brought along an old hat.

Beginning with Decoration Day in 1919, the celebrations in town and at the cemetery were somewhat different. The young men, back from the army camps and the overseas campaigns, wearing their campaign hats and overseas caps, joined the diminishing group of older veterans. We were told about the American military cemeteries overseas—later I visited some of them—with rows and rows of crosses and Stars of David. Some of these bore the name and rank of veterans from Harrison and Daviess counties. We were grateful that the war had lasted no longer than the

eleventh hour of the eleventh day of the eleventh month of 1918.
The American Legion, speedily organized after the war, took up
the cause of veterans and their families in earnest. The Legion also
became famous for holding some of the liveliest, most energetic,
most robust national conventions ever held in the country.

As always, the nation shifted quickly from war to peace, but
with differences. Stores began to sell more cigarettes and less pipe
and chewing tobacco; the convenience of cigarettes for a soldier
on duty quickly made them a manly, not an effeminate, habit. Our
jewelers noted more calls for wristwatches and fewer for pocket
watches. Women's contribution to the war effort, particularly in
industry, gave them a new standing in the country. On August 26,
1920, which happened to be my fifteenth birthday, the Nineteenth
Amendment, giving the vote to women, was ratified.

More than that, however, we felt that the world had been
made safe for democracy, and that this crop of veterans would be
the last. Then came the argument and discussion; even in high
school we debated whether America should enter the League of
Nations, with or without reservations, whether America should ad-
here to the World Court, whether the results of the Disarmament
Conference should be approved. What with the turmoil in Europe,
the shrinking of the market for farm produce, the depression of
the early twenties that utterly ruined so many farm families, the
wave of isolationism that swept the country, we gradually became
cynical about the notion of making the world safe for democracy.
In small communities, each family had to adjust the best it could.

In 1920, Harding beat Cox in a Republican landslide. In the
post-office lobby Wilson's picture came down and Harding's appeared. In their home at the southeast corner of Third and Broadway, the postmaster and the assistant postmaster wryly surveyed
their future. Before long some good Republican would represent
the government's postal interests in Gilman City. In a roundabout
way, we became one of the war's casualties.

19

The Last Days of the *Guide*

The Republican victory in 1920 had been so overwhelming that Father saw little hope of reversing the trend in four years, and perhaps not even in eight. With two growing boys, he could not face the prospect of seeing the family income cut in half. So after ten years, the longest we had lived anywhere, he decided to sell the *Guide* and buy a larger paper.

Most proprietors and brokers who wanted to sell newspapers advertised in *The Publishers Auxiliary*, a trade paper that enjoyed a national circulation. Father described the *Guide* as a live-wire, one-family proposition, published in a thriving and prospering community. *One-family proposition* was a term understood by all as meaning a fine business opportunity for a dedicated newspaper couple willing to work twelve hours a day. We also scanned the other "For Sale" ads and compiled a list of newspapers we might like to buy, also published in thriving and prospering communities. In the twenties, a newspaper was worth what it grossed; Father was interested in buying one that grossed $20,000 a year, four times what the *Guide* was doing.

The choices narrowed to two: the *Schulenburg Sticker* and the *Osceola Tribune*. Schulenburg was a town with a population of fifteen hundred in southeast Texas, and Osceola with twenty-four hundred in south-central Iowa. We studied sample copies and other pertinent information.

You can imagine the discussions we had about whether to seek our fortune in Texas or Iowa. Both papers were weeklies. Each had a vigorous competitor. The *Sticker* had a Linotype, the *Tribune* a Linograph, a simplified but not too successful linecasting machine. The *Tribune* was a better-printed paper, with a greater assortment of type fonts. Either could be bought for a down payment of $5,000, and paid out at $1,000 a year, the interest rate being 5 percent on the unpaid balance.

Father did not have the $5,000, unless he could sell the *Guide* for that much cash, which was extremely unlikely. Even so, he did not seem to worry about the financial angle.

The intangibles were important. Texas was a long ways off, a distant frontier, a different place to live from what any Reid had ever experienced. It was normally a solidly Democratic state, a positive advantage since the county officers would be sure to be Democrats, and would award such lucrative county printing as the court docket, the board proceedings, and the sheriff's sales, to the Democratic paper. The mechanical equipment, however, was only fair.

The *Tribune* was located in a Republican town, a Republican county, and a Republican state. Its competitor, the *Sentinel*, was solidly established and enjoyed a bigger business, including the county printing. But the *Tribune*'s fine presses and wide range of type styles especially appealed to me. I loved machinery and agonized over the *Guide*'s poor equipment—the Country Campbell that was tricky to operate, the Intertype that had both acute and chronic spells of distributor trouble. I did not especially worry about the problem we would have as Democrats in Iowa.

After much family discussion, Father decided to begin the search for another newspaper by taking the train to Osceola and interviewing the *Tribune*'s proprietor, C. M. Gates, a newspaper broker who had long followed the practice of buying a paper, building it up, and then selling at a profit. Gates was not too disturbed that Father did not have the full $5,000, as he liked the idea of income from the interest. After much haggling the two finally made a deal, so when Father returned he could bring word that we were the owners of a new paper, even though we had not yet sold the *Guide*.

I have sometimes wondered what would have been different if we had gone to Texas instead of Iowa. Don and I would have attended different schools, married different girls, had a different set of children and grandchildren—in short the human race would have been pretty badly messed up. However, one should never look back. We were happy with the decision and looked forward to going to Iowa. It was then February of 1921, a month before the Harding inaugural. Father needed to go to Osceola at once to take over the *Tribune*, but he arranged with the post-office department to have Mother appointed as acting postmaster until a

Republican could be selected. Don was to join him at the end of the winter semester. Mother and I thought we could be free of newspaper and post-office responsibilities at least by the time school opened in September.

A newspaper that misses publication dates loses a good deal of its value, so we needed to keep the *Guide* alive and well. In a few weeks, Father leased it to L. E. Shields, so for a while we had a reasonably carefree existence. We quickly perceived, however, that Shields was having a problem. As he had no family, he needed to hire a printer, but he tried to do all the work himself. The machinery worked no better for him than it had for us. The paper came out on time but showed hurried editing, meager advertising, and faulty makeup and printing. Mother overheard complaints that orders for job printing were being delayed. One Monday morning she noted that he had not shown up for work at all. By noon she started making inquiries and learned that he had left town altogether. Entering the office, she found a note in which he expressed his regret at departing so suddenly, and his hope that money due the paper from advertisers would offset the unpaid bills left behind.

There was nothing for us to do but reopen the office and print the next issue. My holiday was suddenly interrupted and Mother's workweek was suddenly rearranged by the need to sell ads, write stories, set type, and get the pages on the press. I was so upset that I wrote a sharp news item to the effect that a hobo printer by the name of Shields, who presumably had been the publisher of the *Guide*, had suddenly left town. Wednesday night we finally got the issue printed and got it in the mail. Thursday Father came from Osceola, after publishing the issue there, and looked over what we had done. When he saw the piece about the hobo printer, he came to a full rolling boil. You cannot, he explained, call a person a "hobo printer." By so doing you are likely to make yourself guilty of libel. It is difficult to prove that a man is a hobo. Now we have not only got ourselves involved with two newspapers, but we may have a libel suit on our hands as well.

I felt sure that I had brought about the ruin of the family. I confidently expected that any day Mr. Shields would walk in and confront us with the grisly fact of my felony. When two or three days passed and he did not appear, I could only conclude that he had not yet seen the paper. Maybe he would never see it. I began to relax. Then on Monday the famous "Missouri Notes" column of the *Kansas City Star* reprinted my squib in full. My agony was rekindled; Shields would certainly now see the item. Then I had the second thought that if there were indeed to be a libel suit, the resources of the *Star* would be nice to have alongside those of the *Guide*. Next came the notion that if the piece actually had been libelous, the *Star* would never have reprinted it. Finally came the glowing reflection that it was gratifying to be associated with the editors of the *Star* in any connection whatsoever.

Father sold the *Guide* a second time to Mr. and Mrs. Jack Stevens, both hard-working, experienced newspaper people. Their first issues contained both bad news and good news.

The bad news was that the Gilman Mercantile Company had gone broke. Ever since its founding at the turn of the century, this large firm had changed hands every few years. Gradually it had lost its buggy-and-wagon business to the automobile people. Its brisk trade in collars, saddles, and harness degenerated into a repair activity, which also steadily diminished. County-seat dealers took over the business in farm implements. Young couples moved away and bought their "outfits" of household goods elsewhere.

The Hotel Harmon hung on, but it, also, had a struggle. At least a dozen people had tried to make a go of it: among them a real-estate man, a school principal, an insurance agent, a farmer. It had never developed a good restaurant or banquet business, considered a profitable part of hotel operation, and it rented steadily fewer rooms. Once its paper-hanger manager had fallen into conversation with a garage owner. One result was to trade the hotel for an old Buick. The new hotel man worried himself sick over the lack of business and did not especially like looking after the few patrons he had. The new Buick owner had trouble getting the car started, and, besides, snapped a connecting rod. A week later they met again and traded back. "I got all the hotel I wanted," said one; "I got all the car I wanted," declared the other. In a noticeable way the hotel, the town's most imposing structure, reflected the changing times. Now the *Guide* was reporting still another change of ownership.

The good news, however, was promising. The possibility of a new $125,000 school building seemed assured. The light plant had bought a new engine, so that the community could have service two days a week instead of one, plus the usual evening service. The Methodists planned a new $10,000 church to replace the one that had burned down. A Farm Products Show would replace the annual picnic, which suddenly failed to make expenses. Deposits in both banks were steadily increasing. The $60 million bond drive to "Get Missouri Out of the Mud" was underway. With luck, Gilman City would be the hub, or close to the hub, of a network of hard-surfaced roads serving northwest Missouri traffic.

The 1920 census counted 618 people, the highest ever, and might some day reach 1,000—as Father had always hoped.

In the years that followed, moreover, the community's leaders planned a number of enterprises. The band was reorganized and started giving evening concerts not only at home but also in nearby Brimson. Booster tours advertised the Fourth of July Fair, the Farm Products Show, Dollar Day, or whatever. A typical tour was a cavalcade of automobiles, making a two-county circuit of Mount Moriah, Bethany, Coffey, Jamesport, Gallatin, Jameson, Brimson, and Melbourne. The band played selections to attract a crowd, and Ira Oliphant, once more reelected mayor, made a speech.

Mac McClelland and Shorty started a feed factory, selling bagged feed blended according to the latest research of the University of Missouri and other state experimental stations. Mac, an avid reader and an enterprising businessman, made a good try, but the project fell short of being another Purina. Bill Haines started a mausoleum factory, but people bought Clark Grave Vaults instead of Haines Mausoleums. Floyd Eberhart, whom I knew as cashier of the Citizens Bank, started a hatchery that was highly successful, with an incubator capacity of more than eighty thousand. He was in business for thirty years.

Sunday movies, for long a highly controversial issue, were instituted. Electric power could not be supplied on a daily basis but was increased to two mornings a week as well as in the evenings. The streets were covered with crushed rock, which kept down the dust and the mud. A water and sewer system, however, was still far in the future. One election to issue bonds attracted only fifteen votes favoring the idea.

Excitement was generated when oil developers discovered a

promising structure six miles northwest of town on Judge Marple's farm. They sold stock in the new enterprise and soon moved a drilling rig to dig what was to be known as No. 1 Marple Well, to be the first in a series. Each day the hole went deeper and deeper. Along the way a slight show of oil aroused everybody's hopes. At eight hundred feet the drill entered the Mississippian limestones, as far down as Harrison County soil had ever been penetrated.

People who had never known anything deeper than the end of a spade began to talk about the Ste. Genevieve layer, the Upper Warsaw layer, the Lower Warsaw layer. "I'm going to Arbuckle dolomite unless production comes sooner," declared the promoter, which was roughly equivalent to California or Bust, another slogan frequently heard. At Slick's Cafe, townspeople met in the evenings to discuss their good fortune. Most of them had a few Shirt Sleeve Oil Company shares left over from the previous decade.

In a few days No. 1 Marple brought up samples from the Devonian system, a word that gets into geology books, when nothing more complicated than fish inherited the earth's surface. This was good news because under the Devonian was the Ordovician, the layer that had produced so much oil in Kansas and Oklahoma. The Ordovician contained the Kimswick formation, the promoters explained learnedly, which corresponded to the rich Viola formation found in oil-bearing country. Soon a representative of the state geologist's office came to view the happenings. Nothing of interest, however, showed up in five hundred feet of either Devonian or Ordovician. And in the next two hundred feet the drill hit a rich vein of saltwater, a geological structure that can be recognized by any amateur, so the venture was abandoned and the rig dismantled and moved elsewhere. That was the story of No. 1 Marple. Of course every town, and every person, has a No. 1 Marple.

Two years after we left, fire took one of Bill Noll's many brick business structures and a restaurant. Next year began a series of what became known as the January fires. In 1925, fire destroyed four buildings on the south side of Main. In 1926 the Ford Garage on the north side went. In 1928 another restaurant and a mineral mixture plant burned down. In 1929 three buildings on the north side were destroyed; and a second fire three months later destroyed four more. Most of the school records, stored in a bank, were lost.

As the north side business district was only two or three blocks long, these fires pretty much cleaned it out. About all that remained was the hotel, a garage, a hardware store, and a furniture store.

In 1935 fire on the south side took out the big Combs department store, successor to the Dunn store. Six years later a pool hall, restaurant, and warehouse went up in flames.

The total loss at any one of the major fires averaged from $12,000 to $15,000, a princely sum that would buy two or three well-equipped country newspapers. The insurance covered half the loss or less. In most instances business had been so poor that the owners did not bother to start up again.

Wrecking crews completed the destruction of other landmarks. They knocked down the Citizens Bank building and hauled the bricks to Mount Moriah, big-league pitcher Babe Adams's hometown, to build a filling station. They dismantled the Hotel Harmon, saved in the 1929 fire, and eventually a one-story cement-block structure was erected in its place.

About the time that the Jack Stevenses bought the *Guide*, officials of the Burlington, which long before had taken over the O.K., noted that it was beginning to operate in the red. The clumsy, slow-moving truck was hauling livestock and other goods and commodities that formerly were shipped by rail. Late in the thirties the Burlington people began to think about abandoning the O.K. altogether. *Abandonment*, a strong word that would have been unthinkable in the nineties, was appearing nationwide in the railroad news. In January 1939, the Gilman City Community Club sent Bill Haines and three others to appear at a Public Abandonment Hearing in Kansas City. The Burlington could show that O.K. operations were down to one passenger train daily each way, and only a few freight trains each week. It argued that it had lost money for two decades. In July it received authorization from the mighty Interstate Commerce Commission to abandon 140 miles of track. Few things in life are more difficult than to persuade a highway commission to alter its plans for routing a highway, or to prevent a railroad from reducing passenger service, so no one could have been surprised by the decision. Soon crews of workmen were tearing up and hauling away the rails and ties that "The Picturesque Hills of Chariton" and its crews had laid down in 1897. Telegraph wire was rolled up, poles uprooted, and glass insulators that had survived hunters' target practice and collectors' raids were hauled away. Missouri's railroad trackage shrank to a fraction of its peak eight thousand miles. Even today in that part of the state you can see abandoned track, telegraph wires cut in a hundred places and dripping from the poles, and the insulators gone.

These reverses had a depressing effect upon the business community. The Stevenses finally had to give up the *Guide*, and Father reluctantly took it back and again put it on the market. In the years that followed he tried various arrangements of leasing or selling with various hopeful buyers. In 1927 the *Guide* bounced back during my senior year at college, and Father and I drove to Gilman City to publish an issue. The next year Don accompanied Father on a similar mission. Eventually he was able to sell it outright. In 1931 the *Harrison County Times* acquired it and incorporated the name of the *Guide* into its front-page title. Next year, however, it abandoned its Gilman City office and in 1936 lopped the name of the *Guide* off its front page. For a while the voice of Gilman City was silenced altogether except for weekly newsletters appearing in the *Times*.

Meanwhile the *Gilman City Star* had been founded, but lasted only a brief time. Then came the *Gilman City Tribune*, which was published for twenty-two years, but even it was suspended in 1956. Those were the years when newspapers, like railroads, were abandoned. The four Missouri towns in which Father published newspapers once supported a dozen weeklies and dailies; that total eventually shrank to three. And as each small town lost its paper, life there became less cohesive, more anonymous. Like all small-town newspapers of that day, the *Guide* and its successors gave the community an identity; and, what is more important, a character. Gilman City without a newspaper to proclaim the week's achievements and enterprises hardly seemed like Gilman City at all.

About 1970 the *Guide* building was wrecked; it had stood empty for years and was in bad need of repair. Bill Noll had always been proud of the fact that he had put up twenty-three brick structures. The *Guide* building was the most attractive, perhaps because Bill wanted to adorn the prominent corner at Main and Broadway with something special in the bricklayer's art. It turned out to be one of the last survivors of the twenty-three.

At some point in the twenties or thirties, the small American town began to go into a decline. In Gilman City the turning point came about 1921 to 1923 when the *Guide* editor and a lot of other people found it difficult to make a living. The community lost its heart and sinew when one by one and two by two the people began to move away. Ralph Eckles took his talents as merchant and grocer to New London, Iowa. Ira Hurst moved to Trenton and hung out his shingle as an interior decorator. Two dentists, Lester Eberhart and L. C. Price, successively moved their practices out of town—one to Kansas, one to Gallatin. Dr. Gardner, who had vaccinated us for smallpox, moved his practice to Gallatin, and later, with his sons, went into the drugstore business in Kansas City. The Markeys, the Honans, the Beelers, the Brownings, the Rays, the Crumps, the Thompsons, the Gusewelles, the Reals, and many others moved to various towns and cities. With the exception of the county seat, other Harrison County towns also declined; so many people moved to Kansas City that the annual Harrison County picnic, held at Swope Park, attracted from three to five hundred former residents.

Gilman City's population of 618 dropped to 555 in the 1940 census. In 1960 it was 379. In 1970, 376. Harrison County's population dropped from 19,700 to 10,200; Daviess County from 16,600 to 8,400.

But to go back to our own move. In the summer of 1921, Father and Mother sold our house and scheduled an auction of our household goods. The telephone poles on which so many sale bills had been tacked now displayed bills announcing our own sale. The articles on view in the front yard did not seem to take much room, even though we were not taking much to Iowa except clothes, books, and a grandfather's clock that had been acquired in an advertising deal. Bidding was spirited, and piece by piece our things were hauled away. Among them was Mother's piano. She had seldom found time to play it after becoming a newspaperwoman.

We returned Father and Don to Iowa by train, possibly the last time any of us rode on the O.K. Mother and I got in Old Betsy and drove away at the handsome speed of twenty miles an hour. At Bethany we hit the Jefferson Highway and followed it to Osceola. Mother, always the least-traveled member of our family, never got back to Gilman City.

Don's first move on arriving in Iowa was to join the Boy Scout troop. He qualified in time to take part in a camp-out at the Iowa State Fair, where he and others served as ushers in the big grandstand. For him it was a proud moment. At the *Osceola Tribune* he learned to feed the Huber newspaper press, which was considerably more refined than the Country Campbell. In the fall we entered high school, he as a freshman and I as a senior. We had a wider choice of courses than we had been accustomed to. The students, however, were as friendly, and the teachers as competent, as we had always known.

At the *Tribune* it was still hurry home Wednesday. There were more people to do the work, but there was more work to do. Press Day is inescapable in the newspaper business. But where the *Guide* had been struggling and losing, the *Tribune* struggled and held its own. Later it did better than hold its own. It participated in a political upset, helped get three or four Democrats elected, and got some county printing.

What I have written is about the first twenty-five years of Gilman City's existence. What happened to cut its population in half is the same as what happened to most small towns that quarter century. Some people saw that they could stay and make a living but others saw that they would have to move. New people moved in and stayed but others moved in and left. Now and then those who had stayed and those who had joined them found special ways of beating the drums for new business, but these efforts were sporadic whereas the opposing forces—the highways, the electric lines, the pipelines—those that favored the larger communities— never let up.

While yesterday's small town lasted, it was special. The small town of today is a filling-station town, a grocery and restaurant town, a hardware and feed-store town. It may have another store or two. It does have hard-surfaced streets, clean air, and electricity around the clock. And gas: sometimes from a pipeline, sometimes from a tank. Conveniences like these will help many small towns, like Gilman City, grow larger. But yesterday's small town had a couple of department stores. A pool of half a dozen physicians, dentists, and veterinarians. A couple of banks. A milliner and a tailor. Not only a filling station but an automobile dealer or two.

A couple of drugstores. A furniture store. A movie. A couple of jewelry stores. A hotel.

A railroad and a newspaper.

We would not want to live in the small town of our memories but it would be nice if we could look in on it just once again.

At the city limits.

Acknowledgments

Many of the incidents narrated are reported in the *Gilman City Guide*, from 1904 to 1921, now in microfilm in the library of the State Historical Society of Missouri. I am indebted to the Society for permission to reprint pictures and other materials from the *Guide* and from other newspapers and books in its collection.

Files of the *Harrison County Times*, the *Bethany Clipper*, the *Bethany Democrat*, the *Gallatin Democrat*, and the *Gallatin North Missourian* often had a weekly newsletter from Gilman City, although it was at times crowded out by a heavy run of advertising or legal notices, or by floods that marooned towns and delayed trains. Trenton and Pattonsburg papers also carried occasional news stories about Gilman City. Of course, all papers heavily clipped one another and occasionally a Gilman City story would be widely reprinted.

Father's two books, *Ups and Downs* and *Tarcomeda* ("A Democrat" spelled backwards), contain references to Gilman City happenings, as do scrapbooks he kept many years.

All of the foregoing sources, plus numerous interviews with former schoolmates, have helped pin down many a name and date, although in the main I have relied on my own memory. As a newspaper family must know what is going on, I heard a lot of adult talk, wrote a few stories myself, and as the principal operator put nearly everything in type. Even so, any memory tends to be selective and at times even dead wrong.

The newspapers cited above and the *Trenton Weekly Republican*, the *Quincy Whig*, and the *Kansas City Star*, along with state and county census schedules, are the principal sources for the construction of the railroad between Pattonsburg and Trenton, and the founding and settlement of Gilman City.

I also acknowledge invaluable assistance from:

My brother Don J. Reid, and my aunts, Mrs. Grace Doak and Mrs. Frances Barton, for much supplemental family lore. I especially prize Aunt Grace's long, helpful letters about the family's early years.

Mrs. Flora Maye Dowell Beeler, Mr. and Mrs. Dean Bell, Mr. and Mrs. Forrest Brown, Mr. and Mrs. Hobart Burrell, Charles Doherty, Tom Dorney, Floyd Eberhart, Gratz Hurst, Nylen Lewis, Nellie Lindsey, Bonifant Moulin, Carl McDaniel, Mrs. Florence Dunn Price, Ivan Ray, Mr. and Mrs. Homer Real, Leo Reid, Ervin Thompson, M. Q. Thompson, and Mr. and Mrs. Jasper Vanderpool, for pictures and information about Gilman City people and events.

The Missouri State Highway Commission, with special thanks to Arthur Taylor, Koil Rowland, Ron Clark, and James Roach, for old maps and pictures of Missouri roads.

Faye Simkin, executive officer, New York Public Library, and R. Cragin Lewis, director of alumni relations, Williams College, for biographical information about Theodore Gilman.

Norman G. Hansen, manager, advertising and sales promotion, Mergenthaler Linotype Company, for information about the pioneer Junior Linotype.

Donald H. Neale, manager of operations, Harris Corporation, for a photo of the first Model A Intertype.

Peter A. Briggs, regional public-relations manager, Burlington Northern, for historical material about the Q.O. and K.C.

Mrs. J. W. Albsmeyer, reference librarian, Quincy Public Library, for information about the building of the Quincy, Omaha, and Kansas City Railway between Trenton and Pattonsburg.

Jack Wells, state geologist, for a copy of the official log of No. 1 Marple Well, the attempt to find oil near Gilman City.

Robert L. Gilmore, secretary, Missouri Public Service Commission, for a copy of a map filed by the Q.O. and K.C. showing its route.

John P. Roberts, secretary, National Museum of Transport, St. Louis, for information about libraries with railroad materials.

Alma Vaughn, State Historical Society of Missouri, for endless courtesies in connection with newspaper files and census records.

Beth A. Dewey, public-relations office, Miles Laboratories, Inc., and William V. Rich, retired employee from the Miles print shop, for information about the Miles trade-deal advertising program.

Norman Hilgedick for technical advice in preparing maps.

Donna Moore for illustrative sketches accompanying the text.

Ira Naroian, vice-president, ATF-Davidson Company, for permission to use pictures from *Specimen Book of Type Styles*, originally published by the American Type Founders Company.

David P. Thelen, of the Department of History, University of Missouri-Columbia, and Howard Miller, of the Department of History, University of Missouri, St. Louis, for reading the manuscript and for comments from the point of view of their specialties. Other readers, not known to me, at the invitation of the University of Missouri Press, also made valuable suggestions.

I am especially grateful to the Press for the continued interest taken in the manuscript, beginning with revision and continuing with the numerous aspects of publication.

Illustration Credits

Grateful acknowledgment is extended to the following people and organizations (maps and illustrations not otherwise credited are from author's collection):

Edwards Brothers of Missouri, for *Plat Book of Harrison County, 1876*, p. 11

Northwest Publishing Company, for *Plat Book of Harrison County, 1898*, pp. 11, 116

American Type Founders Company, for *American Specimen Book of Type Styles*, 1912, pp. 35, 66

State Historical Society of Missouri, pp. 41, 46, 47, 51, 116, 194, 199, 214, 228, 229, 231, 254, 255, 264, 265, 270

M. Q. Thompson, pp. 65, 130

Missouri Public Service Commission, p. 70

Harrison School Reorganized District R-4, pp. 17, 78, 123, 131

Leo Reid, p. 86

Donna Moore, pp. 87, 104, 285

Mergenthaler Linotype Company, p. 102

Vera Williams Brown, pp. 118, 156, 239

Purple and Gold, the 1917 annual of Gilman City High School, p. 154

Flora Maye Dowell Beeler, p. 155

American Book Company, *Standard Arithmetic*, 1895, by W. J. Milne, p. 166

Missouri State Highway Commission, pp. 237, 238

Wayne State University Press, *Automobiles of America*, Automobile Manufacturers Association, 1968, p. 240